The LIFE *and* MIND

OF

EMILY

DICKINSON

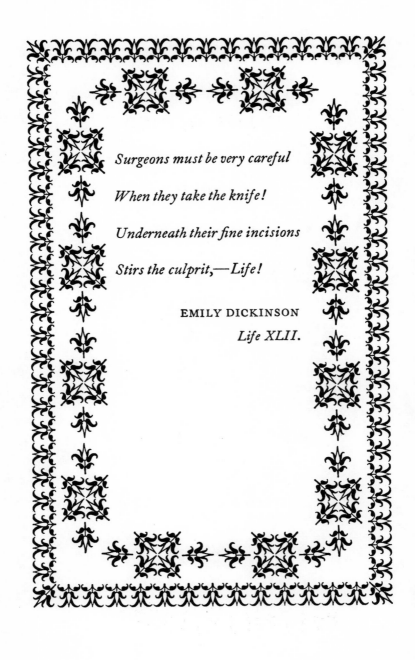

Surgeons must be very careful

When they take the knife!

Underneath their fine incisions

Stirs the culprit,—Life!

EMILY DICKINSON

Life XLII.

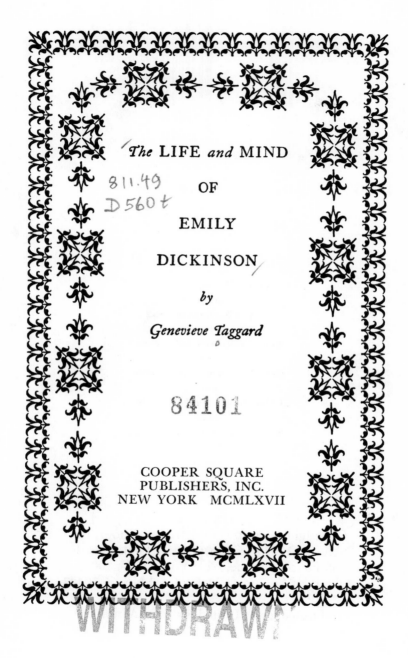

The LIFE *and* MIND

OF

EMILY

DICKINSON

by

Genevieve Taggard

COOPER SQUARE
PUBLISHERS, INC.
NEW YORK   MCMLXVII

DEDICATION

Emily!
The book is bound
The pages cut.
Index says: Emily.
Where are you found?

Deity will see to it
That you never do it.

Deity did.
You are vexed.
You vanish, with a text.

Still you have been
Some months my shy companion. While I wrote
The slow prose,
You watched, alert, amused. Your words
Fell on the page, consenting, with my words.

Index offended you,
The binding, and the print,

The sold book, possession, *the review.*
Emily, where are you?

Go to her verse, reader,
To the great verse.
Here is nothing of hers.

She will elude us all,
Run from any but her own call.
Read her own page, reader.
Wait . . . read the great verse. Do not look up if you
    think you hear her.
Do not for a moment stir.
She will come near, confidently nearer,
Even as I write this, she is here.

ACKNOWLEDGMENT

I WISH TO THANK MR. CARL VAN DOREN, WHO LENT me the 1894 edition of the *Letters* from his library in 1923; and a second time, to take to France for a year while this book was being written; MARY HEATON VORSE for valuable memories; MISS JEANNETTE MARKS for certain significant suggestions; SARA BARD FIELD, for a partial bibliography and many thoughtful and helpful letters; THE JONES LIBRARY in Amherst; MR. ROBERT FLETCHER of the Converse Memorial Library for the Tyler *History of Amherst College,* and the use of files of the *Hampshire and Franklin Gazette;* and the use of an anonymous valentine quoted by the editor of the *Indicator,* the literary magazine, published in 1850, which proved to have been written by Emily Dickinson; and the monthly " Editor's Corner " during 1849 and '50. I wish also to thank MISS BERTHA E. BLAKELY of Mount Holyoke College for material relating to student life at Mount Holyoke during Emily Dickinson's time in the possession of the Williston Memorial Library; MISS SYDNEY R. MCLEAN; and MISS MARGARET BALL of Mount Holyoke College for other material. I am indebted to MR. RICHARD DALE MCMULLAN for material relating to Philadelphia in 1854.

ix

❧ ACKNOWLEDGMENT ☙

I also wish to thank MR. CHARLES F. D. BELDEN and MISS HELEN SWIFT of the Boston Public Library for their kindness in putting the resources of the reference library at my disposal and for permission to use hitherto unpublished material from the Galatea Collection. I also wish to thank CARPENTER AND MOREHOUSE, printers and publishers, for the use of one original picture taken from their *History of Amherst;* MISS GERTRUDE LINNELL, MRS. E. C. DUDLEY, PROFESSOR GEORGE F. WHICHER of Amherst College, MISS CLARA BELLINGER GREEN, MRS. MABEL LOOMIS TODD; MRS. WILLIAM R. HALLIDAY, DR. ERIC ALLING, MISS MARGUERITE HOYLE, and MISS HARRIET WILSON, MISS MARY MAURY FITZGERALD, MISS KATHERINE TOLLES, MISS AGNES REAGAN, and others who perforce must remain unnamed, for assistance in the writing of this book. Certain material in *Emily Dickinson, the Human Background of Her Poetry,* by JOSEPHINE POLLITT (Harper and Brothers, 1930), has been useful in the writing of this book.

I wish to thank as well MISS ETHEL M. SMITH of Amherst, who contributed a great deal of research on Amherst families; MR. WILLARD TRASK, MR. HENRY MEADE WILLIAMS, and HELEN NEUGASS, who read and criticized this manuscript in an early form, and MISS DOROTHY STONER and ELVA DEPEW MATTHEWS, who criticized it as it approximated final form.

And, finally, I wish to thank MISS MANLEY AARON, Mr. Alfred Knopf's secretary, and MR. KNOPF himself for the requisite patience.

A detailed list of sources for this book will be found in the first appendix.

x

FOREWORD

SOME DEPENDABLE LIFE OF EMILY DICKINSON SHOULD have been written thirty-five years ago when her poetry first encountered fame; now, a hundred years after her birth, we realize our loss. Only a small number of the twelve hundred poems catalogued in 1892[1] have been published; a scandal and a lawsuit ended the editing of the poems and deterred the memoir some friend might have written. As for a detailed life, there seemed to be no life to write, in the professional manner of the nineties, and so none was written.

By 1900 the lively memories of the old people ceased, one by one, and those who might have recalled an Emily in a coloured dress gave place to those who could remember only the latter half of her Amherst existence. For these people, some of them still alive, Emily was always

---

[1] "After her death her sister and her friends were amazed at the immense amount of literary material which she had left behind her. Besides the poems collected in the first volume, which is now in its eleventh edition, and in the second series, which has reached a sale of over five thousand since November, there are at least twelve hundred poems catalogued, and no one knows how many more in a mass of notes manuscript found among her possessions — enough to make several stout volumes." — From the *Book Buyer*, Vol. ix, no. 4 (May 1892), pp. 157–8.

xi

just going through a door or into the house as they came near. We do not remember much but legend of a person when we have only half seen a hurrying whiteness.

Where shall we find her, then? Where is she hidden? For there was an Emily Dickinson in the town of Amherst. We can see her own door-posts, and, beside her window, the pine-tree she looked at. And her name is cut in veritable stone in the West Cemetery, to say that she undoubtedly lived before she died. Her words say that she lived — and to her words, nearer to her life than stone and tree, we must return to find her. There is no unspeakable mystery in her words — none was ever intended. On several occasions Emily greatly embarrassed friends by telling more of her life than they were prepared to hear; she told more than the urbane Mr. Higginson told of himself in all his intimate papers, more than Mr. Bowles, "free lance and heretic," thought proper to tell. What has been called mystery is character; and character is the key to this extraordinary story — Dickinson family character and Emily's, at one and the same time the epitome and the antithesis of the family, under the pressure, the light and shade, of the moral climate of Amherst. We have forgotten character, if we have not destroyed it, in our modern study of motives.

When Emily Dickinson's letters are carefully assembled and studied, and three or four downright and candid sentences of her own about herself taken seriously, we have a story which tells itself, and a life the poems verify. Hitherto her letters have been read for their singular "style"; and mystery has been an agreeable accompaniment, in her

poetry, to its "fancy" and its "mysticism." This lazy
poetic inclination in the reader would disappoint an Emily
who seized on essentials. She knew the secret of biography, for she said (and I feel her eyes, large and piercing,
like her father's, upon me as I write):

> *No romance sold unto,*
> *Could so enthrall a man*
> *As the perusal of*
> *His individual one.*

Of her own "romance," whose existence was at times
privately questioned by her friends, Emily grants that it
isn't plausible:

> *'Tis fiction's, to dilute*
> *To plausibility*
> *Our novel, when 'tis small enough*
> *To credit, — 'tisn't true!*

One word of caution to the reader who assumes that he
may with little effort construe a life from Emily Dickinson's own words and by such authority call his version the
correct one. The most common error is to assume that
the positive statements, in the poems especially, should
hold true for a lifetime. We cannot date these poems
exactly; and so we cannot tell which of Emily's innumerable aphorisms came last from her pencil. Obviously, some
of the states of mind shown in poems seemingly written
shortly after her love and renunciation cannot be supposed
to stand for the refinement in vision that continued without
pause for another thirty-six years. And we should remember that poets change their minds; that poets are

capricious; that they often choose odd forms for secret truth. Emily was rooted like a plant in water; she was rooted, but she swayed. We should remember, as well, that absolute statement in poetry cannot describe relative fact in daily life. Another even deeper difficulty comes of assuming that cerebral events recorded in her poetry had always a counterpart in the events of her temporal life. Emily implored Mr. Higginson to remember that the " I " of the verse was a supposed person and not necessarily herself. She would implore us, as well. She was writing about life, not merely, or even left-handedly about her life, much of the time. Another difficulty for the literal-minded reader is the fact that Emily was a symbolist; some readers understand her meaning at sight; others never will. This is a trap for a host of commentators. And, finally, unless the reader is steeped in Emily's ways of thought, he cannot but mistake certain sentences in the letters. Consider Emily's use of the word " love." If a scrap of paper were found tomorrow, in her indubitable script, declaring Emily's love for so-and-so, many would suppose that the old query had at last found an answer. The accustomed reader would know enough to be wary, having already met with the many gradations to her meaning for the word. Only the total Emily will do for our study.

This book tells the story of two lives in one person — lives that interlocked, but did not interfere. Why only two? Were there not many, if more than one? I find only two. And I find the reasons for the two. A central relationship governed and divided this life; the primary impulses were sublimated, intensified, and then turned over to the hidden self. Because her life was forcibly double and her mind divided, Emily's eye saw a double reality; and she was for ever at work to compose that external contradiction into one. It was this troublesome "double" that compelled her to be a poet.

My book starts with a crucial adventure of the note sent with four poems to Mr. Higginson, because at that point, and only that once, did Emily's inner life emerge in action. Thereafter the book is woven of two strands, Emily's outer and her inner existence, the outer becoming less significant, and the inner more so, and often very contradictory, as the story progresses. In telling this story I have had to follow Emily's presentiments and repetitions. I have had to tell the story, not as one draws a line from left to right, marking birth at the left, and death at the right; but as one ponders while he turns a relic over and over in his hands.

> *After a hundred years*
> *Nobody knows the place, —*
> *Agony, that enacted there,*
> *Motionless as peace.*
>
> *Weeds triumphant ranged,*
> *Strangers strolled and spelled*
> *At the lone orthography*
> *Of the elder dead.*
>
> *Winds of summer fields*
> *Recollect the way, —*
> *Instinct picking up the key*
> *Dropped by memory.*

CONTENTS

� CONTENTS ꜰ

ILLUSTRATIONS

ᴛ ILLUSTRATIONS ꜰ

The LIFE *and* MIND

OF

EMILY

DICKINSON

CHAPTER I

ROULETTE, WAR and GHOSTS: 1862

ONE APRIL, PAST THE MIDDLE OF HER LIFE, EMILY DICKINSON wrote a little note, six sentences long, and got someone to post it off before she should change her mind.

Because she had never done anything so perilous before, the letter grew more and more crucial as Emily depicted it on its way to Boston, and by the time an answer got back to Amherst — as if it might be coming from God — Emily had persuaded herself that the verdict would be final.

Meanwhile to the matter-of-fact eye of a gentleman hurriedly scanning his mail in the post-office at Worcester, Massachusetts, where the letter arrived, Emily's was only one of several peculiar petitions.

For twelve years Emily had been cultivating her garden in stoic silence, her face bent to the ground. Two ghosts often came between her and her azaleas, printing thin shadows across her working hands. She weeded and crumbled sod. Although she seemed to be ignoring them while she worked, bending and rising as if she listened to

nothing but the innocent birds, much was exchanged between herself and her visitors without stirring the flowers
on their stems. The first ghost came in 1850; he stayed;
he did not excuse himself and go when, four years later,
the ghost of a man not yet dead entered the plot and interrupted a conversation about poetry between Emily and
the first comer. After a little time the two shades dwelt
together in peace, for although they had the energy of
her memory, they also had its calm. And when Emily
went into the house, they waited outside together.

Inside the house Emily had another life. The winters
were long, and in consequence the other life was often
tedious. But even inside the old brick mansion Emily kept
her soul upon the window-pane and lived, with secret
devices of many sorts, gradually becoming a spinster, a
recluse, one of the queer women of New England. Poetry
had long been self-forbidden. Why? the first ghost wanted
to know. Before he died, Emily aspired to become a poet;
she commenced the process bravely, with a light heart.
And then, abruptly, she stopped. Why? If the first ghost
asked, Emily only shook her head and went on weeding.
Amherst said that she was unfortunate, that she was proud,
that she was a Dickinson. Emily made no comment to
explain why, years before, she had renounced life and —
what was harder — had renounced writing poetry. But
while Emily was refusing to write poetry, she was nevertheless preparing to write it, and her impervious silence
only served to distil what she was thinking about. Bright
flowers spread their petals like fans, vines ran blooming,
and clusters fell in cascades, while Emily carried on a very

4

complicated inquiry which continued for years and years
— twelve years.

The lark argues with God and we call it song. Emily
wished to argue, for she had much to say, and sometimes
she wrote down what she felt, but she did not call it song.
Now and then she indulged in an epigram which budded
before her eyes, growing rhymes and a leafy charm. But
often when she hurriedly scribbled on a scrap of paper and
put the scrap into her pocket or into her copy of Shakspere
— only to take it out again in a minute, and then hide it
again, and then go about humming — usually it was only
a bare little thing nobody would call a poem. Even while
she hummed, Emily did not call it a poem. Still she jotted
the bits down and cherished them. When the temptation
to write grew too strong for her, she weakened and wrote.
But the phrases were quite without ambition; they would
never make their poetic way in the world.

And then a most unlikely event broke her coma. The
twelve years stood up on end and became the past. Emily
began to write furiously. She was thirty-two years old, she
had been quite forgetful of time. The ghosts in the garden
had made her forget and the flowers all about her had
seemed timeless. But the winters had been growing more
morbid, and half the year her garden lay remote under
the snow. Summers, while the ghosts came visiting, were
chiefly the substance of memory; spring and summer and
autumn were themselves ghosts of seasons gone, while each
year closed in nearer, as if trying to behold something
that was happening in Emily herself, swinging back, after
a period of summer exuberance, with skeleton lines and an

5

iron sky. But the winter of 1861 was beyond proportion introverted, bare, and strict; it had a terror unlike those terrors native to the mind. Emily could not cope with it, not put it down in secret; it was the Civil War.

That is, it was partly the Civil War. We shall come to the true trouble slowly. Can anyone long remain fanciful and merely introspective about a war? One morning a man is alive, by noon he dies, " his big heart shot away by a Minie ball." . . . Emily may read about it two days later in the *Springfield Republican*. One battle may stop a war, but nothing can explain why it stops or why it begins, although every pulpit in the country tries each bitter Sabbath to do so. And nobody can put the young men back where they were six months ago, behind the counter and the plough. These very obvious reflections began to clamour in Emily's head during the winter of 1861, and by spring the world was quite changed, and mildew and death hid beneath the spring surface. Let us use the usual language regarding Emily Dickinson: she was an eccentric, a recluse, an old maid, one of the many in New England. She had been living in an enclosed universe and now found the new styles of living and dying troublesome and disorderly. . . . As would be said of any such person, the war gave her something to think about.

We reconcile ourselves with the past because it is past, and nothing can be done about it. The present keeps us in another state of mind. There is the illusion of action; one's contemporaries seem to be making the present, sending it through some sort of machine, from which it emerges, confused and elaborate, in unfinished segments of days and weeks and months, bracketed. All during 1861 the Civil War kept getting bigger and bigger in design, and more people were involved in the pattern daily; the war was both visible and invisible, personal, but like an engine; it was not yet the Civil War of our text-books, where it has what is termed a happy ending. It was unsure, and as yet very unhistorical. And although it was familiar when it came — because it used old bitternesses and the principles expounded, north and south, for years, sending forth with muskets in hand all kinds of old economic anxieties — it was unreal, too, as the present is always a little unreal.

Wars are mutations; epochs pass in minutes. Barefoot armies, battles like Bull Run, and men operated on without anæsthesia are visible bits of a shocking process; war reveals what always lies beneath the surface. The place to be, undoubtedly, is at the centre. Stonewall Jackson, secure in God, even under fire, illustrates Emily's remark that Action is Redemption. Emily was idle.

And violently imaginative. An introverted person (that is, a person with a compulsion to fancy, refine, extract pain and truth and half-truth and lies, all in the experiment of thinking), unless he rushes into the front line of battle, will force himself to see more of the process than is good for him. He will endure in a double existence, consciously and unconsciously, as much as any soldier, in another scale of pain. Emily, ignorant of physical wounds, was to say he endured more.

The war broke her coma. For twelve years she had lived meagrely by a set of axiomatic ideas. The war upset the ideas by which she lived, it tilted life suddenly from a level of understanding to an oblique angle and so seesawed issues which had seemed in equilibrium that she found herself writing without leave, without premeditation, forced to put things down while they still burned. . . . She looked at the rapid lines of script late at night in her little bedroom, read them through once more, changed a word or two as one would tune a machine to top pitch by the turn of a screw — and then hid the papers.

In bed that winter, mingling battlefields with her personal grief, she must have lain stark awake for hours, numb and tired, saying the verse sentences to herself.

She had renounced life, and she supposed that she had renounced poetry.

She had renounced life; but poetry had sprung up out of the impersonal mind, having no relation to any other poetry, and no relation to Emily herself, it seemed, except to use her as a polisher and keeper of the mind. Emily was astonished — and called it poetry, at last. It seemed beyond herself; and yet, like herself, it had no education, and its subjects, its reverences, its poetics, and its rhymes were all heterodox. Still, whether of this world or not, it was by her own definition poetry and an absorbing delight — a new thing, like a child. She wrote it secretly in her chilly bedroom at night when no one could suspect her of employing the black art.

And after writing certain of these poems she had the natural desire to show them to someone.

But not to those who customarily called Emily eccentric, lest they call her poetry eccentric too. Emily protected her poetry from the jury of Amherst opinion; even if she had dared to be a poet openly, as she did not dare, she would have kept her poetry from the verdict of an Amherst that was ready for anything Emily might do — its mind made up. Finally after a long hesitation she took her power in her hand and exported it to a kindly person who loved to discover and abet persons of talent. Everything would depend upon his verdict.

And so one April Emily wrote a note and put four poems in an envelope while the spring campaign was starting on the Shenandoah. Prisoners sometimes make their escapes from jail-cells during earthquakes. And if a subtler chain holds another kind of prisoner, we remember that the bedridden, when a house catches fire, will often rise and walk out of doors, released by the extremity. Nothing had happened to Emily for years; but now she was breaking rules and superstitions right and left and burning candles in her bedroom late every night.

Self-sufficiency began to look artificial by the war's glare; her candle burned, a yellow tulip, itself lit by volcanic red. The practices of a recluse did very well for a rigid life, an almost dead life — a life of undisturbed states of mind. But when Emily began to live and poetry to be written, self-sufficiency seemed false. Except that, as Emily continued to write more poems while waiting for an answer, she grew a little indifferent to anyone's opinion. In a sense it did not matter what the stranger critic might say. In another sense it did.

But she was a little shocked at her boldness. By the time the letter got to its destination, Emily was proposing

9

to herself that she had engaged in a game of chance, a game she might play once only, since — and this made the suspense even greater — everything she had was ventured upon a single throw. She could never do anything like this again. She never did.

The assumption is that Fields, the editor of the *Atlantic*, redirected the note to Worcester. It may have gone direct. Boston is not far, and Worcester is psychologically only a stone's throw from Amherst. Opinion in Amherst agreed tacitly that Emily was that generality *wrong*, and Amherst, by majority, of course *right*. Not in one instance, but in all instances. It was perhaps necessary for Amherst to find this flaw in the proud family, after impeccable Edward. Emily was Edward Dickinson's daughter, Austin Dickinson's sister, a spinster, a town character although invisible, who said things people repeated, wore white, and made superb charlotte russe and julep, who had stopped going anywhere now, even to church. As widening circles diminish, so the more un-Amherst of her friends, who had known her longer than most, tolerated, loved, approved, and even at times would applaud. . . . The modulation of the verdict on her ways of thinking, acting, talking (in short, living), from *No* in Amherst, to *Yes* at other points on the periphery, made the difference between suffocation and breath. This fact she tried long and arduously to deny to herself, only in the end to affirm. There are limits (and Emily knew because she had tried) to a regime of complete self-sufficiency.

Letters had served as a means to breath for a long time. At fifteen she had begun these forays. While she still wore

THE

ATLANTIC MONTHLY.

A MAGAZINE OF LITERATURE, ART, AND POLITICS.

VOL. IX.—APRIL, 1862.—NO. LIV.

LETTER TO A YOUNG CONTRIBUTOR.

My dear young gentleman or young lady,—for many are the Cecil Dreemes of literature who superscribe their offered manuscripts with very masculine names in very feminine handwriting,—it seems wrong not to meet your accumulated and urgent epistles with one comprehensive reply, thus condensing many private letters into a printed one. And so large a proportion of "Atlantic" readers either might, would, could, or should be "Atlantic" contributors also, that this epistle will be sure of perusal, though Mrs. Stowe remain uncut and the Autocrat go for an hour without readers.

Far from me be the wild expectation that every author will not habitually measure the merits of a periodical by its appreciation of his or her last manuscript. I should as soon ask a young lady not to estimate the management of a ball by her own private luck in respect to partners. But it is worth while at least to point out that in the treatment of every contribution the real interests of editor and writer are absolutely the same, and any antagonism is merely traditional, like the supposed hostility between France and England, or between England and Slavery. No editor can ever afford the rejection of a good thing, and no author the publication of a bad one. The only difficulty lies in drawing the line. Were all offered manuscripts unequivocally good or bad, there would be no great trouble; it is the vast range of mediocrity which perplexes: the majority are too bad for blessing and too good for banning; so that no conceivable reason can be given for either fate, save that upon the destiny of any single one may hang that of a hundred others just like it. But whatever be the standard fixed, it is equally for the interest of all concerned that it be enforced without flinching.

Nor is there the slightest foundation for the supposed editorial prejudice against new or obscure contributors. On the contrary, every editor is always hungering and thirsting after novelties. To take the lead in bringing forward a new genius is as fascinating a privilege as that of the physician who boasted to Sir Henry Halford of having been the first man to discover the Asiatic cholera and to communicate it to the public. It is only stern

PHOTOSTAT OF THE UNSIGNED ARTICLE THAT IN-
STIGATED EMILY DICKINSON'S PRIVATE CAREER
AS A POET. CF.: "TO TAKE THE LEAD IN BRINGING
FORWARD A NEW GENIUS IS AS FASCINATING . . ."
— *Reproduced from a Photostat*

THE COMMON *with the Academy at the right*
— *From an OIL PAINTING in the possession of the* AMHERST HISTORICAL SOCIETY

sprigged muslins and went to parties, it was possible to
write witty and effusive epistles and not be considered too
literary or too unduly ambitious. All young ladies learned
to write stylish little letters, just as they learned penman-
ship with flourishes of doves' wings and how to work
needle-books and watch-cases; as they learned to play on
the piano — not well, necessarily, but pleasingly. It was
pre-nuptial employment, and it suited the basques and the
Empire gowns, the bonnets, shawls, and Mount Vernon
bandboxes, the old silver, snowy blankets, lace, and fine
linen that belonged to a girl as her trousseau and dowry.
A woman who didn't have too many children would go
on exercising herself as a letter-writer for ever. Many
spinsters kept journals; lacking the joys of wedded life,
they were permitted some of the frills and furbelows of
Victorian authorship.

Emily did not indulge in the sententious habit of the
journal, but she liked writing letters. She liked sketching
a series of epigrams in half-rhyme, down the page — the
nimbler the sentiment, the better the phrases ran. With
a pencil in her hand Emily's fancy would drive words into
delightful designs; the design was speedily past the requirements of letter-writing — Emily posted her enigmatic essays to friends, who must have found the task of
answering in kind a very considerable effort.

When it came out in speech, her family found her wit
a little too witty; father would silently leave the table
when Emily's talk escaped bounds — his displeasure
numbed her manner, but could not change its flavour. The
exercise of her powers in letters and conversation had its

checks and hurts. Emily went over everybody's head when
she had poetry to show.

> *The soul selects her own society,*
> *Then shuts the door;*

says poem XIII. She selected Thomas Wentworth Higginson.

> *I've known her from an ample nation*
> *Choose one.*

It was an ample nation. Why choose Mr. Higginson?
There was Emerson. Emerson had said of himself disguised as Osman: " . . . yet there never was a poor out-
cast, eccentric or insane man, some fool with a beard or
a mutilation or pet madness in his brain, but fled at once
to him. . . . And the madness he harboured he did not
share." She might have written to Hawthorne. Or why did
she not send Mr. Thoreau the poetry she had written in
solitude? He was a solitary; the only dogged solitary New
England had. There were such poets as Lowell and
Holmes — Emily had memorized their writing in her
Academy days. All these men came from the same strain
as Emily, and any one of them might have seen her greatness through a fancied resemblance to himself. Her choice
was erratic. The poem implies as much, and continues:

> *Then close the valves of her attention*
> *Like stone.*

Emily chose, as she describes the soul doing, and then
she closed the valves of her attention. It is perfectly literal.
But the poem has a middle stanza which is not literal,
which never happened. Emily put the stanza in only be-

cause it belonged — because although it did not happen to her, it does happen in the metaphysic of the perfect event. The middle stanza is about the fame that never arrived:

> *Unmoved, she notes the chariot's pausing*
> *At her low gate;*
> *Unmoved, an emperor is kneeling*
> *Upon her mat.*

(This poem is a great piece of writing, one of Emily Dickinson's greatest. As a poem it is quite apart from her life — it exists in itself. She wrote in order to establish the existence of things in themselves. Only in the relative world, in the hurly-burly, does it have the significance given above. We should never care to tell this story if this poem and others merely aided biography.)

In Emily's life — which we must remember is a poor thing compared with her mind, and only attached to it by a small taut thread — Mr. Higginson never did kneel and there never was an emperor. But Emily did not need fame in order to make clear what she would do with it.

After her letter went off, just beyond her reach, so that she could not snatch it back again, she experienced all the sensations of a gambler and she must have fully enjoyed them. And she perhaps wrote during the interval two poems in the gambling metaphor. One is entitled *Rouge et Noir*, and the other *Rouge Gagne*, both from roulette.

The more explicit is one of her least poems:

> *'Tis so much joy! 'tis so much joy!*
> *If I should fail, what poverty!*
> *And yet, as poor as I*
> *Have ventured all upon a throw. . . .*

This state of mind, manufactured at the expense of the innocent gentleman of beautiful letters.

She had never done anything so perilous before; her life revolved round the little note. Our story revolves round it. Since it was then and is now so important — just how peculiar did it seem to Mr. Higginson at first glance?

He describes the handwriting within, saying that it looked like a series of minute bird-tracks, and he remarks the fact that Emily put her name in pencil in a very small envelope, as if to hide her identity until the last moment; but he says nothing about the outer envelope (which is now lost) or the handwriting upon it, and so we assume that there was nothing peculiar about it. . . . There might easily have been. At times Emily felt an overwhelming aversion to putting her handwriting on the outside of a letter; it was herself, her naked hand. She disliked enlarging her script for postmasters; she disliked having her immaculate characters stamped and smudged. Her sister often addressed her letters — for the aversion became an eccentric practice in time. When Lavinia was busy, names were clipped from newspapers and box-numbers, and the city and state assembled and affixed, too, from bits of print. Did the highly peculiar hand which wrote the note and the verses address the envelope, too? Presumably Emily took all the risks this time, composing six short sentences, selecting four poems, and writing Mr. Higginson's name with care. But beneath the care the aversion remained — and the aversion returned with redoubled power after the note went its way; the rest of

Emily's life was obedient to it. All the more wonder that Emily did once venture to send four poems out into the void she mistrusted, asking in her little note to know if her verse was alive. The letter went its way stamped by one postmaster; it was restamped, sorted into a pigeon-hole, and then drawn out and torn open.

Again we ask, because the question persists, why did Emily choose Mr. Higginson? Was it entirely hit or miss? A blind gesture?

Imagine a spot of light, like that intense flake cast by a hand-mirror held at an angle with the sun, playing zigzag over the earth's surface. For a time it lingers over little places in the West, quivering while it waits, from the hand that guides it; then it swoops off to strange lands in pursuit of a person who has gone to foreign places on the map; it follows his movements from city to city. At last the light comes carefully nearer home, covering its object; it rests over a city not far distant — that is, it rests over the city of Worcester, for there the person whom it picks from the darkness has come to stay.

After ten years' absence a tall, young, slender, and already rather stooping figure walked the streets of Worcester. Emily's attention focused there in brightness.

And so, as if irresistibly attracted, her poems went to Mr. Higginson in Worcester. Whether Emily's missive went direct to Worcester or not we do not know. She had read an anonymous article entitled " A Letter to a Young Contributor " in the April *Atlantic*. How did she know that Mr. Higginson was its author? How did she know that he lived in Worcester? Did the tall young man recommend that Emily send her poems thither? Did the tall young man know the versatile Mr. Higginson?

Or was Mr. Higginson to be imagined obliviously passing the tall young man with the poems rustling and living in his hand? Whatever our conclusion here, we may rightly suppose that it was Emily's fancy in the spring of 1862 to have to do with Worcester.

Mr. Higginson wrote his mother on the day that the supplication arrived:

Worcester, *April 16, 1862*

72° in the shade — windows open.
Dear Mother,
I never saw such a spring. We have stepped from February into June.

Was Emily remarking the miracle of weather? Was she saying the same words with an overtone of special meaning: *" I never saw such a spring. We have stepped from February into June "* ? Now that hope was budding like a lilac, now that life, twisting underground in a tree's root, persuaded her of life, did Emily accept the omen?

Superstitious Emily, she invented omens when there were none. She fancied connexions between discontinuous worlds; she had a passion for turning omen into truth.

And the windows were wide. Did the sunlight shine with manifold clearness during those days when a very long winter seemed to be over? Certainly, after so many ghosts of seasons, this living June, wedging its way like a current of blue water into a drab sea, must have been quick with new life and promises, while everything hung in the balance.

"A blue and gold mistake," she called the same illusion — the cheat of enchantment — at the other curve of the oval year when she wrote *Indian Summer*, later.

It was about time for the first arbutus. About time . . .

CHAPTER II

THE BUSINESS OF BEING DICKINSON

TIME IS NOT CLOCKED IN THIS STORY; AND SO WHILE Emily's letter is going slow-motion-wise to Worcester, we will prolong the pause to find the first de Kensons in Yorkshire and come with one of the boldest of them on a little giddy ship to America — watch his sons establishing Hadley, laying out Amherst, and rearing more sons and daughters, with crops of wheat and apples and corn, fighting the Indians, the French, the English, and the Hessians, fighting each other in Shay's Rebellion, after the Revolution; then being rebuked and drawn to complaisance by the prosperity that ripens with peace, emerging finally, energetic and headstrong, in characteristic individuals — Oliver, Reuben, Squire Nat, and Samuel — and at length emerging in one, Edward, and then one, Emily; bring her to the verge of the Civil War and show her sitting in her upper room, blowing her nails to keep her hands at work, writing verses for herself — all this before Mr. Higginson opens the note.

An ancestor had a manor in Yorkshire which he or someone of the line got, so genealogists say, from William the

18

Conqueror at the time of the Conquest. His name was Walter de Kaen-Manor, later de Kenson. The name reappears in Johnne Dykonson, described as a freeholder of Kingston-upon-Hull, Yorkshire, who married a woman named Margaret Lambert in 1260 and died in 1316. There they are, Johnne and Margaret, the people of Chaucer's day. . . . What shall we imagine of them? Shall we fill the gap in what we do know with a throng of English associations?

Whan that Aprille with his shoures sote
The droghte of Marche hath perced to the rote,
And bathed every veyne in swich licour,
Of which vertu engendred is the flour . . .

This is the story of the flower of the vine. . . .

Other Dickinsons lived in Leeds, in Cambridge, in Bradley, Staffordshire. The first given names were William, Hugh, Anthoyne, Richard, Thomas; and surnames were spelled de Kensen, Dykensen, Dykonson, Dykensonne, Dicconson, Dickingson, Dickerson, Dickinson. Thomas was an alderman and afterwards mayor of Hull in 1443. The twelfth in line, Nathaniel, born in Ely in 1600, married a widow when he was thirty years old, and came to Watertown, Massachusetts, with her shortly afterwards — in 1634, to be precise.

After this leap across the ocean it is only eight generations more to Emily; but the span of salt water on wee ships, and eight lifetimes of slow toil on the raw land, served to erase England from active memory. England must be for us as it was for Emily herself — far and indistinct, but a place from which, nevertheless, she had something familiarly her own, nearer than hands and feet.

Nathaniel and his sons came to Hadley in 1659 and took up home lots. We see them in the pantomime of toil and ease: the man surrounded by his sons in the field, his daughters in the crude kitchen. These Dickinsons were a stalwart part of the first settlement which worked its way up from Hartford, led by its minister, Mr. Russell, who found the new-fangled preaching of the Hartford church intolerable; they more than assented in petitioning the "pious and godly government of Massachusetts" to allow a company to take up a plantation on the river, east and north of Northampton. Dickinson babies played with the flint arrow-heads they picked up out of the mud near the doorway. For six years Hadley prospered and cut six crops of corn; then the arrow-heads, like teeth of the dragon sown in the ploughed field, sprang from the ground fully armed. Philip, chief of the Wampanoag Indians, secured the pledge of the chief of the other tribes to exterminate the settlers and their prosperity on his Connecticut River. Indian wars lasted pretty nearly ninety years. At the outbreak, in the autumn of 1675, a double row of stakes ten feet high were driven into the ground round the town of Hadley for protection against the attack. In Hampshire County that year one hundred and forty-five white people were tomahawked.

A generation grew up during the next ninety years which believed the Indians to be children of the Devil; it was the Devil who fought them; it was the Devil who put his head in suddenly through the window behind ma's back. One of the devils fell last Saturday in the woods, only to rise again in one hundred new devils and jump on a man ploughing within sight of his own chimney-smoke. Theories of evil had their daily illustration. Sarah Henry of South Hadley killed a rattlesnake and exclaimed when she dispatched him: " I have killed the Devil." The very soil of the new continent was bad. Witches flourished within the community to prove it. No wonder gentle England vanished. Anxious, morbid people fought invisible foes, felt the air inhabited by pale shapes, found the earth treacherous. . . .

In 1684, " Philip Smith, a judge of the court, a military officer and a representative of the town of Hadley (an hypochondriac person) fancied himself under an evil hand, and suspected a woman, one of his neighbours, and languished and pined away, and was generally supposed to be bewitched to death. While he lay ill, a number of brisk lads tried an experiment upon the old woman. Having dragged her out of the house, they held her up until she was dead, laid her down, rolled her some time in the snow, and at last buried her in it and there left her, but it happened that she survived and the melancholy man died."

This was New England. Nehemiah Dickinson was appointed town measurer and laid out Hadley for its proprietors. Did Nehemiah remember the angel in the book of Revelation measuring the new city with a reed? The cultural past was wiped out — only the Bible remained. East Hadley became Amherst, named after Sir Jeffery Amherst, who fought the Indians. Sergeant Reuben Dickinson, one of Emily's ancestors, fought in the Bloody Morning Skirmish of 1757, and then vanished and brought his men safe home through the woods rather than wait for transportation. He got back to his crops in time, and the crops were good that year. But the anxiety whereby they grew did not dissipate easily. Certain savageries were essential to the fighter of Indians. These settlers were strung up between two extremes of living . . . to survive they needs must drop the English character, or, at any rate, modify it greatly. In such an effort to cope with facts the *American* was born. Reuben is remembered for the soft tread of the fine woodsman. . . .

In 1772 Amherst was listed as a town. It had had its bloodshed, a plenty; now it was to be called, with satisfaction, "peaceful, wide-streeted, river-encircled."

This, then, was Amherst; this, then, New England. A stage rattled into town; there was a tavern. Saddle-bags smelling of tart apples were slung on the bar; the men talked politics, drank, swore, spat, and went to church for fourteen hours on Sunday. Families swarmed with young.

Amherst had a representative in the legislature. His name was Nathaniel Dickinson, junior. He was the first Amherst boy to go to college; he set a precedent for education and ardour. " Many traditions of his eccentric character and earnest temper are preserved among his numerous descendants." So goes the chronicle.

Nathaniel studied law at Northampton after Harvard and went to the first three provisional congresses. One morning at church, " when the Tory minister, Parsons, compelled to read a proclamation in the pulpit by the new government with the usual formal conclusion: 'God save the Commonwealth of Massachusetts,' added: 'but I say: "God save the King."' The young impulsive Whig lawyer sprang to his feet and cried out: 'I say you are a damn rascal.'"

He was a rich man. He had two horses, two oxen, three cows, four swine, eight sheep, and one hundred dollars at interest. These possessions so awed his townsmen that he was able to establish the integrity, arrogance, ability, and eccentricity of the Amherst family. Everybody called this man "Squire Nat."

The Dickinsons had always been a little odd, even before they became ruling class. They often emerged with red hair and the Celtic temper — the Yorkshire Celts had long ago seen to that. Now their nature was to do just as they pleased; to speak outright, to care for no convention if it hindered them, and to carry themselves well in their own eyes. Captain Reuben, who was of the people, fought at Lexington and Bunker Hill, but he turned round next to join Shay's Rebellion with sixteen other hard-headed Dickinsons who wanted to know what they had been fighting for. The Rebellion failed; and Reuben in 1787 took the oath of allegiance to things as they were going to be.

Oddest of all, Oliver, called Land-od Dickinson for the tavern he kept, donated eight hundred and eighty hard-earned dollars to the parish fund and then built his fellow-townsmen a church when they wanted one in North Amherst. To cover his investment he rented the pews or sold them outright at seventy-five dollars apiece, and finally sold the very pulpit to the ministers and deacons for a good sound silver dollar. The farmers paid with cords of wood and yokes of oxen.

Small record remains of the women of the line. Each new female Dickinson had, of course, some other name except for the rather frequent instances when Dickinsons married Dickinsons. The women lent themselves to the labour of the men; and if they were frail and could not keep the cradles full, there were many others to become wives and subdivide the burden. All that we can be perfectly sure of about the women is that they bore a great many children. One of these, a little schoolgirl, by the name of Hannah Dickinson, wrote a composition on the town of Amherst in 1813. Her statements are numbered from 1 to 13. Statement No. 4 is: "Amherst contains about 250 houses and 1600 inhabitants." No. 5: "The people in Amherst are generally avaricious; they want to get as much property as they can; they are generally honest, but tight in their dealings."

The schoolgirl hand continues, unshaken in its candour, to talk of Noah Webster: "There is one person employed in writing a very large dictionary. This man is probably better acquainted with languages than anyone else in this country; he is the author of several useful school-books. There are six schools kept in Amherst about three months every winter. . . . Almost every family in this town manufactures clothing for its own use, and some manufacture for other people." No. 11: "There are two distilleries in town, one at the south part and one at the middle of the town. In these are distilled great quantities of spirituous liquor from cyder and grain." No. 13: "The buildings of the north and south parts of the town are in general not very elegant, though there are some in the middle of the town which are built in a neat and elegant style." " There are in town four lawyers," wrote little Hannah, bound to tell the truth as she saw it with the impartiality of the historian, "neither of whom is very distinguished in his profession."

One of these lawyers was Emily's grandfather, and before he died, he had somewhat altered Hannah's verdict in his favour. He altered Amherst.

It took one hundred and fifty years to make an Amherst that should in turn make itself a college. The Dickinson story is bound up with both. Elijah Dickinson gave the land on which the college stands, and Emily's grandfather, Samuel Fowler Dickinson (one of the four undistinguished lawyers), ruined himself in the struggle to build it. Over and over again he pledged what fortune he had not given outright in the first place; he kept the project going by first-hand methods; his horses and his labourers were donated to the job; he himself was donated. His wife and daughters toiled and slaved to keep the men fed, and Samuel neglected his law-office to tramp about with the workmen and to help raise the first beams of the new building.

In his youth Samuel had put his hand to the plough and then had looked back — as they phrased it then. That is to say, he had resolved to be a minister and then had interrupted his preparation to practise law. He was a good lawyer (despite Hannah) — it was declared that he " did more business than any man in Hampshire County and was the best lawyer." But he seems to have been driven by some anxiety; he had a terror of wasting time. "He would catch up his green baize bag and plunge out of the house to walk to Northampton, exclaiming: 'I can't wait to ride'"; and he never allowed himself to sleep more than four hours a night. It was a tradition that the Dickinsons loved to "live well," but it is said that Samuel limited himself to a diet of apples, cheese, coffee, and cider, which he took before the family breakfast. In *The History of Amherst College* the author remarks: "The conversion of the world often pressed heavily upon his mind."

He believed that the millennium was only about seven years away. Child of the Revolution, born in 1776 on a farm in East Amherst, the youngest of the family, he was sixth in line from that Nathaniel who first came to Hadley. In the midst of an illness in his youth, with the fear of death upon him, he had been converted to, and thereafter practised, a kind of hysterical personal religion of his own. So ardent was he that he was elected deacon of the West Parish Church at the age of twenty-one and remained in that office for forty years. With his older brother, who was an ordained minister at Holliston, he began the study of theology and planned to enter the ministry until, "finding that he needed a more active life," says one contemporary, "he turned his attention to the legal profession."

Samuel had a large family of nine children and he wanted them educated where he could keep an eye on them; and so, as a leader of the unit of town affairs, religious, educational, and local, he, with a few others, first established Amherst Academy in 1814, erected the build-

THE DICKINSON ARMS

Dickinson

THE BUSY CORNER OF TOWN AS IT LOOKED WHEN EMILY
DICKINSON WAS TEN YEARS OLD. THE HON. EDWARD DICK-
INSON'S LAW-OFFICE WAS DOWN THE BLOCK TO THE RIGHT.
— *From an* OLD PHOTOGRAPH

ing, and furnished it splendidly for the scale of the times, and then combed the state for good teachers. Soon there was talk of moving Williams College to some central location, and the Amherst fathers agitated to secure it for Amherst. Having once begun to dream of a college in Amherst, Samuel could not bear to give it up. With what energy Samuel built his dream! A list still exists of the contributions gathered in sums starting as low as one cent and running up to one thousand and five dollars (a very large sum indeed for the time), which Samuel donated. Later he was one of nine men who pledged fifteen thousand dollars between them. His neighbours agreed that he was the " highest style of man." *The History of Amherst College* gives him this credit: " With all the zeal and efforts of numerous friends and benefactors the work would often have stopped, had he not pledged his property until the money could be raised. His own means at last began to fail. His business, which was so large as to require all his time and care, suffered from his devotion to the public. He became embarrassed and at last actually poor. And in his poverty he had the additional grief of feeling that his services were forgotten, like the poor wise man in the proverb who ' by his wisdom delivered the city, yet no man remembered that same poor man.' "

Samuel's eldest son, Edward, Emily's father, came back from Yale Law School in 1823 just in time to save his father's law-office, to put it to rights, and to get it running again. Three years later he became the practising lawyer of the firm. Samuel had no longer any interest in his office, nor any interest, for that matter, in the struggle in Amherst. The college had opened its doors in 1821. The battle was won. Samuel resigned as college trustee in 1824. Three years later he served a term in the state Senate and then at last went west with his wife and left his children entrenched where he had dug so many ditches. First he was steward at Lane Theological Seminary, at Cincinnati, Ohio, and later at Western Reserve College, at Hudson, where he died in 1838. " His body," says the chronicle, " was removed by the filial piety of one of his sons and buried in the cemetery at Amherst."

This son was of course Edward. Edward had stepped into his father's shoes at the law-office, but he refused to inherit his temperament. Perhaps Edward in his frosty formalities was somewhat more Montague than Dickinson. His mother, Lucretia Montague Gunn Dickinson, had been a tall, spare woman with a witty tongue. Edward was tall, but he was not witty. He had certain memories of his mother, who was termed a natural aristocrat by her neighbours, toiling to cook for the college labourers, under Samuel's ardent spell. When Samuel went west, she accompanied him. Her eldest son, Edward, grew up to school himself in a cool, proud manner, correcting the paternal errors of impetuosity. Like a pious son, he undertook his father's projects, but in a rational fashion. He would never impoverish his family, nor would he run to the law-office, seven miles away, full of the terrific zeal of endeavour in the new morning of the world, in the new morning of the short day. There were better ways of managing such things, Edward implied by his stately pace. He was less credulous and more conservative, with all the

28

abilities of a resolute man in the second stage of an accomplishment. Fittingly enough, the old Samuel went west; the young Edward stayed under the elms in his little town. Seven years had passed and no millennium. Samuel was in error. It remained for Edward to settle himself to a more thorough program, a heftier load. Awkward as it was for his social position, Edward refused to become a hysterical Christian — in fact, to become any kind of orthodox Christian. He did not join the church until 1850, at middle age, and then as if by concession to some inward need. He laboured for the church, ran it, hired and fired its preachers; very simply, he would do anything for it but join. What was this silent young man to do, as he grew older, to exceed the power of these negative acts of his own soul? Samuel prayed over him with a full, terrified, emotional heart before he went to Ohio. But Edward allowed his father to die and to be ten years in the grave before he felt ready to come to the Lord. Nothing could hurry him. Only now we wonder if these deliberations of his have not a nervous, careful air, as if he, too, felt some of his father's anxieties trembling within him even while he resolved to keep them down.

Samuel and Edward contrasted at nearly every point. How strange, then, to hear their daughters' voices chiming so similarly in daughterly judgment upon them:

"I never saw my father laugh but once in his life," said one of Samuel's daughters.

"My father would have died for us, but he never let either of us know it. He never kissed either of us goodnight in his life," said Vinnie, Emily's sister.

29

CHAPTER III

A JEALOUS GENTLEMAN, GOD

ANY NEW ENGLAND TOWN IS OLD ENGLAND IN PLAN, a unit transplanted, the little geometry of village green, church-spire, outgoing streets, and cubes of houses set on a New World contour, and the virgin hills are still seen through a mist brought inside the mind from the old country.

But this patch of a great continent could afford to wait; while men were calling it *New England,* the words were changing flavour on their tongues. In two hundred years the climate had eroded a good deal of imported temperament, and the country was having her own way slowly, altering people by the habits she forced upon them. First, she changed the farmer, because she had him most in her power; last of all she stopped the mouth of the fanatic preacher and wrinkled the ground under a wall or a boundary, to undo the work of the lawyer who had brought over codes that dated back almost as far as Magna Charta.

"Sending a frozen ground swell under it," the country levelled the criss-cross of worm-fences and stone-piles. The national block of a continent must be studied all of a piece; the whirls and eddies of emigrants drained from one corner filled another; gold had only to be discovered in California to change the wheat crops in the fields of Massachusetts. Very soon the great wealth of the land and the conditions of getting it were to make the wars, culture, government, and national beliefs of these Americans.

Their faces would change; and their handwriting.

New England, the wide continent's advance-guard, had some of the speediest victories; she produced new temperaments from the chemicals in her soils, working in invisible ways; she disciplined here a little, and there she let loose things hitherto bound. The Puritan farmer staked her out, ruled her slanted sides, yanked her trees out by the roots, took off the top layer of stone, and made walls which never quite fell down. . . . Townspeople planted English gardens and transplanted their elms with the old pattern in mind, congratulating themselves on getting things so neatly into shape; but about the time their great-grandchildren were writing " Year of Our Lord 1800 " on their school slates, by the persistent instruction of evening sky, line of hill, wine of air, and innumerable conditions of the earth, the country was producing a Hawthorne in Salem, an Emerson in Concord, and a Thoreau near Walden.

Emily Dickinson's father, Edward, yielded as little as possible to the ragged land.

He established a formal existence in rustic Amherst, walking to and fro from the house to his law-office four times daily, dressed in black broadcloth, with a gold-headed cane in his hand, lifting his glossy beaver hat very gravely to his friends and colleagues, the good men of the town, as he met them; going to church with his flower-faced wife and his three children, sitting aloof and listening, deep creases forming between his terribly piercing large eyes. Squire, they called him; the farmers and tradespeople in their rough homespun sensed England and the solid old order they had not seen, but about which they could feel almost pious when they saw Edward.

Not even the preacher compelled this reverence for his person; it was Edward's manner. Edward seldom spoke, and everything he did was already ratified. The preacher gazed down on Edward as he preached, perhaps fearing him a little for his power, his silence, and his law-office filled with the facts of the town-life, knowing as he stood above Edward in the high pulpit of the meeting-house that he could not overawe Edward; that Edward was saturated already with the precepts of Calvin and, in a sense, could remain immune from belated admonitions, carrying his upright and blameless life before him like a shield. Nobody could find any fault with the Squire. Edward had joined the church late, just as he married — deliberately, when he got ready, in order to secure for himself a good life and formal relationships which suited him. He was a slender, sedate, handsome man, and after he married, in 1828, and settled his bride in the old mansion built by Samuel on Main Street in Amherst, he walked, very formally and elegantly dressed, the few blocks between his house and his office over Palmer's store as if he lived at the core of the world's affairs, as if he were not going into the Hampshire County Court House that afternoon to present a little wrangle about a yoke of strayed cattle, as if he did not have to listen daily to the recitals of illiterate clients about bungled boundaries and Indian land-grants. Still, law was a factual profession, less hysterical than preaching. Mortgages, wills, and codicils, with their seals, stamps, and flourishes of the pen, gave life a gravity Edward greatly enjoyed.

As formally as he might, Edward walked down the main street of the little Amherst made and sustained by people of his name since its foundation — as if America were not a young wilderness still, imperfectly pegged down here and there by townships and farms, and Amherst only a speck on the uplands of New England — ignoring the muddy streets, the people in homespun, ignoring the hardship that still prevailed and the slight lessening in respect towards himself as he grew older and times sharpened and changed. Edward's people were old stock and freeholders before they came to Massachusetts; they could trace the family line for a long time back; and if they had not always been as prosperous as they aspired to be, that did not keep them from thinking in terms of gentry, in terms of people with property. Now Edward was called Squire and acted the squire part, and he took up his little town and held it in his hand because he had the economic right to — because property was his concern now, his legal concern.

His face is terrible by reason of its fineness and its sadness in a portrait when he is still a young man. An archaic pain shines in the austere eyes; for his eyes' sake a person would be more gentle with Edward than Edward would be with him. The forehead is high, running into the hair at the sides and bringing it down curving between; the eyes seem to change at second glance and belong to an upright judge bent on ignoring the humanity of a culprit — they remain large, dark, and knowing, under eyebrows that mark a level line above them, drawn together in a prolonged moment of scrutiny. . . . The nose is long, straight, and not painfully fine, a little widened over a hidden nostril; the mouth wide — as drawn together as the eyes, with a long upper lip and a chin that asserts and verifies the righteousness of all the other features. Sensitive and stern, the head sits erect on the body; if it were not for the eyes and a certain beauty somewhere about the width of forehead, we should shudder at the face and the soul in the face and demand of it its right to gaze at the world with such accusing frigid calm.

Before she could speak, Emily Dickinson saw this face and had it designated to her as " Father."

Nothing ever becomes in life more intimate than the face of our dominant parent, seen in the blurred dream we begin in. The reconnoitring child, and above it in the firmament the parent's Face too alone for any dimension . . . beginning to learn very slowly, by an almost stupid study, the child's soul allows itself to take small trips away from that Face as centre; even late in life the Face, remembered, means something near and strange, unutterable. We cannot tell all that Edward's face meant to Emily; but even in a portrait Edward's image is potent for us; he perfectly represents, he perfectly seems to have and live, the fastidious and formal authority, the probity, the will to righteous order which was a Puritan ideal.

This person, merely by his silences, controlled the child climate.

Whatever had been ruddy and expansive in a Dickinson in Yorkshire had been scaled off now, to give Emily a father in Edward, whose heart was a little bleak and whose love was hidden — a power, not a sentiment.

This man, in his black gentleman's attire, walked high above Emily in her infancy, large because she was small, but large also because Edward willed to be large in the minds of his children. At home he eased his formality a trifle; with his children he was stern, shy, and consistent. Edward undoubtedly held up the sky over little Amherst; mother treated him as if he did; everybody looked to him; he was just — a quiet tyrant — and while she was little, Emily beheld big brother Austin always punished when he showed signs of becoming more human than Dickinson.

The gold-headed cane went and came down the main street of Amherst for nearly fifty years; at home it stood in a corner next the cape, the shawl, and the glossy beaver; the children grew and were obedient, as they could not help but be in a well-knit society where everyone obeyed the Squire.

But Edward, who had married sedately, as he did everything else, found intensities in his home he had not reckoned on.

He began to live in a network of intimacies with his daughter Emily. Austin had come first and had given him a male of the line; two daughters would add to Edward's home a demure charm. He counted, doubtless, on two flower-faced daughters if he was to have no more sons. But Nature so long put off by this man's deliberations, fashioned him a girl-child next who should have his dark red-brown hair and his pallor; who should have also a certain wildness that failed of being decorative; who should not be pretty at all, but original and strange. The likeness to Edward — to an inner Edward — was not merely physical. Austin was his father's son, but his spirits were robust; he was more of a boy than his father had been. No, in a strange way Edward saw something, hitherto unacknowledged in himself, escape into Emily and shine there, and flash at him, so that he loved Emily only as he loved himself, and a little more because she was more than he.

An extremity of temperament lurked in Emily, which her father only indicated by his silence. But in place of Edward's inarticulate soul, which could do nothing but blaze in his eyes, here was Emily, who spoke inpertinently and nimbly — and sometimes incessantly, having the gift of speech. Of course, Edward at first wanted to annex Emily to himself. As all parents try at times to use a child as an extension to their wills, Edward tried hard. Just when this proud, stiff man learned his first lesson we cannot tell — it may have been very early, and both, doubtless, forgot the small tussle promptly. It must have been a hard lesson for Edward to learn even partially, for no one had said him nay for a long time and he permitted the pious flattery that surrounded his person.

To this static man was born a child who was all games. "You know he never learned to play," said Emily in middle age. Precision in the details of life took away Edward's flexibility; he did not need it greatly, for everyone came to rely on his inability to give way. A tyrant has his uses. And the tyrant formed the child. Emily's portrait at the age of eight shows a bright, inquisitive, tender, eight-year-old face. Here is a person already acquainted with the salient objects in the only life she was ever to know. She had inspected her universe of seventy houses; her birth- and death-place, with its common — a mere pasture and frog-pond — its dame-school, its miniature American main street, as modern to contemporary eyes in 1838 as any main street now. On her way to school she had stopped to see the flash and stir that greeted the stage from Northampton to Boston when it dashed up to the tavern every morning. Inside the door at the bar was the familiar picture of Uncle " Lijah " Boltwood setting out drinks for the travellers, mixing spring bitters for town folk all the year round. She had had all the required illnesses of childhood, and Dr. Gridley had given her as much of his ration of wormwood and calomel and boneset as he contrived to give to Helen Fiske, or to Eliza Coleman. One of the memories of the children was the great fire of 1838. This little town will grow as Emily grows; and its replica will stand in heaven.

One or two legends picture Edward and Emily together in this early period.

One Sunday morning, so the story goes, Edward announced that everybody in the house was to be ready to leave for Sunday-school in ten minutes. Emily had been contriving to stay at home on various pleas and excuses. Emily vanished, as if in obedience to the decree, but could not be discovered when ten minutes had passed. An extra ten-minute search failed to find her. The family left the house and returned in two hours or so, after Sunday-school and church, to continue its search. . . . Emily was eventually found in the entrance-way of the cellar — a position technically not "in the house." Such a tendency to engage one's father in legal quibbles before putting off the pinafore boded nothing but ill.

Another legend tells the tale of the nicked plate. Twice Emily set such a plate before her father when laying the table; and twice she was reprimanded. The plate disappeared with the culprit, and she was found out behind the barn smashing the troublesome thing into a thousand bits.

Legends include only the slender face of Emily's mother, looking on, at these domestic encounters. And a long time later Emily was to say, when her idiom in hyperbole could be divined: "I never had a mother." Of the gentle person who bore Emily and gave her her first name, the only remaining epitaph now to be found (aside from Emily's own letters) is the remark that she was "oppressively tidy."[1] Father raised Emily.

In letters to brother Austin when she is a young lady, Emily sometimes suggests the true nature of the struggles at home. To Austin she could write without betrayal of the family pride; Austin was the other male in the group; although still a stripling, he would understand. After

[1] It is worth noting, nevertheless, that Austin, Emily, and Lavinia were all named Norcross family names.

Austin went to Harvard, Emily missed his ruddy disposition. With Austin gone, life was pretty sober. Emily says: " It is all pretty much ' real life ' " — and she adds under her breath: " Father's real life and mine collide sometimes but as yet escape unhurt."

As yet.

Did Edward blame Emily's excess of temperament on her flighty sex; or did he conclude that, after all, her age . . . ? In a way as quiet as his own, Emily contradicted everything he did. She was a fanatic for some as yet undisclosed end. Did she resemble her grandfather Samuel, who believed in milleniums? But there was a mockery in Emily that Samuel had not harboured, that Edward abhorred, that her mother grieved over. An excess of vitality, perhaps; an excess of sensibility.

Emily controlled the rest of Edward's life; and Edward's life controlled Emily's. With incredible greed he started while Emily was young and insouciant to preserve her for himself; the unspoken intimacy under the guise of filial and paternal love held them in a vice, making his future and hers coincide.

He was jealous of everything — his jealousy can be seen in his eyes. He was even jealous of Santa Claus. Santa Claus was papist; Edward, although " a little late in joining," clearly ranged on the side of Calvin. That innocent myth of the children's saint was banished from the Squire's house. How could Edward permit the image of a jolly, fat old gentleman to take hold of his children and divert their infant esteem from himself? Only father was allowed the role of giver of good gifts, dispenser of worldly blessings.

He was jealous of Emily's playmates — boys and girls, and later men and women, cousins from the South who flirted with Emily, and cousins from the next town who probably bored her; he was jealous of schoolmates who begged her to come visiting; he was jealous of her teachers at the Academy, and of the men of affairs he brought into his home, who liked Emily immediately, who wrote to her, and with whom she shared witticisms. He was even jealous of her books. If God had not been an adjunct to himself and he in a position to gain from the alliance, he would have been jealous, too, of God.

All through her childhood Emily had trouble with clocks. She explained the beginning of her difficulty once, saying that when she was very young and very timorous, Edward had resolved to teach her to tell the time and, calling her to his knee, snapped open his thick gold watch, which hung on the heavy chain. He explained everything just once — once was enough — showed her the hour-hand and the minute-hand and pointed out that we say it is twenty minutes to twelve when the long hand arrives inexplicably at the figure 8. As a result Emily did not learn to tell time correctly until she was fifteen. Higginson has the tale from her.

" . . . as she had been afraid to tell him that she did not understand, and also afraid to ask anyone else lest he should hear of it."

The omniscient and, as Emily once exclaimed, the redoubtable God!

As Emily neared young-ladyhood, Edward, who had had an ordinary life without suffering or terror, now began to live in a fever of daily anxiety lest she fall in love and marry. A spinster daughter was a misfortune to some men, but Edward began to require Emily to become a spinster daughter, a daughter devoted, although not demonstrative, a daughter who should cling to home and weep at the thought of leaving even for a fortnight.

Gaiety and independence suited Emily too well; gaiety she could make, and independence have, at least so she seemed to be resolving:

" I have perfect confidence in God and His promises — and yet I know not why, I feel the world has a predominant place in my affections."

With a small air of challenge, Emily spoke in those days many little sentences derived from this conclusion; Emily could glance at her father capriciously, as if to say that she could run whenever she chose, where he could not catch her and bring her back; this merry Emily might so easily slip away oblivious of her father in a romantic attachment over which he could have no control . . . her head would fly back and her hands up in the excitement she always showed with a person she adored — she would escape him, she was always escaping him.

Her mother tried, he tried, to teach her to be demure. She learned — but Emily knew that hers was not a muslin soul, as she put it. Round the edges a game of defiance darted in and out. She was good, Edward knew that she was good; the trouble was that she was gifted, too, and being gifted elevated goodness to a plane Edward found as dangerous as wickedness. She was a wild, precocious little girl, as shy as her great father, but, under the shyness, twice as bold. Edward, disguised to himself as the good parent, set about making it impossible for Emily to commit the outrage of marriage — instilling in her in innumerable ways the idea that she was too small, too fragile for life. While Emily was hopefully planting seeds in her father's garden, her father was planting in her mind the suggestion that she could never exist outside his domain. He schooled her in disdain, in a disbelief in authority beyond his own. And the lesson she tried not to learn before her twenties seems by her thirties to have been perfectly imbibed.

No one rose up to contradict father. An uncle who could run counter to him, or even a strong-minded aunt, like Emerson's Aunt Mary, might have been a great blessing. If Austin, the eldest, had set his face against his father's mode of life, or even his manner of arguing a case or wearing a hat, Emily might have seen some crack in familiar divinity before it was too late. But we find that Austin dyed his hair red, as a young man, because his own tow hair seemed un-Dickinson, and he wished to have red hair like father's. Later in life Austin wore a red wig for the same reason. And as a child it was clear that Austin would never either satisfy or withstand father. Mother, as delicate as a bird, only safe in a nest, assented to father's absolute rule, and no one came bearing tidings of great joy, declaring that the world could be employed for the purposes of living.

No one in the monarchy but Edward himself had any knowledge of the world. If he chose to say that the world was evil, his testimony must be allowed to stand, for lack

of an opponent. And he could say that the world was evil
with evidence, because he practised, weighed, explored,
and gave decisions on matters of evil. It was not hard for
him to say because he was in a humdrum and not a spiritual
or an ethical relation to his neighbours; he saw the seams
in the structure of daily life and had very little to say concerning those unreal motives, those dubious values, that
all persons of a higher nature stress so earnestly. It was
not hard for him to represent the world as evil in the contrasted haven of his home, where his wife and his daughters
lived in a beautiful innocence. Generations had said it with
less motive, although with greater fervour, before him.
Now as a just and judicious man who put his cane in the
corner with an air of finality when he came home, he said
the world was too evil for his Emily.

How can we be sure? Because we find Emily arguing
with her father in her letters. The idea had been planted
and had to be treated, solved, and clarified before she was
through with it. Whether she replied to her father in real
life beside the hearth and over the dinner-table cannot be
discovered. She answered him in her writing, where all the
elements of her mind were engaged in a deft war. It is a
monologue when pieced together: one-sided conversation
with Higginson, a cousin, or an old schoolmate — the one-
sided thinking in private of a baffled child resolved to be no
longer baffled. Did Emily know that Edward's picture of
an evil world was painted with an emotional motive?
Emily knew almost everything before the end; but formality forbade applying to father the results of her illumination.

At home, while the contest was fresh, Edward must have been even more severe than customary. Emily and sister Lavinia learned doubtless to give the subject a wide margin. Could anyone get through the bog of Edward's violent feeling on the subject? It was best to skirt the subject nimbly; Emily was tender with her father — she never surrendered to him; but always she loved and revered him. Still, any hypothesis advanced as a description of the world had to be tested. Emily's mind worked that way. She has a great reputation as a recluse, but a close study of her method makes her more curious, active, and " scientific " than, let us say, such a vigorous hysterical creature as Margaret Fuller, or such a humane liberal as Thomas Higginson. In parable form she writes Mr. Higginson that when she was a little girl she was told that in the woods she might be kidnapped by goblins or bitten by a snake or poisoned by a flower. Instead, she says, trying to put it graphically, she met only angels, who were far shyer of her than she was of them.

Of the lurking powers of darkness known only to men of the world and lawyers Edward failed to convince his little daughter, the disturber of his peace. Emily was a brave person. Bravery is a willingness in impulse to sacrifice self to some desired good. Emily was not " afraid." But Edward did succeed in his wish to keep Emily, by chaining something deeper than her mind, something with which the mind often waged a piteous war. Emily feared the world because of her father's suggestions, but her fear was not a reasoned belief, as was his. It was a reflex.

At fifteen Emily hadn't felt the little cobweb chains around her.

" Please send me a copy of that Romance you were writing at Amherst," she implored her dear A. " I am in a fever to read it. I expect it will be against my Whig feelings."

She was writing compositions and poking fun at young ladies who tried to be " poetical." And, besides, studying mental philosophy, geology, Latin, and botany. That fall she began in good earnest the little airs of a provincial young lady. " I have grown tall a good deal, and wear my golden tresses done up in a net-cap."

Music lessons at the piano, and Sunday-school singing to improve her voice, went with young-ladyhood, poised for flight.

" I expect I shall be the belle of Amherst by my seventeenth year," writes the giddy girl. " I don't doubt that I shall have perfect crowds of admirers at that age."

Such frivolity about the house can make an adult father ridiculously miserable.

As only a gushing girl can, Emily loved everything worthy of the slightest love — her teachers, each and nearly every schoolmate. . . . She adored music and worshipped the romantic poets and characters in fiction, scanning the horizon to find some sufficiently compelling person, like a person in a book, to drag her outside the magnetized area around her father. Edward would often sit and look at her, doubtless, those winter evenings of 1846, frowning at his rebel, at her vitality and avidity for life. Where would it take her? In his own mind he felt he had a right

45

to do anything he could to hobble Emily's absurdities. Across the hearth a sixth sense in Emily doubtless told her exactly the shade of severity in her father's face (for sixteen years she had been the clever prognosticator of father's feelings), but she doubtless kept her eyes to her reading, and even turned a page.

His voice would interrupt the tension.

" Put down your book, my daughter, and let us hear you perform the *Lancers Quick-step* on the piano."

Anyone could see that almost hysterically the girl was trying to escape. Her gentle mother probably hoped she would, beholding for Emily a normal life of marriage and children which would silence some of her girlish vagaries. Her father intended silencing her vagaries without the help of anything so unnecessary as a normal life.

Emily at sixteen was imploring life to end this act and begin the next one. She was anxiously waiting to see whether her whole span of years was going to be spent, as she sometimes suspected, here in this circumscribed spot, walled with the usages of this domesticity; or whether life was going to give her all the major things grown-ups enjoy — among other releases, a sense of distance from the old child-life. Emily could not get a sense of distance now; the shine of the hair sofa and the tail of the lion rug had the intolerably familiar look of things that have been seen from childhood until they are no longer objects in themselves, but a series of recalled sensations. At sixteen Emily had the fierce need to sever herself from the lion rug and her mother and father — most of all from her silly little infant self. What many people gain by going to college, or starting on a career, Emily could not gain, except by patient years of inner separation. The comfortable sitting-room must have been in the secret, its rocking-chairs and tables and rugs and its family portraits must have grimly known that Emily, for all her struggle and fluttering, would grow old and die in their presences — that there was going to be, so far as material things went, no " other life."

Other life? The swiftest way to annul father and secure another life was to substitute another man for father — marriage was the only exit over which father could have no economic control. This economic power was hidden, to be sure, vested in father's person. (To live then, as now, without money was of course impossible, but that fact, which now can be isolated and so to some extent solved by itself, was for Emily and Edward incorporated with everything else in the absolute of masculine dominion.)

Emily played the *Lancers Quick-step* dutifully. When she grew older, she might improvise soundlessly, in her upper chamber, experimenting with words. Now she might not improvise. She was playing for father, and in father's morality experiment was wicked. She played the notes as they stood, submitting. Mother and Lavinia listened. Father could not be said to be listening; he was simply waiting for Emily to finish. At the instrument Emily in her full skirt, her head covered with auburn curls, her girlish shoulders seen from behind, became for a brief time the satisfactory decorative picture of the daughter Edward had had in mind when he procreated her. He often

requested his daughter to play for him, but he seldom betrayed any undue pleasure in the repetition of her notes.
Asking her to play was Edward's way of bringing Emily
back when she escaped, absorbed in a book.

Still, it is also just possible that Edward liked music.

Emily played. Sometimes, as if at a party, Lavinia sang.
His daughters performed for an audience of one. If he
enjoyed them, he concealed the fact, and he did not, when
he heard her, enjoy Jenny Lind. . . . The long winter
evenings were unhurried. Darkness stood at the windows,
and the variations of Nature were blotted. Father and
mother, and Austin, when he was at home, listened or
merely sat in a stiff reverie. Until this generation the Dickinsons had permitted themselves no reveries. They had
worked for themselves and the Lord. They had starved
the Senses, lest they clog the Abilities.

Family portraits hung on the walls of the sitting-room
and added, while Emily played, their coloured squares of
identity to the living company. There was father in the
flesh, and father in the portrait, a double, an altered, an
omniscient image. There was mother — the mundane
mother sewing primly below, and another mother like a
grace-note flown up in the air above the breathing-level.
There were the three offspring at an arbitrary age: Austin
a four-square little boy in his Sunday attire between the
round faces and fixed gazes of two leaning little sisters.
Vinnie held a rose, and Emily a book.

What imp helped a book into Emily's hand when her
portrait was painted? Did the provincial painter, dodging
the difficulty of the hand's anatomy, employ a book to

48

cover his lack of skill? Or did he find that a book flattered
the usual common-school parent? Did Emily hold a book
while she posed? And did she covertly peep into it? Or
was it simply painted in? Emily was eight years old when
the travelling portraitist came and unscrewed his tubes and
daubed out his colours; she was old enough to know that
Edward could not abide the sight of a book in his children's hands. Not merely novels and romances — any
book except the Bible. Edward eyed a strange volume as if
it were a coiled serpent; books contained subtle poisons;
books negated paternal sway. Books brought the absorbed
look of the hungry reader to the child's face. Even for
himself and his wife Edward was careful to a fault,
perusing in the evening only such papers, Emily declared, as he was well assured "had nothing carnal in
them."

Higginson's account fits many details:

" He did not wish his children, when little, to read anything but the Bible; and when, one day, her brother
brought her home Longfellow's *Kavanagh,* he put it
secretly under the pianoforte cover, made signs to her, and
they both afterwards read it. It may have been before this,
however, that a student of her father's was amazed to find
that she and her brother had never heard of Lydia Maria
Child, then much read, and he brought *Letters from New
York,* and hid it in the great bush of old-fashioned tree-
box beside the front door. After the first book, she thought
in ecstasy, ' This, then, is a book, and there are more of
them.' "

Although she does not look at all like the tenth muse

lately sprung up in America, Emily was painted with her small symbolic book. When she was devouring forbidden pages with a beating heart in that same sitting-room a few years later (near enough the pianoforte to use the cover for a checking place), did she enjoy the fact that her prim little self at the age of eight held a book into which she might not look? Life would have been fatal and stale, like other people's lives, if Emily had not relished such situations. Father accepted the painter's job and had the portraits framed and hung. The discrepancy stood.

Books were full of lies. So Edward said. Emily found in books, nevertheless, the hope by which she lived. The hope, to put it plainly, implied a man with whom Emily might fall in love; he and nothing else would make possible the ecstasy of the poets Emily read. *Jane Eyre* said it all for her. Rochester's cigar-smoke became the odour of hope. Emily wanted without contradiction both the passion of the romantic poets and the mystic unity of religious love; at sixteen she was not yet reading Browning, but she was living for a Browning event. Love, as every literary mouthpiece of her time declared, might be single, flawless, might last a lifetime, bloom into spiritual passion, and take up its theme in heaven almost without pause for the details of death. Beyond all else, it would save one from a humdrum existence. Italy! Or anywhere but here!

Emily was imploring destiny to be saved.

Perhaps Edward told himself that he could tolerate for Emily an alliance only if it were made with a sobriety like his own. Emily Norcross of Monson had come to him with her dower loaded on oxen and he had set the tone for a life of entire rectitude by writing her just before the wedding ceremony:

" Let us prepare for a life of rational happiness. I do not expect or wish for a life of pleasure. May we be happy and useful and successful and each be an ornament in society and gain the respect and confidence of all with whom we may be connected."

This is exactly what Emily hoped to avoid.

That summer of 1846, when she was sixteen, Emily won a small and signal victory; her father consented to let her prepare to enter South Hadley, as it was called, or, more correctly, Mount Holyoke Female Seminary, where Miss Mary Lyon was training young ladies for the career of Christian gentlewoman. And then, after consenting, Edward took Emily to Boston, where she visited Bunker Hill and Mount Auburn, the Chinese Museum and Horticultural Exhibit. She heard two concerts; but in spite of her hours at the piano she seemed to like the Chinese best of all: she could hardly keep from laughing, she says, when one reformed opium-eater — Emily calls him an " amateur " — played and sang. She admired the fine brush-work of the calligraphist and she secured one of the Chinese cards to bring home to Vinnie. Heedlessly father prolonged their stay in Boston until it was too late for Emily to enter Academy for the fall term, when she should begin, as she proposed, the new program of preparing for Mount Holyoke. After she got home, she writes, with some show of self-control, that she " has made up her mind " to stay out of school until the winter term, after Thanksgiving.

Clearly father's tardy return was a great blow to Emily's career as she had designed it for herself; and every letter reiterates: " You know what it is to ' love school ' "; and: " I have been an exile from school two terms on account of my health."

But a year later Edward let Emily go to Mount Holyoke in spite of her health. Something displeased him; and he hoped, doubtless, that a year in a female seminary would straighten Emily out.

CHAPTER IV

THE 1850 VALENTINE

THE EXILE WAS A FAILURE EVEN, PROBABLY, FOR Edward.

Except that Emily came home contrite, with tears in her eyes.

Two young men had appeared on the horizon; they came home with Austin frequently and gained sometimes invitations to supper. Two young men were observed to be listening intently in the sitting-room below for Emily's little footstep on the stair. Emily was accordingly enrolled at Mount Holyoke Female Seminary.

It was not the school discipline that Emily could not abide. Miss Lyon's sternness could never distress Emily as father's distressed her. Miss Lyon's might touch the outer person. Father's touched the soul. The long arm of father's will reached all the way from Amherst through the Notch. Going nine miles away failed to annul him. It is better to be under the throne than on the periphery of power.

She had gained her point; the battle was won, and here she was, just where she wanted, now, not to be! Perverse

53

child! — so father's silence may have addressed her. Had Emily wanted to be educated? Very well, let her be, in all good earnest; drop now, Emily, this novel-reading and all this romantic talk of nature and poetry and apply yourself to your own self-improvement. If Miss Lyon is right in contending that women really have brains, prove it, my child. Pass your examinations!

And so Emily wrote: ". . . but I hope, to use my father's own words, that I shall not disgrace myself."

Miss Lyon's energetic bonnet-strings bobbed in and out of class-rooms in hourly admonition. How very like old Samuel Fowler she was! Emily had been cut off, we feel, from the tide of energy in her ancestors. Edward's isolating powers were very great. He stood too imposingly, a step behind his children, for any glimpses over his shoulder at kinsmen and kinswomen. Emily's only environment was her father — as she was now learning.

She did not feel quite herself without him.

How live if this were true? If Emily had been like her class-mates, with the hope of an open life before her, this extrovert energy, this air of great endeavour, might have served as a good beginning. It served for many of her friends; it served for her cousin Emily. Good girls graduated from the Fem. Sem — Miss Lyon's Missionary Rib Factory, as it was called — and were, according to popular account, immediately married to foreign missionaries and sent away into an even more glorious exile to live for the rest of their days far from the paternal door-step. Emily tried to be a good girl, but she was more interested in cir-

54

cuses and valentines than in missionaries. She wept a good
deal at Mount Holyoke when she was supposed to be in
her closet engaged in prayer.

Cousin Emily Norcross of Monson, who was Emily's
room-mate, inquired, we may be fairly sure, for news of
one of the nicest young men in Amherst, now a sophomore
at college, who had been in Monson for four years attending Academy. If Emily Dickinson blushed, for reply, or
if she promised teasingly that Cousin Emily should see
him at Thanksgiving time when they rode home through
the Notch, or if she simply remarked that he was Austin's
friend, not hers, we do not know. When Austin came to
drive the two girls back, he tucked them in with buffalo
robes and, being brotherly and obliging, probably answered
all their questions. It was a stormy day; the rain fell in
torrents, and the wind howled. The next evening the girls
put on their best merino wool dresses and shawls to go to a
candy-scrape party at Mrs. Deacon Mack's, where there
was " quite a company of young people."

The Amherst sophomore, who was too far away
from home to spend Thanksgiving with his own people,
doubtless pulled taffy with all his might and main
at Mrs. Mack's party, target of the eyes of the two
Emilys.

The wintry trips across the Notch, the shuttle back and
forth between Amherst and South Hadley, rebuked Emily
so thoroughly that she caught a cold and failed to shake
it off.

Another circumstance beset her seminary life. She was
not a professing Christian. The group that had not con-

55

fessed Christ was segregated, prayed over, and constantly worried. Susan L. Tolman, who writes the account of this period to a missionary graduate in Persia, remarked that in 1847 she had never seen Miss Lyon so anxious to save souls. " It seems," said Miss Tolman, in entire sympathy, " as though she could not rest."

There were feverish meetings three or four times a day. Prayer-circles having met at seven and a half in the morning, the Impenitents were brought together at four and a half every afternoon at the beginning of the term. Miss Tolman remarked: "There seemed to be solemnity at least, on everyone present. Some were in tears."

And again: " The other large class [referring to the Impenitents] were divided between Miss Scott and Susan L. Tolman. The subject was Human Depravity." After a preliminary drubbing by these teachers, the group was turned over, tired and weary, late in the evening to Miss Lyon. After her meeting with the whole group Miss Lyon requested those who felt the spirit working within them to write her notes stating their condition and to meet her later in her own room for further prayer.

The old legend that Emily rose in the morning meeting to protest against Miss Lyon's announcement that Christmas was to be observed as a day of fasting seems, in the light of this just-discovered material, to have some foundation. The only false impression given in the tale as formerly told lies in the implication that Emily was the only Impenitent in the school. She may have been, as the legend relates, the only student bold enough to rise before the terrifying austerity of Miss Lyon; but clearly, from this record, about half the school was with her in spirit.[1]

Shocking as this religious coercion seems to us now, we must allow a little for the spirit of the times before we visualize the situation. In 1843 a tremendous wave of conversion swept the country. Emily was thirteen then; she saw what happened; she knew the manners of religious zealots before she came to South Hadley. By her time at Seminary the intensity had ebbed, and the Devil was supposed to be again very busily engaged, holding many a soul against God.

Let us return to the metaphysical climate of Emily's childhood. In 1831 a little book was published, entitled *The Child's Book of the Soul.* A copy with Mary Lyon's name in it is now to be seen and studied. Most New England infants were taught to follow its reasoning. A few years before, Jonathan Edwards had characterized the unsaved child as a " little demon spitting its venom at God." The Preface of this primer is very gentle and rational, by contrast. It says: To teach a child, that he has something within him, distinct from the body; unlike it; wonderfully superior to it; and which will survive it after death, and live forever; — is the simple elementary principle of all religious instruction."

On this thesis Mary Lyon harried her pupils morning and evening.

We read in Miss Tolman's Journal of 1847:

[1] Mrs. Henry S. Jones, ex-'51, still living, of Ludlow Center, Mass., does not remember any such story concerning Emily Dickinson and Mary Lyon.

Dec 20. I have just come from Teachers Prayer Meeting. It was a good one. . . . Friday of this week is to be observed by the church as a day of fasting and prayer. Before our prayer meetings of last eve, Miss Lyon requested each teacher to learn how her circle felt about observing the day in connection with this people. Tonight at the meeting all mentioned that they found a desire in their circles for the observance of the day. We shall probably take it. Miss Lyon's meeting with the Impenitents yesterday was of interest. There is attention and some awakening but little *deep* feeling, yet. She spoke to them more solemnly than at any previous meeting. She addressed them in regard to the salvation of their own souls, of seeking it in earnest and now. I am more and more convinced of the exceeding hardness and depravity of the heart, as I see how little effect, truth presented and applied in her forcible manner has upon those who listen. . . .

Dec 22. Miss L. spoke again this A.M. on the observance of Fast Day. Said there had never probably been one observed in this family when some soul had not been born again. . . . Nearly all of the family observe tomorrow, the exceptions are few.

Dec 25. Attended to our usual business today. There has been a good degree of quiet. I have hardly heard one Merry Christmas this morning.

In the middle of the spring semester, very broken in spirit, and with the cold, which now alarmed her father, Emily was fetched home.

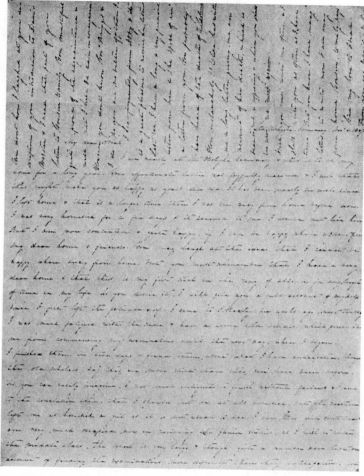

EMILY DICKINSON'S HANDWRITING AT THE AGE OF
SEVENTEEN
— *From a letter in the possession of the* WILLISTON MEMORIAL
LIBRARY *of* MOUNT HOLYOKE COLLEGE

MARY LYON, FOUNDER OF MOUNT
HOLYOKE FEMALE SEMINARY
— *From an* OLD STEEL ENGRAVING

MOUNT HOLYOKE FEMALE SEMINARY
— *Courtesy* MOUNT HOLYOKE COLLEGE *and*
MRS. WILLIAM R. HALLIDAY

On May 16 Emily wrote her dear A.: " Father wishes
to have me at home a year and he will probably send me
away again, where I know not. . . ." At this point the letter has been edited.

In such a fashion would Edward treat a recalcitrant
child. He had given her Seminary as he had given her a
dose of nasty medicine left by Dr. Gridley when she was
little, holding her nose to make her swallow — as a determined parent will when he must.

One of the young men in Amherst was Leonard
Humphrey. He came to Amherst to enter college when
Emily was twelve. He was her first friend. For years he
was merely a face at church, or at lyceum, or on the Common, before he came into the position of friend. When the
girls wandered the woods, looking for trillium and arbutus, and when cattle-show cluttered the Common, Emily
encountered, among other faces, his. He was collecting
geological specimens; Emily was making an herbarium.
But only after four years did the face seem to catch a
glance from hers and send it back. She was such a little girl
when he first came, Helen Fiske's satellite — her hair
down, her dresses up — too small for the importance of
college gazes. But one day Leonard Humphrey did behold Emily; and Emily beheld him, strange in familiarity.

In telling this story we must use the method of the artist
who cuts a wood-block for each colour in his picture. Across
Leonard Humphrey's story we will print a bolder and
clearer one. But the second story will profit by the first.

Higginson, the last " teacher," was freely told the little that we know. And on the evidence of a few sentences

59

and a few tiny known events we must design Emily's first joy and her sorrow. Young Leonard Humphrey was graduated from Amherst College in 1846, where he belonged (we learn from old records of the time), with his friend, William Howland, who was also Emily's friend, to the Alpha Delta Phi fraternity and the Alexandrian Literary Society. He registered from Weymouth, Massachusetts, the same little town where the boy Hazlitt had lived for a time during 1785 and '86, before the Reverend William Hazlitt despaired of securing the Unitarian pulpit in that place and returned to England. Humphrey had no Unitarian taint; but he was a well-read young man, fond, it seems, of moral philosophy and hair-splitting dissertations, one of which, " The Morality of States," was his commencement oration. The two young friends were equal in scholarship when they graduated together, and Mr. Howland gave the salutatory and Mr. Humphrey the valedictory address of the occasion, one hot August afternoon. The Common was full of carriages and carryalls, and a great supper was spread under the trees — joints and tarts, as they were sometimes still called, topped off with American water-melon. Faculty wives waited beside their cookery, fanning away the flies; while everyone else in town, even the store-keepers, and especially the young ladies, turned out for " commencement."

Of course Emily went to the exercises; it was the year's event. For this occasion new bonnets had been brought by stage all the way from Boston, and new muslins had been displayed for several weeks in Palmer's Store. Now the hands that had been so busy shirring and seaming lay still in their little mitts, while rows of young ladies listened to the capable orations of the young men.

Being valedictorian, Leonard Humphrey was the hero to the girlish fringes of college life where Emily dwelt. One hot twilight of that same commencement week he came to the annual party at the Deacon Mack house, where Emily poured and passed and chatted with the lions of the hour. Susan Gilbert was most likely there, and Vinnie, too, with her younger friends. The zealous men of the faculty, with their wives and sons and daughters, came, as to harvest home. It had been a hard, lean year for all of them. Emily's mother with the women of the faculty had gathered many an evening at Mrs. Hitchcock's house to patch the elbows of a good many student jackets. The instructors eked out a living on nothing at all, resolved to pull through. In place of President Heman Humphrey, described by his contemporaries as a man of a " well-balanced bilious temperament," President Hitchcock, a scientist and a liberal, held the college together. Now that Hitchcock was in the chair, endowments were rolling in — the debt which had so furrowed Edward's forehead, was being lifted, and he watched over the incoming dollars as earnestly as old Samuel had ever hoisted beams. A brighter time seemed to be coming, in the service of the Lord.

These young men for whom so much patching and mending and saving and scraping and begging and praying was being done were naturally the centre of the life of the townspeople. Their fortunes and their personalities coloured the seasons, and college was small enough for everybody to know the names and the faces of the bright young strangers who went and came according to the seasons. The nine men on the faculty strove to treat the nineteen seniors as their own sons.

As sons of a large family, they were on this occasion being fed and applauded and 'a little adored by Emily, who wore the quick inquisitive look of a young man's sister when he came from college, back home.

But the news flew about almost before Humphrey had taken the stage-coach down for Weymouth that he was coming back next fall, incredible good fortune, to become principal of the town Academy, with his brother James, who was to be his assistant.

Edward, who had so much to do with matters like these, may have brought this about. Until then the young people at the Academy, the juniors, who watched college life at the respectful distance, had had chiefly old men and maiden ladies as their preceptors. Humphrey was destined to become a very precious possession of the young folk. For in those days a young man with a flare for oratory was the equivalent of our football hero. Humphrey's pupils would toil to distinguish themselves in his eyes.

Emily's desire to toil, shared with all her friends, suffered a serious check in September when she found that the trip to Boston cost her her first term under the new teacher. All the other girls went to Academy under the new teacher and came home doubtless with glowing tales, so that Emily felt defrauded as she listened to the plans for a new literary society and a new school paper. How she ached to be in the first row, and to be the brightest pupil! Instead, at father's signification, she was learning to make good digestible bread, at home.

But after Thanksgiving she was permitted to enroll, and there she studied with all her wits and senses, algebra, Euclid, and ecclesiastical history. She read Watts, *On the Mind*. She toiled. Her pleasure had to be cross-grained and hidden, and she quickly found that she must not be too rapturous at home, nor too devout even at school. After mentioning Leonard Humphrey once, she leaves him out — or an editor has left him out — but she describes in a letter to her dear A. every detail of the appearance of a Miss Woodbridge, and concludes:

" Forgive my glowing description, for you know I am always in love with my teachers."

What must have happened that winter, punctuated by the study of ecclesiastical history and algebra, comes out in little hints in the poetry and letters for thirty years. Humphrey was an exceptional person to have been given one of the best academies in New England to rule over at the age of twenty-two. He seems to have been both devout and brilliant; he seems, as well, to have been unusually alive. Young and old alike acknowledged this. At the Literary Society, which met weekly, this young man, who was only six years older than Miss E. Dickinson (who had just put up her hair in a net cap, and who lived on elation from morning to night), focused the group. He could quote poetry from memory long after the poetry books gave out, doubtless; and if he was like the other young men of his time he read Emerson and *Jane Eyre* without turning a hair. Later it was said of him in the stilted language of the public prints:

" Possessing a mind exact and logical, yet tasteful and elegant, his productions were always rich in delight and beautiful in form."

From which we conclude that there were writings of some sort — " productions." Emily merely remarked: " We now have a fine school."

After a year as principal of the Academy, Leonard Humphrey went away to enter Andover Theological Seminary, the stronghold of Puritan orthodoxy, resolved to become a minister. His was the only, the universal choice of gifted youth in New England. Those who cared for books and the things of the spirit were perforce ministers. In a year he returned, seeming to have abandoned his choice. Did he find his choice a misfit; or did he return to his college to teach for lack of funds? Or did he come back in the fall of 1848 when he heard that Emily was no longer attending Mount Holyoke Seminary, because he was already in love with Emily, his pupil? Back he came, at any rate, whatever his reason.

Evidently Emily was not in love. How trembling and delicate and ideal an attachment this had become is difficult now to tell. But during this friendship Emily began to live as a poet. The young mind dreamed deliriously of its powers; it had a teacher, a trainer, a friend, an audience.

And Emily was at home again, where she knew how to map and control her privacy and her dreams. To be sure, she could see Leonard Humphrey less often now; he was tutor at college and had boys for pupils now; but she could know what was happening, and Austin and Vinnie saw everyone and knew everything of daily moment that went on. Father permitted Emily to enter the harmless Academy. She was like a bird with a twine on its leg, of course — at any moment in danger of being jerked home. Nevertheless, Emily flourished. She, too, felt tremendously alive. She was writing the humorous column for *Forest Leaves,* the school paper; and there was another Literary Society, where the members imitated and parodied poems by Holmes and Lowell and Moderwell. And there were parties. Noah Webster's granddaughter (the Mrs. Gordon L. Ford of the *Letters*) gave P. O. M. meetings, which turned out to be Poetry of Motion meetings when translated into action — that is to say, dancing, real dancing, forbidden by most of the autocratic fathers of the town. It was a gay winter. Austin with his class-mates came to dance with the younger girls.

Gaiety Emily could make and independence have. Or at least she seemed to be still resolving.

In January 1850 Emily wrote a long and wordy letter to her old school friend, Mrs. Strong (dear A.), which begins with a little dissertation on God. . . . God, it seems, is sitting right near, He knows everything that she does, He watches her while she writes; she dares not look at Him, she says, for fear she will die. The letter mentions that she is writing while all the folks are away for the afternoon and she is alone in the house. On and on go the sentences — one impulse is to confide a secret; some other cautions that it dares not, with God sitting right there. But a little slips out:

" If you were here I would tell you something — several somethings — which have happened since you went away."

And the letter concludes, as is inevitable under the circumstances:

" Your very sincere and *wicked* friend. . . ."

You cannot know all about what Emily considered her wickedness, perhaps; but it is clear from the letters of the period that something very exciting was going on. Mrs. Ford, years later, remembered the stir and flutter of the spring of 1850 and attempted to put down her memories for Mrs. Todd. That she was inaccurate is indicated by the fact that she says the young people discussed the latest issue of the *Atlantic Monthly* in 1850, seven years before it was founded. Still, her memories are worth something, and when she recalls that Emily's poetic quips from the humorous column of *Forest Leaves*, the Academy paper, were read and admired and " One bit was stolen by a roguish editor for the College paper where her touch was instantly recognized," we grow curious to know what Emily was writing then, twelve years before her note to Mr. Higginson.

Curiosity fades into mystification with the " production " before us. And the circumstances which surround its writing — its place in *Forest Leaves*, and the larceny of the college editor — make it more of a puzzle than ever.

The editor says, by way of introduction: [1]

[1] From the *Indicator:* A Literary Periodical; February 1850.

﹁EMILY DICKINSON﹂

Editor's Corner

But St. Valentine's Day, although as rough as the blasts of Siberia, brings fun and frolic enough along with it and this year brought *quantum sufficit* to us. Many a chary epistle did we receive, and many did we send — but *one, such* an one! I wish I knew who the author is. I think she must have some spell, by which she quickens the imagination, and causes the high blood " run frolic through the veins." Yes, the author, of such a gew gaw — such a frenzybuilt edifice — I should like to know and talk with, for I don't believe her mouth has any corners, perhaps " like a rose leaf torn! "

But I'll not keep you in the door way longer, but enter the temple, and decipher the thought engraved there.

ATTENTION

Valentine Eve

' Magnum Bonum,' ' harum scarum' zounds et zounds, et war alarum, man reformam, life perfectum, mundum changum, all things flarum?

Sir, I desire an interview; meet me at sunrise, or sunset, or the new moon — the place is immaterial. In gold, or in purple, or sackcloth — I look not upon the *raiment*. With sword, or with pen or with plough — the weapons are less than the *wielder*. In coach, or in wagon or walking, the *equipage*, far from the *man*. With soul, or spirit, or body, they are all alike to me. With host or alone, in sunshine or storm, in heaven or earth, *some* how or no how — I propose sir, to see you.

And not to *see* merely, but a chat sir, or a tete-a-tete, a confab, a mingling of opposite minds is what I propose to have. I feel sir that we shall agree. We will be David and Jonathan, or Damon and Pythias, or what is better than either, the United States of America. We will talk over what we have learned in our geographies, and listened to from the pulpit, the press and the Sabbath School.

This is strong language, sir, but none the less true. So hurrah for North Carolina, since we are on this point.

Our friendship sir, shall endure till sun and moon shall wane no more, till stars shall set, and victims rise to grace the final sacrifice. We'll be instant, in season, out of season, minister, take care of, cherish, sooth, watch, wait, doubt, refrain, reform, elevate, instruct. All choice spirits however distant are ours, ours theirs; there is a thrill of sympathy — a circulation of mutuality — cognationem inter nos! I am Judith the heroine of Apocrypha, and you the orator of Ephesus.

That's what they call a metaphor in our country. Don't be afraid of it sir, it won't bite! If it was my *Carlo* [1] now! The Dog is the noblest work of Art, sir. I may safely say the noblest — his mistress' rights he doth defend — although it bring him to his end — although to death it doth him send!

But the world is sleeping in ignorance and error, sir, and we must be crowing-cocks, and singing-larks, and a rising sun to awake her; or else we'll pull society up to the roots, and plant it in a different place. We'll build

[1] Named for the dog, Carlo, in *Cranford?*

Alms houses and transcendental State prisons, and scaffolds — we will blow out the sun and the moon, and encourage invention. Alpha shall kiss Omega — we will ride up the hill of glory — Hallelujah, all hail!

                                    Yours, truly,

                                         C.

[Editor's Comment]

Now this is, after all a very ingenious affair. If it is not *true*, it is at any rate philosophical. It displays clearly an inductive faith; a kind of analytic spirit, identifying each independent truth, and fixing it as a primary essence, which the author had known, and felt. There is no desiccation of humor, no magnetic sleep of intellect, no spasmodic movement of thought. The author, however, has not (it is plain to see) told the half of her feelings! It were impossible! To work out such subtle ideas into form by means of words, is like the effort to " forge silver flowers with the large forehammer of the blacksmith "   QED.

It is significant of these young people of Emily's group, and Humphrey's, that they choose to name their magazine after Leigh Hunt's London weekly of 1819.

But for Mrs. Ford's stray assertion and the reference to Carlo, the name of Emily's dog, so often mentioned in her letters, no one now would seek out or identify this piece of writing as Emily's. What is the point of this schoolgirlish epistle? The roguish editor — and who was he? — remarks: " The author has not told half her feelings."

Paraphrased, the passage is giddy with innuendo.

Sir: I desire an interview; meet me at sunrise, or sunset, or the new moon . . . with soul or spirit or body — they are alike to me. Somehow, or nohow, I propose, sir, to see you. And not to see you merely, but to chat. I feel, sir, that we shall agree. We will be David and Jonathan, or Damon and Pythias. Our friendship, sir, shall endure till sun and moon shall wane no more. . . . All choice spirits, however distant, are ours, ours theirs. . . . I am Judith, the heroine of Apocrypha, and you the orator of Ephesus. . . . We'll pull society up by the roots[1] and plant it in a different place. We'll build alms houses and transcendental state prisons. . . .

Indeed, this is very serious; and it was this that was going on, with such concealed elation!

How came this in *Forest Leaves*? How came it in the *Indicator*? Only a vanished situation could tell us that.

The situation is not so simple as it might seem. For whether written to him or not, the man Emily is said to have later loved and renounced, who is commonly supposed to have first met and fallen in love with Emily in Philadelphia, was one of the five editors of the Indicator!

Emily was twenty that spring. In May she wrote:

" When I am not at work, I sit by the side of mother, provide for her little wants, and try to cheer and encourage her. I ought to be glad and grateful I *can* do anything now but I do feel so very lonely. . . . At noon . . . I heard a well-known rap, and a friend I love *so* dearly came and asked me to ride in the woods . . . and I wanted to

---

[1] Obviously Emily wrote " by the roots."

exceedingly. I told him I could not go, and he said he was disappointed, he wanted me very much. Then the tears came into my eyes, though I tried to choke them back, and he said I *could* and *should* go, and it seemed to me unjust. Oh, I struggled with great temptation, and it cost me much of denial; but I think in the end I conquered,—not a glorious victory . . . where triumph would come of itself, faintest music, weary soldiers, nor a waving flag, nor a long, loud shout. . . ."

That fall, in the middle of November, after the crucial May, Leonard Humphrey went home to Weymouth.

Twenty-four years later, two months after the death of her father, Emily wrote:

" My earliest friend wrote me the week before he died, ' If I live, I will go to Amherst; if I die, I certainly will.' "

Whatever made young Humphrey talk so serenely of death was part of the manner of his dying. He was not yet twenty-six years old, and he was in some kind of profound and yet lucid despair. After going home he wrote, a week before he died, telling Emily that he was about to die. Is this not extraordinary? Telling her, too, that she should surely become a poet. Why such compact prophecy? The illumination of a peculiar state of mind?

And the effect of these two statements is found everywhere in Emily's memory. Emily's friend, like Tennyson's, and Milton's, and Shakspere's—like the numerous " friends " who haunt the pages of biography—bequeathed some special life to the poet, in the act of dying. Humphrey is involved in some very vital way with Emily's existence as a poet. The *vita nuova* began in the mourner. Humphrey played a perilous part; he taught *immortality*.

But was it Humphrey who begged her to go for a ride in the spring woods? We cannot be sure. I think not.[1] She always refers to him as " friend," a term used interchangeably with lover, even for a married friend's husband. The term is the gentle understatement, perhaps first employed with father in saying: " He is my *friend*, we are friends, father. There is no harm in being *friends*, is there? "

Saying Emily *could* and *should* go sounds like the language of the final sentence, threatening to be in Amherst one way or another in spite of Squire Dickinson. Still, there were several determined young men in Amherst. Leonard Humphrey may have been only a spectator, a witness to Emily's regard for another person.

But clearly somebody almost broke the enchantment.

On November 30, 1850 Humphrey was dead. He fell on the street of his town with congestion of the brain. Arthur Hallam died of the same ruptured blood-vessel as he lay asleep one afternoon in Vienna. Humphrey was like Hallam in life and death and influence. And, like the young Tennyson, Emily was to keep silence for ten years, for a sign — although she took no vow.

" But when the unreconciled spirit has nothing left but God, that spirit is lone indeed," says Emily, amazed at Death's brutality.

---

[1] *Emily Dickinson: The Human Background of Her Poetry*, by Josephine Pollitt, states (p. 68) that Humphrey was engaged to be married to some young woman in Amherst. It is evident that Emily was not this person.

CHAPTER V

LEGEND AND A LIVING GIRL

When Sappho was a living girl,
And Beatrice [1] *wore*
The gown that Dante deified.
Facts, centuries before.

FROM 1848 ON, LEGEND WRAPS THIS STORY IN A thick skein, spun around and over, in and out; it is even hard to say whether or not incidents accepted and printed as literal are not also one kind of legend woven over the gaps in another. Legend grows overnight in New England, like the lush grass in soggy spring, like ghost flowers in the dark woods, and vermilion parasites from rotting tree-stumps of half-cleared land that has fallen back to brier and small timber again. Legend pushes up around any New Englander who does not first speak for himself. It is hysterical country. The Puritans had a remarkable aptitude for the truths of character, but large sections of the self had to remain unconscious or suffer a keen mortification. Legend resulted — an attempt to explain troublesome behaviour.

[1] Intended to be pronounced with four syllables, not three.

73

Emily spoke for herself, but too late. The letters and the poems show the actual Emily Dickinson, about whom legend was busy long before she surrendered to death. The poems have an edge as shining sharp as a scythe — they alone can cut the tangle of undergrowth. This story must use the knife of the poems against the accumulations of falsification. If you let the undergrowth stand, it will choke the flowers of poetry, for most of the legends make Emily's poetry obscure. Whereas if you begin for the sake of the poetry to clear the land, the obscurity will fall down like the thistle that grows in neglect.

There are local legends and literary legends, both vulgar. Most critical writing about Emily's poetry in reference to her life has accepted the vulgar legend, just as Amherst over its tea-cups while Emily was still alive helped the stupid legends to grow. For the nurse-maids of Amherst Emily was the Woman in White, who had a red carpet spread down before her when she ventured into the garden. The carpet is derived from a red blanket Emily used to sit on, dewy evenings. One red blanket accounts for many a legendary crazy quilt.

Children for a generation were frightened into obedience by the mere utterance of her name. Nurse-maids made her into a contemporary witch for their convenience, and critics of literature have been not unlike the nurse-maids in their use of the legend.

It was legend adjusted to current taste that helped to sell Emily's poems after she died; the poems found a momentum not their own; they reached some readers on

AMHERST ACADEMY (AT THE LEFT) IN 1847
— *From an* OLD PHOTOGRAPH

FRATERNITY ROW IN 1850. THE ALPHA DELTA PHI FRATERNITY OCCUPIED ROOMS ON THE SECOND FLOOR, ELEVENTH AND TWELFTH WINDOWS FROM THE RIGHT

— *From an* OLD PHOTOGRAPH

the interest of a quaint news-story and gave Emily a fame
of which in anticipation she could write:

> *Unmoved, she notes the chariot's pausing*
> *At her low gate;*
> *Unmoved, an emperor is kneeling*
> *Upon her mat.*

We thank the legend for helping the poems and the
person out of oblivion.

But the legendary half-light has lasted too long; and
now we have found the poems superior to the legend. As
commonly visualized, Emily Dickinson's life is little more
than fifty-six years of sweet fastidious nothingness, in the
midst of which the poems explode without a fuse. Only
one cause is commonly assigned — her virtuous renunciation of a married man, to whom she remained wedded in
spirit for the rest of her life. In a study of genius one cause
is as good as another; it gives the baffled mind something
to fiddle with, but the truth is that there is no cause, there
is only the intricacy of being. We must try to touch the
veritable Emily; and her acts and the events that befell
her are a part of and have to do with her genius, not as
cause, but as material.

If we deduct the known taste of the period from the
total legend, we shall get something like the life itself.
First we remove the Victorian varnish; underneath is the
grain of the wood. Like all poets' lives, Emily's was
rubbed up for the needs of the sovereign reader — his
easiest least vital need, his floating emotion. Queen Victoria stamped a standard of conduct for poets as well as
for sentimental scrub-women, and the period, when it

found that Emily Dickinson had humanly loved and renounced and remained true, embroidered the theme with
the silk floss from Victoria's sewing-basket.

But Emily's poetry sprang from an earlier period — a
period nobody in 1890 wished to remember. Life during
and just after the Civil War, while the industrial boom in
the North was not yet seriously debauching the remains of
the aristocratic tradition, had its odd moments — 1890
could just remember. By 1890 Edgar Allan Poe was a
genius. Middle-class taste in Poe's time had been as bad,
although not so rampant, as the same taste later that certified him. Poe (although he boasted an aristocratic start)
was not immune from all the chromos that hung in small
sitting-rooms, east and west — chromos composed of the
graveyard, the weeping willow-tree upon which the
equally weeping maiden reclined by moonlight, murmur-
ing, according to caption: " And Art Thou Gone Yes Thou
Art Gone Alas." From such surroundings Poe derived
many an impulse and when *Annabel Lee* and *Ulalume* and
The Raven worked the familiar sentiments up into more
elaborate art-forms, an audience was conditioned and able
to take the next step.

There are three excellent occasions for romantic mischief in the telling of Emily's life, but the strange thing
is that only one of them has been used for the purposes of
legend. Emily herself took advantage of none of the
themes. Edward is an excellent occasion, in the role of the
Unfeeling Father — which happens to be the sub-title of
the everlasting popular best seller of the period, called
Alonzo and Melissa. Humphrey's early death is a second

76

excellent occasion; it suits the theme of the chromo. Emily grieved over Humphrey, and she must have felt the distressing parallel between her real grief and the conventions of grief, cheap and lurid all around her — discovering that irony of living in seeing the resemblance between the plain truth and its cheap and lurid copy. Emily grieved, but she did not have time for attitudinizing.

These two first occasions for mischief are all but obliterated in Madame Bianchi's *Life* — a twenty-five-thousand-word sketch which she published with the revised edition of the *Letters* in 1924. Not so the third. Emily, speaking when she has natural cause to speak in her letters, informs us of her father's and Humphrey's place in the graph of her life. Her poems and the workings of her affections confirm their stated and implied importance. But never are they given the slightest indulgent significance by Emily, who tells her own story gravely, aware of its unlaboured drama. " My life has been too simple and stern to embarrass any. ' Seen of angels,' scarcely my responsibility." She did not romanticize, as she might easily have done, at least for a short time after 1850.

The period before Emily's poetry, when she was still a young romantic girl, was drugged with notions that resemble Poe almost more than any period should resemble a poet to his credit. But when the third occasion arose for self-dramatization, Emily, although she knew Poe and in a letter writes a sentence about a " phantom niche " which is suggested by Poe's Helen lyric, showed no inclination to relax into a convention of grief. She everywhere avoided such convention as falsification. It was her life's avoidance.

77

Not so her niece and biographer.

The story of Humphrey has been almost wholly erased. Only those who own a copy of the rare 1894 edition of the *Letters* have any opportunity to follow the slender sequence of events. It is hard to understand why Madame Bianchi has been at such pains to obliterate Leonard Humphrey. At first one wonders if he was more important in Emily's life than even her phrases indicate; but on second thought it seems more likely that Humphrey's story is involved with another's. This would account for Madame Bianchi's avoidance of him and still leave Emily's testimony intact.

Madame Bianchi makes no mention whatsoever of Humphrey in her account of Emily's school-days, omits the few letters that awaken an interest in him, and only once in the 1924 *Life and Letters* lets his name appear, and then only as casually mentioned.

Emily contradicts her:

January 2, 1851

. . . it was once my study hour — my master has gone to rest, and the open leaf of the book, and the scholar at school *alone*, make the tears come, and I cannot brush them away; I would not if I could, for they are the only tribute I can pay the departed Humphrey . . . .

You have stood by the grave before; I have walked there sweet summer evenings and read the names on the stones . . . but I never have laid my friends there, and forgot that they too must die; this is my first affliction, and indeed 'tis hard to bear it. To those bereaved so often that home is no more here, and whose communion with friends is had only in prayers, there must be much to hope for, but when the un-reconciled spirit has nothing left but God, that spirit is lone indeed. . . . I will try not to say any more — my rebellious thoughts are many, and the friend I love and trust in has much *now* to forgive.

Either Madame Bianchi has not pondered very deeply the mesh of Emily's life and feelings, or she has deliberately wished to elide Humphrey's importance.

In her Introductory to her edition of the *Letters* Mrs. Todd said:

" It was with something almost like dread that I approached the task of arranging these letters, lest the deep revelations of a peculiarly shy inner life might so pervade them that in true loyalty to their writer none could be publicly used. But with few exceptions they have been read and prepared with entire relief from that feeling, and with unshrinking pleasure; the sanctities were not invaded."

Such is the attitude of Emily's first editor.[1]

But Madame Bianchi's narrative contains many discrepancies which make us wonder how much patching has gone into the writing of her unconvincing *Life*. Some of these errors seem to be carelessness. No one could miss the significance of the little outcries of 1851 if he cared to ponder the letters that contain them. Carelessness will account for the mistakes in the dates of Emily's birth and

---

[1] Mrs. Todd is said to have said: " I told as much of Emily's life as the family wished me to tell." The reason for caution in 1894 will be clear later.

her death; in the wrong middle name ascribed to her, even possibly for the "Winter and Spring" of 1853 in Washington and Philadelphia, which turn out to have been really some time after March and before June 1854. But we are constantly meeting with imperfect fact which does not seem to be mere carelessness. What, for instance, shall we do with the incident given on page 47 of her book, in the chapter entitled *The End of Peace*?

"But only a few days later Sue looked up from her sewing to see Lavinia, pallid and breathless from running, who grasped her wrist with hurrying hand, urging: ' Sue, come! That man is here! — Father and Mother are away, and I am afraid Emily will go away with him! ' "

The implication is that sister Sue, Austin's wife, was next door, that Vinnie ran through the hedge to get her. All this in 1854. Austin was not married, the Italian villa next door was not built, and Sue was not sewing next door in Amherst until 1856.

In later editions of her book Madame Bianchi has attempted an explanation of this very obvious difficulty; but it remains unexplained.

It is clear, then, that we must class parts of Madame Bianchi's *Life* with the unauthentic material relating to Emily's life. It will have to be inspected with care and rejected if it does not harmonize with the letters and with other material.

But to return to the story of Leonard Humphrey, whose death had such a lasting effect on Emily's mind.

A notice in the *Hampshire and Franklin Express* tells us a very little more of his personality:

"Death of Tutor Humphrey! — Leonard Humphrey, A. M., Tutor in Amherst College, died very suddenly in North Weymouth, at the residence of his father on Saturday last, after an illness of ten hours, in the 27th year of his age. He left town on Wednesday of last week, in his usual health, but was taken on Saturday with a severe pain in his head and died in a few hours of congestion of the brain.

"Thus suddenly has passed away one in the midst of life and in the fullness of hope. Mr. Humphrey was a young man of great promise, highly cultivated and of fair attainments. As a Scholar, few at his age stand higher in the number and value of their acquirements.

"He was patient, accurate and thorough in his investigations. Possessing a mind exact and logical, yet tasteful and elegant, his productions were always rich in thought and beautiful in form. Few possessed the power of more deeply interesting by their exhibition of truth than the deceased.

"But it was not as a Scholar, merely, that he won others to himself. There was a delightful combination of qualities in his character that made him beloved by all who intimately knew him. To those who met him in the social relations of life it need not be said that there was a delicacy and refinement of perception visible in all his intercourse with others, an easy, natural regard to their wants and wishes. Religion had shed, also over all his natural endowments her chastening influence. . . ."

The morbid little outcries in the letters of 1851 and the years following were first severely winnowed by the

editors in 1894. Everything that remained was discarded
by the second editor in 1924. But Emily escapes distortion,
in the so-called enigmatic fragments left to speak for her.
Her girlish letters of grief for her dead teacher are the
melancholy musings of any young person of her time;
but the girlish melancholy deepens with the years, showing how great the shock had been from the first. All her
life long, Leonard Humphrey's death was one of the facts
she found too stubborn to understand. It happens that her
testimony to Mr. Higginson, which is the most forthright
of all her remarks about herself, could not have been
omitted very well by the editors in either edition, because
Mr. Higginson had already published Emily's letters,
evidently to the annoyance of some of her family, in the
Atlantic, in 1891, and by 1909 republished them in *Carlyle's Laugh.*

We must be wary of legend; it contributes very little
and is often false or obtuse. But even legend will serve,
where Madame Bianchi's narrative will not, to suggest
possibilities, to supplement the few facts of which we are
sure. One legend, still extant in Amherst, says that Emily
became a recluse on a vow taken in a moment of outraged
pride. In the garden one evening Emily and a young man
with her turned suddenly to see Emily's father standing
over them with a lantern, ordering her back into the house.
Emily is said to have replied: "Very well, father, if you
do not trust me out of your sight, I will never leave your
garden again."

Is the legend true? Was the young man Humphrey, or
was it some other young man, or was it simply the instru-

ment of a contest between father and daughter? *On prin-ciple.* Is the legend only a folk-way of telling what all the neighbours knew to be true — that Edward was devoured by jealousy so acute for any prospective son-in-law that he would use his prerogative as a father to get him off the premises and banish even the possibility of others?

We cannot tell. But after Humphrey's death the relent-less situation slowly warped and hemmed in any way of escape. Humphrey was dead; with him certain ways of living seemed to die. In reality they never died. It was not just his personal loss — no loss of a friend is ever merely personal. People stand for things in our hearts, if we love them. We have seen what Humphrey stood for. Remarkable young Humphrey, who had sensed his im-pending death as well as Emily's destiny! No one who ever came near her again had such a luminous power of observation and prophecy. And, dying, he seemed to be-queath his great power of knowing to Emily; from then on she is inhabited by a spirit like his — an added insight that came to wed hers, because hers drew it down.

"If I live, I will go to Amherst; if I die, I certainly will." That threat extended his presence; there are many poems that mention his ghost. And Emily working in her garden in stoic silence had his words to think about. Emily lived with the accusation of her father's eyes upon her, she lived in the consciousness of guilt, because she carried Humphrey with her in her mind and was still cruelly be-traying her father in the privacy of her mind. Father claimed her fiercely now, although tacitly, brooding doubt-less over Emily's long and stubborn infidelity, which was now invisible, but which at times he must have suspected in despair. It is difficult to be jealous of the dead or to forbid them to enter your house; they seem to have rights for having forgone the flesh. Humphrey did come to Amherst just as he had said he would.

This attachment had been a deeper violence to Edward's egotism than mere customary love and marriage would have been. Humphrey had taken a position none but father was supposed to occupy . . . he had used authority in matters of poetry — audaciously requiring Emily to be a poet — that must have irritated Emily's father. The result was that father indicated to Emily that he would prefer her to leave poetry alone.

The beloved teacher became, then, an alternative for a lover. And the beloved teacher usurped a father's position when it extended past the scope of fatherhood. Emily's creative self had found a symbol that should serve against a father's too intimate love. Father, alas, stood barren in crass authority. Twelve years after Humphrey's death, when Emily was still trying to establish a relationship with a beloved teacher, by enlisting Higginson against the authority of heaven, she writes, and the pattern is still plain, and exactly what it had always been.

With Humphrey's death, when she was just turned twenty, Emily was ready to become a recluse. Life sickened her. In so far as she could forget and resist Humphrey, she could regain her childhood's peace. She saw bitterly enough that she might not even be a poet openly now without adding to the score of crimes already counted against her. To be a poet in secret seemed cowardly —

impossible. Death had chilled her. To Austin she wrote: "If I hadn't been afraid that you would 'poke fun' at my feelings, I had written a sincere letter, but since 'the world is hollow and dollie's stuffed with sawdust,' I really do not think we had better expose our feelings. . . ."

A melancholy settled over the household, emanating from Emily. The graveyard and the curious phenomena of death had fastened on her mind. It was reality, not a chromo. She was herself in a sort of grave at home, or so it seemed, after a girlhood of expecting the abundant life promised in the Gospels. All her symbols, all her obsessions, start from this year of hallucinations, 1850. Death had italicized everything, life itself. For twelve years Emily was a poet, practising in the quiet of her mind, and yet she wrote hardly a word of poetry. In the passage describing the invitation to ride in the spring woods, she prefigures in prose several poems later to be written and almost literally sketches *To fight aloud is very brave.* Death, God, and the Soul have begun to rehearse for the allegorical roles they later enact.

Knowing now the expanding pain of the rack, Emily tried numbly, no doubt, to atone to her father for the hurt she had given. He saw his daughter coming nearer him, her orbit returning, to maintain again the relationship so strong in her childhood. Her father did not know that Emily failed to tell the time all during her childhood because she saw his face between herself and the clock whenever she looked at it. She turned the child countenance towards him again, as a careful planet keeps the correct side of itself towards a star.

85

Hungry and stricken, Emily saw that any life except one of renunciation on her part would be painful to her father. She turned inward on herself, not from obedience, we suppose, but from love, wishing whatever part of herself might still be offensive to become as small as possible, unnoticed enough to go unmolested.

But, having renounced life, Emily had an experience in store for her which she spends the rest of her life trying to articulate. . . . She began to live with trebled intensity. In the bright spot of her imagination the realities Humphrey's death and her father's life had forbidden came back enlarged a hundredfold. Having experienced this, Emily had a philosophy. At first she calls it *consolation upside-down,* and she may have at times recognized its resemblance to Mr. Emerson's doctrine of compensation. It is the core of her gospel; it is the good news of spiritual poverty and deprivation; it is the great Puritan metaphysic, born from a dual view of life — anti-rational, anti-material, and yet so axiomatic when expounded that it sounds like a law of science, and bears none of the hallmarks of the vision of a mystic. Consolation upside-down, in other words, was a fact of Emily's experience, and she worshipped a world which could show her such a fact. She worshipped her experience, and so we must call her experience intensely, searchingly religious.

It states itself in a hundred versions, and nothing Emily ever wrote was uncoloured by her conviction — forced upon her, to be sure, but tested in the extreme zone of her years of deprivation: *Know light by knowing darkness, know fullness by hunger, and taste by desire, know suc-*

cess by defeat; and the corollary: *Nothing can limit the soul from what it may need to know.* Over and over she begins a poem: "Take everything away," or "To know the transport by the pain," or "A prison gets to be a friend."

There are sixteen poems on the theme of starvation; eight on the theme of imprisonment. Emily mentions, and for more reasons than one, *The Prisoner of Chillon.*

She was a prisoner. Stone walls do not a prison make, nor iron bars a cage, she mused to herself, but she did not quite know the nature of her chains; they were real, but invisible. Father and daughter were exceedingly reserved; what went on in their minds came out in a glance of the eyes, perhaps — visible for an instant to the other — but never in speech. Edward knew, now, that he suffered if Emily carried on with young men, and that he would prefer her not to marry in any haste. More than this he could not guess about his scrupulous self, for the rest was unscrupulous. Emily knew that something in her drove her to defy her father, and something else revolved her at a distance of reverence, held and established in relation to him, as a planet relates its motions to the central sun. By this we may observe that the relationship between Emily and her father was a primitive one.

They were both compelled to act as they did. For many reasons it was to become a truism in America, to be confirmed by the experience of numbers of generations, that children, however they may love their parents, are obliged by something greater than their love or their parents to dissent from authority.

Despite the gaps in fact, and the workings of legend, we can, then, glimpse something of the young woman who lived in a suspended world peopled by two or three personalities, until the crisis of her love-affair. We cannot tell when this came or where it came. That Emily was by no means morbid during this period of four years, several valentines testify. Because they have been taken as little love-letters, we shall have to examine them. The first mention of them comes in a letter to Austin written on February 14, 1848. Emily explains that they are forbidden at Mount Holyoke Seminary. She adds: " I am sure I shall not very soon forget last Valentine week, nor any the sooner the fun I had at that time." The passage is edited after this reference. The Valentine week of 1849 has left no echoes. But during the week when she wrote her prose epistle " I am Judith the heroine of Apocrypha, and you the orator of Ephesus," in 1850, she wrote as well a valentine in verse for Mr. Bowdoin, who had lent her *Jane Eyre* and so inoculated one more young New Englander with " *Jane Eyre* fever," as it was called at the time. Mr. Bowdoin was a law-student in father's office; it was he who had put Lydia Maria Child's *Letters from New York* in the great bush of old-fashioned tree-box beside the front door. Emily's seemingly sententious note of thanks for *Jane Eyre* becomes rather droll and understandable at the mention of this tree-box, for the note read: " If all these leaves were altars, and on every one a prayer that Currer Bell might be saved, and you were God — would you answer it? " The book was accompanied with box leaves plucked from the guilty tree.

Mr. Bowdoin's valentine is an entreaty that he quit bachelorhood for a more blissful state:

> *Oh the earth was* made *for lovers, for damsel, and hopeless swain,*
> *For sighing, and gentle whispering, and* unity *made of* twain.
> *All things do go a courting, in earth or sea, or air,*
> *God hath made nothing single but* thee *in His world so fair!*

Six true and comely maidens are eligible for his advances, Emily implies:

> *There's* Sarah, *and* Eliza, *and* Emeline *so fair,*
> *And* Harriet *and* Sabra, *and she with curling hair.*

Several things are worth noting here. First the opening lines of the valentines have been deleted. Why? Second, the verses are teasing, but evidently Emily is ridiculously anxious, in spite of her levity, that everybody be in love. . . . Any other state seemed unnatural to her. It was a prolific season. If she wrote two such outbursts, she evidently wrote others, for Mr. Bowdoin was not a very dear "friend," and she lavished a good many lines on him. Forty, to be exact.

Two years later she wrote another valentine in verse to Mr. William Howland, who had been Leonard Humphrey's dearest friend — the lines employed the same silly use of Latin phrases that Emily used in the prose valentine; but it is not a love-making verse. One stanza goes:

> *Unto the Legislature*
> *My county bids me go.*
> *I'll take my india-rubbers,*
> *In case the wind should blow.*

This effort of Emily's was evidently admired — for some-one sent it to the *Springfield Republican.*

It is the last of the valentines that have come to light. The prose epistle of 1850 is the only declaration of affection among them, and it was not published with Emily's prose.[1] The jesting verse-valentine of the same year, which is, of course, the merest frivolity, and a paraphrase at the same time of Sir Philip Sidney's famous verse on amorous nature, receives this comment from Madame Bianchi: "Emily had about this time *quite a spicy affair* with a young law student in her father's office, an habitue of the house who was bewitched with her and certainly added quite an amount of variety, if only as another objective for her own mental sallies. He became a con-firmed bachelor, but she assailed him with a valentine unique in that Saint's calendar. . . ." The italics are mine.

Madame Bianchi places the writing of the valentine in the period of 1862; she implies that the man was a bache-lor because of a passion for Emily, although he was mar-ried two years before the incorrect date, and although the subject of the poem shows that he is already somewhat determined on bachelorhood in 1850; and she uses one of the most peculiar phrases yet coined in the craft of biog-raphy: " quite a spicy affair."

From 1848 on, legend wraps this story in a thick skein spun around and over, in and out. Let us cut it by asking: " Who was the other young man? "

[1] I found it in 1929 while searching the files of magazines published in Amherst.

AMHERST COLLEGE IN 1848. GEORGE GOULD LIVED AT
MIDDLE COLLEGE. (CENTRE, DURING HIS SENIOR YEAR
— *Courtesy of* AMHERST QUARTERLY

"SAINT" AURELIA — OR MRS. AURELIA HINSDALE
DAVIS   — SEE SWORN STATEMENT

CHAPTER VI

"VOLENS ET POTENS"

A TALL SLENDER BOY, IN AN ILL-FITTING SUIT OF
clothes, came to Amherst College the fall after
Leonard Humphrey was graduated. From the first
he was singular. He was six feet eight [1] and wore, even as
a freshman, his " usual abstracted air." Although he stayed
for four years, the gentle singularity of his manner did not
wear off; indeed, it grew.

We are told that he was poor, and before we have time
to infer that he was proud, we chance upon the fact that
his middle name, his mother's family name, linked him
with the first orator of the Revolution and the first governor of Virginia — Patrick Henry. The boy fancied himself of direct descent, although he wasn't. " *Volens et
potens* " was written on the family arms. Through these
same Henrys he was said to be related to the Montagues;
and the Montagues, as everybody knows, were related to
the Dickinsons. Was he a very distant, an unencouraged,
cousin of Emily's?

If he was, he shut his eyes to Dickinson connexions in

---

[1] The college student's report may have exaggerated.

this Amherst of theirs; he stood on his pride and remembered Patrick Henry, and the old South, from which he liked to fancy his mother came, and the family coat of arms, a sledge-hammer in a powerfully uplifted hand. It was Scotch blood in him; it was pride.

His rhetoric remembered his ancestor, for his rhetoric was more golden than anyone required. The music of his words was a "fault." If Tutor Humphrey took him in hand when he returned from Andover, it was of course with the intention of teaching him restraint and a little of the schoolman's logic. Even when the young Henry was a senior, a class-mate dared exclaim: "Hold on, you plugless word-spout."

He had a hard time getting as far as Amherst; but he had come. When he left home for the Academy at Monson, four years before he came to Amherst, after being for some time an apprentice to his uncle who had a harness and carriage manufactory at Oakham, he prided himself on being able to make an A number 1 whip-lash. He prided himself on having walked the twenty-five miles from Oakham to Monson with a bundle swung over his shoulder, doing chores for food, and sleeping in kindly barns. He prided himself on being one of the best pupils of Dr. Hammond, whom he later described as the Dr. Arnold of Rugby's counterpart in Monson. He had, indeed, no other resource than to retain at every step all that he could of his pride, for he was being sent to college by the generosity of the daughter of Dr. Fiske of New Braintree. When he came into Amherst, a few days before college opened in September 1846, a gawky figure of a boy in a suit made by the sewing-circle back at home, he was perfectly capable of calling on his very distant cousins the Dickinsons, at the Deacon Mack house, and presenting (if Joel wrote such a letter) a letter from old Joel Norcross of Monson, to his daughter Emily, Mrs. Edward Dickinson. Joel had founded Monson Academy at about the time that old Samuel Fowler Dickinson had founded Amherst Academy. Here was a bright lad, and related, too. Such a letter would not be an unnatural thing for anyone to write; such letters were being written every fall, carried in breast-pockets of home-made jackets — letters asking someone in the next town or so to look out for some worthy boy in his effort to get an education; passing him on to higher things, with best wishes and a blessing.

Emily was jingling into town on the stage from Boston at about the time that young George Gould was perhaps arriving on foot. A hay-wagon may have picked him up; or a pedlar, peddling suspenders and bright tin pans — some tonguey auctioneer, full of Yankee notions. He could tell George Gould about his high-born kin in the big Deacon Mack house. Or if, perchance, Edward rolled by on the top of the clattering stage, returning from Boston in time to get back for a meeting of the trustees, before college opened, the pedlar would be able to point him out in his wide-brimmed black hat. "The one setting up so straight. . ." Everybody near by was telling the story of the professor who was showing a visitor through the college-buildings. The professor's young son was with him and wanted to know who owned it all. He asked his father and pulled at his coat and asked again: "Pa, who owns Amherst College? Pa, who owns Amherst College?" "Ed'ard Dickinson; now hold your tongue."

Emily had just seen Bunker Hill and Mount Auburn and the Chinese Museum. Amherst would look small from the stage window; diminutive, a comic little town where life went on and on and on like the humming of bees, as monotonous as the clapping of horses' hoofs, the lifting and falling of little hills and little dales for setting.

But to George Gould it would be constructed of glamour and desire. The elms would have dignity, and the classic hall on the hill would symbolize something that bright boys worshipped in 1846. Nevertheless, if the pedlar had him in his cart, George would take some pleasure in showing him that in spite of all his education, past and to come, he could braid an A number 1 whip-lash.

Poverty had some sting, but no stigma in 1846. George Gould was soon elected to membership in Alpha Delta Phi, the fraternity to which Leonard Humphrey belonged, to which Austin was at the same time elected. After all, he was a Henry, and the Henrys were related to the Montagues, and, as everybody knows, the Montagues were related to the Dickinsons.

When the sewing-circle suit wore out, he had a chance to be charming. Evidently he was. Evidently Emily thought so when Austin brought his fellow freshman and fraternity brother and distant kinsman home to dinner. Father looked him over and saw at a glance that he would have to be a minister — the boy had no legal timber in him — that was certain, from everything about him. He was an emotional type — cared for the things of the spirit. The family would have one more poor, underpaid preacher to look out for; one less upstanding burden-bearer on whom to rely. Father doubtless asked about some Aunt Sally or other and went on about his business.

Slowly, however, it became evident in spite of the handicap of poverty that George Gould would be something better than an underpaid preacher. He was a theologian, a poet, and an orator. New England cherished such young men and put them before her largest audiences and in her highest pulpits. They performed an office no other might perform — they made the word of God fluid, the word of Christ, the poetry of living. Such young men were the strength of the people, a reserve for the country-side, a storehouse of spiritual energy, in which the fagged layman might be baptized week by week, in order to continue to live by faith and good works. The poet of God was cherished because he could quicken. The golden torrent of words, the bright uplifted countenance, was given for a sign to the Lord's anointed. While such young men were preparing for this sacred function, they were given an intense, an almost unhealthy, stimulus, fed on a passionate bread from the beginning, watched by the community, and tended by teachers, so that in time of great need they might be sufficient for the task of keeping the community alive. George Gould was singled out to become an "inspirational preacher."

And so the brightness of George Gould's face, abstracted as it was, meant more than his tattered jacket.

And innocent pleasures and high spirits surrounded

him, and surrounded Emily. Austin brought his friends
home to dinner and willingly supplied fraternity brothers
for all his sister's parties and all his sister's best friend's
parties. In this world of witty young people Emily began
to sparkle; she was radiant with pleasure and hope and
belief in her own destiny. Father found her too radiant
and sent her away; but soon she was back again, and when
she came back, she and Tutor Humphrey and George
Gould constituted a quorum.

During '48 and '49 and the first eight months of '50
the three friends read and discussed the same books.
Emily and Leonard and George shared *Pickwick* and
Tristram Shandy and *Kenilworth*, Emerson and Poe, the
Fable for Critics, Washington Irving, Chaucer and Mrs.
Hemans, Burns and Horace (in bits), Longfellow and
Oliver Wendell Holmes, *Jane Eyre* and the Preface to
Lyrical Ballads. Longfellow's *Kavanagh* they took as a
tonic, against like absurdities in themselves.

Among themselves how they differed! Emily flew
through books, flew to conclusions; Leonard Humphrey
kept a note-book full of sedate meditations, and his little
paragraphs were "rich in thought and beautiful in form."
He talked less than did George and Emily; he went home
to read again the passage in Ruskin or Wordsworth that
needed re-reading; he came back to the next conversation armed with dicta with which to confront his young
pupils. George Gould talked, deliriously, in repartee with
Emily. They made a world of their own and believed it
durable.

By his senior year George Gould was chairman of the

board of editors of the literary *Indicator*. It was a dizzy height to reach, the apex of college ambition. Several times he had come near having to leave college, despite the kindness of Dr. Fiske's daughter in New Braintree. College expenses had gone up:

"The people of the village were still friendly to the college . . . but they could no longer welcome and cherish its two hundred and fifty students as pets or wards in their own families; the halcyon days of primitive and almost pastoral simplicity, when their apple-orchards and walnut groves, their parlors and fire-sides, their homes and hearts were open to the members of the college generally, almost as if they were their own sons, had gone, never to return. Board was perhaps fifty percent higher than it was at the opening of the college. The influx of wealthy students, by changing the tastes and habits of the community, had increased in a still greater percentage the incidental and unnecessary expenses. . . ."

Still, George Gould managed to stay in college and to keep alive. "His diploma was won at Amherst only after a bitter struggle with poverty. In the face of difficulties that would have deterred an ordinary man, he fought his way step by step, until after four years of struggle he was graduated with honor."

Is this the equivalent of several miles of shovelled snow-paths every winter, evening and morning "chores," schoolrooms swept out, and fires built to a sleepy scholar who tries with a heavy mind to remember the chapters from Plato or Dugald Stewart or Emerson that kept his lamp burning until nearly dawn? We know that George

97

Gould was an early riser from necessity, and that at Amherst College he studied himself into some kind of nervous ill health which followed him all his life.

These years were intense ones for Emily; and for her two friends life was grim. One friend was struggling with disease that ended in death; the other was engaged in a hand to hand combat with poverty. For all the time that Emily knew George Gould in Amherst, poverty had the upper hand.

" We only say," says one of the facetious editors of the *Indicator,* in the last number of the paper before commencement, when George Gould was graduating with honour, " that he has spent the year in a fruitless attempt to combine the philosophy of Dugald Stewart with that of Ralph Waldo Emerson. His little success in this affair has so often given him the ' Blues,' that his friends have serious fears lest he should commit some outrage on himself. Burdensome duties have worn him away until he has become;

A meagre, muse-rid rope, adjust and thin."

And so we catch our chief contemporary glimpse of George Gould through the pages written by one Obadiah, of the *Indicator* staff — an extravagant fellow who delighted in farcical accounts of the editorial meetings. The attempt was Dickensian on Obadiah's part; he loved Jingle's stenographic talk and tried to reproduce it; he tried caricaturing his fellows — George Gould's long legs, and lazy Bonniface's spittoon and cigar, and another editor's " beaver." The hilarious slap-stick serves very well; we see George Gould, who was nicknamed Nathaniel Winkle, walking and running up and down dormitory stairs and pounding on doors, calling meetings of the editors, scowling at stale jokes, and criticizing bad poetry. He was the captain of the "quill-driving fraternity," and very busy.

This is Obadiah:

"It was the sultriest hour of a warm Saturday's afternoon, and the manifold progeny of our Alma Mater, from obsequious Fresh to stately Senior were gone their several ways to such occupations as their own inclination or a more peremptory master had prescribed. We of the *Indicator*, too, had yielded slightly to the somniferous influences of that melting season. Winkle was pacing the walk (we call it such) in front of the Chapel with his usual abstracted air occasionally casting a furtive glance at the old college clock, which told him unerringly that the hour for Editor's meeting would soon arrive; Van Twiller was stretched supinely in the lee of old Middle, charming sundry Sophs and Freshmen with a recital of stirring vacation adventures; the Corporal was surfeiting upon a huge pile of exchanges; Obadiah was no doubt benevolently employed somewhere, and Bonniface, who had spent the ominous space of thirty minutes in rioting upon his dish of greens, was now safely brought to anchor in his favorite armchair, pumping away quite otiosely at the fag-end of the last Havana. . . . No thought of unwritten Indicators for impatient and fastidious readers was suffered to disturb the serenity of that blissful hour. . . . Here loud steps were heard to approach the door, followed by a still louder rap. . . ."

It was Winkle, wanting to know if Bonniface would be so good as to come to editorial meeting and bring six bottles of Dr. Townsend's sarsaparilla, for the afternoon was hot and there were many manuscripts.

It is impossible to fit the nicknames to the real editors. None of the articles were signed, and the names of the editors only appear in the final issue in the following order:

CHAIRMAN, GEORGE GOULD

JACOB M. MANNING

JOHN H. THOMPSON

HENRY SHIPLEY

DANIEL W. FAUNCE.

Manning, one of George Gould's best friends, and Faunce became ministers, Thompson later became a lawyer in Chicago after work on the *Springfield Republican*, and Shipley was a newspaper man who died in California nine years later. We cannot fit the nicknames to the actual young men; for us it is only perfectly clear that Bonniface was lazy, that the Corporal had " a military career " in prospect. Fortunately George Gould is identified in numerous ways. He is designated as chairman and given the name Winkle; he is the orator of the group, and he is constantly depicted as six feet eight inches high.

" In a retired section of the premises is seated, or rather lodged, the Chairman of the corps. . . . There is . . . a kind of pensive dignity brooding over the man, as though fully conscious of the high responsibilities of the hour. His personal appearance is rather impressive. . . . His corporeal capacities are rather longitudinal than expansive; and his locomotive members (of which Nature has been wonderfully lavish) enable him to take a high stand wherever he goes. Some regard him as ascetic in his habits. Others believe him mischievously disposed towards the frailties of his fellows. Our own opinion is dubious. His friends have stigmatized him with the classical sounding title of Winkle — if it please thee, reader, we will call him thus."

Fortunately Winkle had a sense of humour. If Obadiah was heavy-handed, Winkle was mischievous. If the other editors were a little dull and lazy or wearisomely schoolboyish, Winkle could be remembered for nearly fifty years as the best wit of the day.

" I recall so clearly," said Daniel Faunce in 1900, " the tall straight figure of Gould; his flashing eyes as he discussed college questions, and his happy way of retort when closely pressed."

Faunce pointed out that, aside from his charm and wit, it was Gould's " mingled philosophy and practicality of the fact " which distinguished him from his fellows.

After the Fourth of July celebrations someone wrote of Winkle's speech in Northampton:

" We are told that Winkle, irresistible as usual, made a deep impression on the hearts of the young ladies of N —. We have forgotten at this moment, whether six or sixteen was the number of hearts broken upon this occasion."

Winkle's speeches continue to be satirized:

" Winkle — we have dubbed him the great-toe of our

editorial corpse — has given us a lengthened account of
his adventures, which we hope he will transcribe for our
next number. . . . His habits of early rising have followed him . . . his mornings have, we understand, been
occupied in composing one of those amphibious orations
which will answer for almost any public occasion; if the
word 'Anti-Slavery,' be used in certain vacant places of the
manuscript, it may do for a 'Free Soil' speech at the next
election. The word 'peace' substituted, and it will go far
to allay the war-spirit — except that the comparisons like
those of most other peace orations, are entirely from the
battle-field. For an address on the 'Glorious Fourth,' it
would be grand and absolutely magnificent."

Yes, George Gould's rhetoric was a campus joke; it was
his chief pride; on the platform his humour vanished, and
the words grew golden and round and sonorous. Off the
platform he was invulnerable and one wondered sometimes how serious he was. On the platform he remembered Patrick Henry.

*" I am Judith the heroine of Apocrypha, and you the
orator of Ephesus."*

And so Obadiah parodied, for the amusement of *Indicator* readers, the well-known style of the orator of the
hour:

" Rome," said he, looking calmly round, " Rome is
fallen — Greece is no more, as also Palmyra with its
hundred gates. Carthage lies in ruins, but Mary Huss no
longer weeps over its ashes, for the American Eagle has

arisen into lumeniferous ether, while the eyes of an astonished universe are gazing upon the transcendent spectacle. . . ."

" The orator," says Obadiah, " then proceeded to divide his discourse into the following general divisions: —

1st. The American Eagle as it was.

2nd. The American Eagle as it is.

3rd. The American Eagle as it will be.

4th. The American Eagle considered in general.

5th. Moral Reflections.

" The reader will see at a glance what a field was opened for one of Mr. Winkle's powers. And in fact Mr. Winkle outdid himself," concludes the satirical Obadiah.

After oratory came poetry. With Emily and Leonard Humphrey it came first. Oratory was the Lord's and the fullness thereof; poetry, so George Gould evidently thought, lacked the swing and thunder of great periods. It lacked the Lord. Poetry had grown stale; it had fallen into a decline; it failed in invention; it lacked wit; it lacked the heroic and golden colour of great words. Either Leonard Humphrey or George Gould gave Emily a copy of Shakspere all checked and underlined. On that book they could all agree. Shakspere with Emily and George and Leonard made a quorum!

The second number of the *Indicator* records that Winkle rose to his feet and made the announcement at one of the meetings that the editors had been called together to " take in consideration the alarming retardation and unprecedented decline of the poetical talent in this college; and to devise, if possible, some effective measures whereby we can resuscitate and breathe a new life into this sinking department of literary effort."

The poetry continued to be as bad as ever. Winkle, in criticizing the few creditable performances and the " usual quantum of pathos and bombast " in the speeches at commencement the year before he was graduated, dismissed the whole spectacle of the gaping audience and the crude elocution in lines that appear to have been invented to describe the situation. He felt very much the same way about poetry, and even sometimes about his own future:

> 'Tis wonderous fine I calculate,
> To sit upon an oak;
> And hear ten thousand bull-frogs join
> In one almighty croak!

Is this a forerunner of " *I'm nobody. Who are you?* "

By February we have signs of a real flirtation. What else was Emily's valentine? It was doubtless written to George Gould — even now, with the little we know, we infer that. How provoking, and how like Emily, to put it in *Forest Leaves*, declaring her feelings, as always, round about and round about!

George thought so, and he paid her back in her coin. " Many a chary epistle did we receive, and many did we send — but one, *such* an one. . . ." Here the jest has meaning for all the young people in the secret: " I wish I knew who the author is. I think she must have some spell, by which she quickens the imagination, and causes the high blood 'run frolic through the veins.' Yes, the author, of such a gew gaw — such a frenzy built edifice —

I should like to know " — here the jesting would delight
Emily — " I should like to know and talk with, for I
don't believe her mouth has any corners, perhaps ' like a
rose leaf torn.' "

With a beating heart Emily read that number of the
Indicator when it came off the press. Would father hear
about it? Would Austin keep her secret? All the " fool-
ing " in the world could not hide the exhilaration bursting
forth afresh in Emily, the exhilaration that her father so
discouraged, so silenced, when he was able, by a meticulous
remark. Ecstasies and reveries (father pronounced it
rev-e-ries), were as unbecoming to Emily as a low-cut
dancing-frock.

If she could not dance except in prose, she would do it
there. If she could not flirt behind a fan, she would do it
with a silly valentine. And while everybody was suspecting that Emily, like George Gould, was not quite serious,
she was writing in desperate fancy:

" But the world is sleeping in ignorance and error, sir,
and we must be crowing-cocks, and singing-larks, and a
rising sun to awake her; or else we'll pull society up by
the roots, and plant it in a different place. We'll build
Alms-houses, and transcendental State prisons, and
scaffolds — we will blow out the sun, and the moon,
and encourage invention. Alpha shall kiss Omega —
we will ride up the hill of glory — Hallelujah, all
hail! "

No wonder if, shortly after, George dared to kiss the
mouth that was like the rose-leaf torn. That was a mar-
vellous spring, but Emily renounced a ride in the spring

woods, and other things. The sadness, the denial, began; it was a doomed love from the first.

> *O Rose, thou art sick!*
> *The invisible worm,*
> *That flies in the night,*
> *In the howling storm,*
>
> *Has found out thy bed*
> *Of crimson joy;*
> *And his dark secret love*
> *Does thy life destroy.*

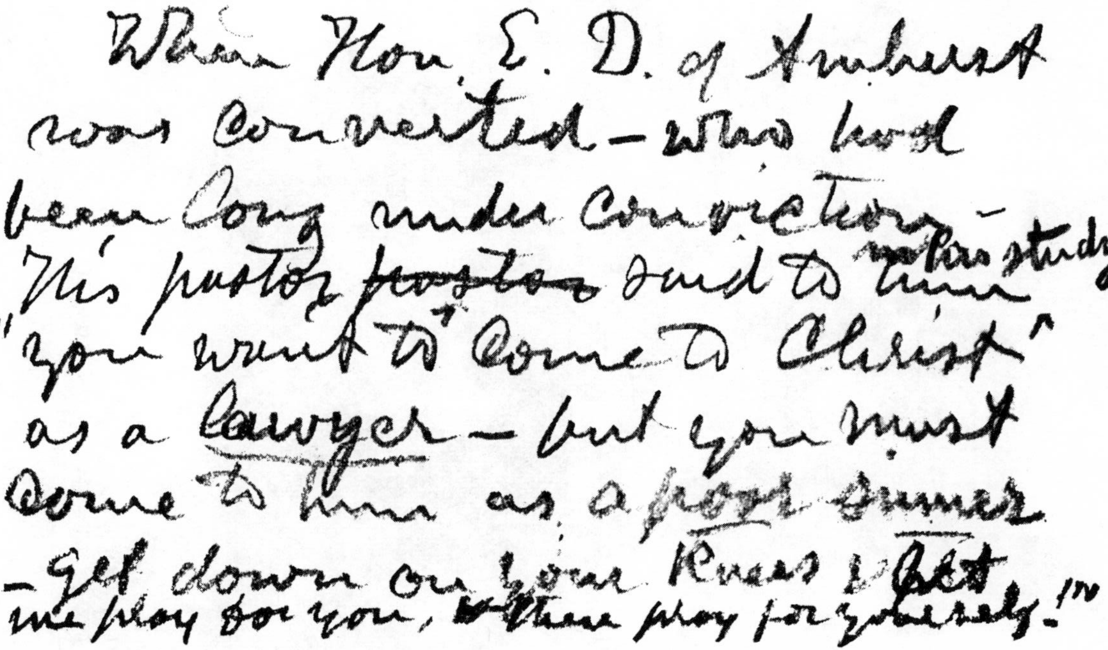

[handwritten note, difficult to read]

When Hon. E. D. of Amherst
was converted — was lost

been long under conviction —
His pastor forgave God to turn study —
"You want to come to Christ
as a lawyer — but you must
come to him as a forgot sinner
— Get down on your knees I fell
not him for you, either may for you say !"

FROM THE NOTE-BOOK OF THE REV. GEORGE
H. GOULD, DATED SEPTEMBER 14, 1877
— *Courtesy* MRS. JOHN W. GOULD

GEORGE GOULD
— *Courtesy of* MRS. JOHN W. GOULD

CHAPTER VII

SWORN STATEMENT

AFTER DISCOVERING THE PURLOINED VALENTINE IN the files of the *Indicator* one summer afternoon of 1929, almost seventy years to the day from the time that George Gould began to edit the second volume of the little magazine, I waited in a prolonged suspense, pondering Judith, the heroine of Apocrypha, and the orator of Ephesus, hoping to know more. Then, with a sigh, I gave up the attempt to reconstruct such a gossamer past upon a plane of blanks and queries.

Some time later, during the period of the sigh, I found a letter in the morning mail written in a delicate and regular nineteenth-century hand. The writer had known Lavinia Dickinson intimately before she died; had indeed once copied the entire volume of the book now known as *Further Poems* at Lavinia's request. Bit by bit this person gave me a story which has every sign of being the truth. I quote from a letter and append a sworn statement:

". . . He[1] decided when this young man, who was to become a minister of the Congregational faith, began to show a decided fancy for Emily, and she ' was willing

[1] " He " refers to Edward Dickinson.

to have it so ' — that the affair must end, and so he forbade Emily to see the man. He, Mr. Dickinson, was in a habit of inviting the faculty of Amherst College and some of the seniors, if not all, to a reception at his home, in June. The year Emily's lover was to graduate, a few seniors were invited, not all, to the annual reception. Emily sent word to her lover to meet her at a certain hour, in a part of the grounds, after the reception was over. She was dressed in white, and when her lover appeared she told him that her father had forbidden her to see him, or to write to him, and declared that love was too vital a flower to be crushed so cruelly. She promised to love him as long as she lived, said she would answer every letter he wrote, arranged to have Mr. Sweetser receive and deliver the letters to Maggie, told him she would dress in white, fall, winter, spring, and summer, and never again would go outside the gate, but live the life of a recluse — for his sake. This promise she kept. Maggie told me the same story, not knowing Lavinia and Mrs. Davis had already done so — and you are the first person to receive this confidence. . . . And now, in secrecy, I give the name of the lover as given to me — Rev. George Gould. He preached for years in Worcester, Massachusetts and I heard him several times, in my early years, when he seemed very old to me."

This person later consented to the publication of this name and signed the following statement:

I do solemnly swear, being in my right mind and in full possession of my faculties, and do willingly give to Genevieve Taggard for use in her book, *Emily Dick-inson*, and to the world in general, this statement: that three persons, Mrs. A. B. H. Davis, Mrs. Maggie Mahar, the servant in the Dickinson family, and La-vinia Dickinson who was Emily Dickinson's sister and my friend, told me that the man Emily Dickinson loved and renounced was Mr. George Gould, (later the Rev. George Gould), who graduated from Amherst College and later became pastor of the Congregational Church in Worcester, Mass. And that I was told that Emily Dickinson's father forbade the match.

On no account shall my name be used in any connection with this statement while I am living.

Signed

X^1

Let the reader discount something for legend; forty years is a long time, even in that curiously timeless house which Emily and Vinnie shared alone, after Austin married and father and mother died. Nevertheless, forty years after 1850 Vinnie told this story of the sister she served and adored. The renunciation occurred forty years before, but the love evidently was a reality to the very end. It was the reality of which Vinnie spoke. At about the same time she was writing to Mr. Higginson:

"I have had a ' Joan of Arc ' feeling about Emilie's poems from the first. Their reception convinces me I was right. As all Emilie's possessions were given to me before

---

[1] See Appendix III for a statement from another person, denoted as Z.

her death, I recognize the right to magnify her name as she deserved."

One does not falsify a sister and magnify her name in the same breath. One does not tell idle tales of a cherished memory. Vinnie, then, knew and confided that the man " Emilie " loved and renounced was George Gould. His picture is said to have hung in an oval gold frame in Emily's bedroom, and the family is said to have marked its presence there with respect. And so in spite of the fact that Madame Bianchi claims that only sister Sue knew, we maintain that Vinnie is a qualified witness.

This revelation, from Vinnie, via one other person, is the single fact we have so much needed to know in order to simplify Emily Dickinson's life, cluttered as it now is with absurd and unnatural suppositions. With this name it may be possible to bring the life back to the austerity of the poems.

Emily's voice mingles with Vinnie's:

" When a little girl, I had a friend who taught me Immortality; but venturing too near, himself, he never returned. Soon after my tutor died, and for several years my lexicon was my only companion. Then I found one more, but he was not contented I be his scholar, so he left the land."

This is Emily's story to Mr. Higginson. The flirtation and the valentine of 1850 may have covered or followed or evoked avowal. But I think it unlikely. Emily's words imply that the crisis came several years after 1850. George Gould, with nothing to offer but poverty, with three more years of struggle ahead before he should even be ready to begin his own self-support, could easily have been warned off the territory of the garden by the flash of Edward's lantern.[1]

Commencement found George Gould on the platform before his fellow students, facing the trustees, the faculty, and the oval faces of those young ladies who had made such an occasion of the day. Austin Dickinson spoke sixth on the program on " The Elements of our National Literature." Sixteenth, after an interval of music, came tall George Gould: " The Relation of Self-Reverence to Christianity." Prayer and poetry and oratory were all one, perhaps, under pressure of the excitement. For weeks he had been singing one hymn at senior prayer-meeting; it haunted and disquieted his class-mates, and one of them noted the discrepancy between the new romantic tune of *Naomi,* fitted to the old words of resignation:

> *Give me a calm, a thankful heart*
> *From every murmur free.*

Then he went away to Union Seminary, in New York City, and Emily was very much alone. The little group dissolved, and the spirit that had dictated the *Indicator* vanished when the magazine went out of existence. Humphrey lay dead under the incredible snow; Austin was studying law at Harvard and teaching Irish boys to figure; George Gould vanished into the tall world of theology. No wonder that Emily turned to Noah Webster's dictionary, her lexicon, her only companion. The lovers of words were elsewhere. In the middle of the year George Gould left

[1] See Appendix IV for material from the *Indicator.*

Union, to attend Professor Park's brilliant course of lectures on systematic theology at Andover. He, like Emily, was prone to an undue attachment for his teachers. First it had been Dr. Hammond at Monson Academy, referred to as the " inspirer of all the ambitions of his life "; then at Amherst it had been a Dr. Smith. " Drs. Gould and Manning were wont to say that they owed more to him than to any other professor at Amherst. . . ." Now it was to be Professor Park. And for him George Gould would change schools.

Emily wrote Austin letters that had little edges of ice after he left; nearly always on a Sunday evening, or Sunday afternoon.

" There has been not much stirring since you went away — I should venture to say prudently that matters had come to a stand — unless something new ' turns up,' I cannot see anything to prevent a quiet season. Father takes care of the doors and Mother of the windows, and Vinnie and I are secure against all outward attacks. If we can get our hearts ' under,' I don't have much to fear — I've got all but three feelings down, if I can only keep them! . . ." (Letter edited.)

Two paragraphs on, Emily set down the passage explaining that she would write a sincerer letter except for the fear that Austin would poke fun at her feelings.

Edward marked 1850 by joining the church, under the Reverend Aaron Colton. He had hung out alone, with his sedate and fiery power, remaining always a little wary of God, standing on the dignity of the individual soul. Nearly twenty-five years after the religious exhortations of Samuel, his father, he felt the need, and he tried in vain, to come to God on his own terms. Should one of the most zealous and righteous men in all Massachusetts have to humble himself now that he was ready?

That drama was a supreme one for Edward, as it must have been for spectators who knew Edward. George Gould knew the significance of this conversion, for he puts down twenty-seven years later:[1]

" When Hon. E. D. of Amherst was converted — who had been long under conviction — his pastor said to him in his study — ' You want to come to Christ as a *lawyer* — but you must come to him as a *poor sinner* — get down on your knees and let me pray for you, and then pray for yourself! ' "

Another letter from Emily to Austin ejaculates: " Oh, I am so lonely! . . ." and then is edited, perhaps for having been too specific. " I miss you very much," says another letter — " I put on my bonnet to-night, opened the gate very desperately, and for a little while the suspense was terrible — I think I was held in check by some invisible agent, for I returned to the house without having done any harm! "

Emily's letters show that she went down to visit her dear romantic brother, as she called him, in September 1851. She and Vinnie stayed at Aunt L.'s. Her letter indicates that they went and came back on the " cars " alone; father and mother stayed in Amherst. Austin, who dearly

---

[1] From George Gould's note-book, Worcester, Mass., September 14, 1877. These note-books are in the possession of Mrs. John W. Gould of Worcester, Mass.

loved Emily, and who knew and doubtless liked George Gould, may have arranged a meeting for George and Emily in Cambridgeport. In 1851 George Gould was preparing to go north to Andover, not south to Union, and he would of course go through Boston. The renunciation, which is supposed to follow the visit to Philadelphia, may have taken place in Aunt L.'s garden or her parlour.

Emily was, indeed, " held in check by some invisible agent."

" Oh, Austin," goes another letter in December 1851, " you don't know how we all wished for you yesterday. We had such a splendid sermon from Professor Park — I never heard anything like it, and don't expect to again, till we stand at the great white throne, and ' He reads from the Book, the Lamb's Book.' The students and chapel people all came to our church, and it was very full, and still, so still the buzzing of a fly would have boomed like a cannon. And when it was all over, and that wonderful man sat down, people stared at each other, and looked as wan and wild as if they had seen a spirit, and wondered they had not died. How I wish you had heard him — I thought of it all the time . . ." and more editing.

So Emily, after hearing George Gould's new teacher, " that wonderful man." A letter records the fact that Deacon Luke Sweetser stared at her so at church during 1851 that she had to discover " Nothing, up in the Sky somewhere."

When he was graduated from Union Seminary, in August of 1853, a flattering offer came from the Reverend Albert Barnes of Philadelphia, asking George Gould to come down on trial for a few months, to preach in the Presbyterian Church on Washington Square. We cannot prove that George Gould went down, but we do know that the work of collegiate pastor was offered him some time during the year.

Emily went south, too. If she had made a vow not to leave her father's garden, could she have broken it, in the hope of seeing George Gould? Or did he come to see her, before he left for Philadelphia after visiting his " folks " at Oakham, near Worcester? Father was in Washington after the first of December, bound up with the politics of the Thirty-third Congress. Father could not be sure that Emily would go; we see his uncertainty from a quoted bit in his letter. It sounds like the memory of a vow. Emily went; of that we may be sure. In Washington she wrote Susan Gilbert a letter, which we know only in paraphrased form; but its meaning has not been destroyed. I quote Madame Bianchi, *Life and Letters* (page 46):

" It makes the grass spring in her heart, she wrote, and the linnet sing to know that one she loves is coming there, and for one look of this friend she would give all the pomp, the court, the etiquette of the world."

Edward was too busy, just then, to keep track of young George Gould, who had been studying and preaching for three years. Gone he seemed to be, at any rate, if not quite forgotten.

All the tonics in the world failed to bring Emily back to her better spirits. Father sent her off to see the Hollands in Springfield. They always cheered her. The girl was not quite well. Perhaps Edward was beginning to wonder if he had not merely curbed Emily's wild spirit, but broken it. She seemed in a quiet " decline." He was famous about the country for his fast horses and prided himself that he knew how to treat a high-bred, high-strung creature. Home was painful now, with Emily silenced. Had Edward managed to kill the very thing he most prized in his young daughter — had he checked her galloping wit and her wild spirits and ruined her pace? Congressman Dickinson went to Washington and in March wrote his son at Harvard to bring Lavinia and his mother, and Emily too, if she would come, although (knowing the power of all he had so long insinuated) " he would not insist on Emily coming." Emily was being coaxed out of her young melancholy. Let her come down to the capital and see her father at the core of the world's affairs, let her watch her father acquit himself like a man of importance in the big world. Let Emily forget the young men who had read her poetry.

Daniel Webster was responsible for father's entrance into politics. First Edward went off to the Whig convention that was going to nominate Daniel Webster for the Presidency. Then Webster died. Edward went to the Thirty-third Congress. In 1853 he was one of the forty-four Northern Whigs who voted against the Kansas-Nebraska bill. The capital seethed with new political alignments. Father was in the thick of things; he was busy. " The bill " precipitated things.

" On the morning after the passage of the bill, a meeting of about twenty members of the House was held, at the suggestion of Israel Washburn, Jr., of Maine, at the rooms of Edward Dickinson and Thomas D. Eliot, of Massachusetts; and after some discussion and a little talk of trying to identify the Whig party with the cause of freedom, it was generally agreed that the only hope of victory lay in a new party, for which the name Republican was judged appropriate." [1]

The family, guided by Austin, arrived, after many trials, by train and coach. The world, which had such an ability to become both big and quaint before Emily's eyes, obliged her to stare at its ingenuity and its variety. Washington shimmered with warmth and ballooned with white muslin. Women dressed, and flirted and chatted and curtsied. Black faces mingled with southern faces. Parasols tilted and swayed, and tall silk hats gestured greetings.

The family stayed at the Willard Hotel and Emily seems to have taken almost her mother's place as her father's hostess when guests came to dinner. For here Emily's demure mother could only smile her cameo smile, antiphonal to Edward's silence. Father did not leave the table to indicate his displeasure now; he allowed Emily to jest about hell-fire when it arrived on plum pudding — in the presence of dignitaries.

Emily was doing very well, indeed. She went out to see Mount Vernon. The little patriot burned into sentiment, in a letter to the Hollands. She doubtless met Lieutenant Edward Hunt, the husband of the Helen with whom she had played in Amherst under the syringa bushes. Later she remarked that Lieutenant Hunt " interested her more than any man she ever met." This has been construed to

[1] From the *Life and Times of Samuel Bowles*, by George Merriam.

117

mean that Emily fell desperately in love with her friend's husband. Lieutenant and Mrs. Hunt were busy people, and it seems unlikely that a person as wholly devoted to scientific speculation as Edward Hunt appears to have been would neglect all the eminent scientists gathered for the meeting of the American Association for the Advancement of Science, men he was overwhelmingly eager to meet, in order to take the time to talk with, or fall in love with, a not-pretty-at-first-glance young miss from his wife's home town — particularly when he was already only two years married to the fascinating Helen.

Meanwhile she waited " for someone she loved very dearly." After three weeks Austin took them on to visit Eliza Coleman in Philadelphia. There she was to meet the Reverend Charles Wadsworth, with whom she was later an ardent correspondent. As they went north, spring softened the latitude by opening into flower.

The pattern is clearer now. Can anyone credit the likelihood that a married minister would fall precipitately in love with a visiting young lady who lived surrounded by friends, a sister, a mother, and a brother, who stayed as a guest for two short weeks and whom he saw at the most not more than half a dozen times? Ministers of the gospel live perpetually in a feminine world; they do not lose their minds and pledge their futures and desert their divine callings at the first arrival of a visiting young lady, however extraordinary. Lonely men living under unnatural conditions fall in love in this fashion; cowboys and Oxford students and explorers, and missionaries who go alone into exile, often find themselves desperately in love at a glance; but Emily Dickinson was not Zuleika Dobson, and, by her own paraphrased letter, she was expecting to meet someone she already knew.

Whether she was already in love with George Gould or not we cannot tell. Whether she had been on the verge of love ever since the 1850 valentine or whether she had already denied him is all conjecture. But to encounter each other after four years — in a new city, on a new footing — George Gould released from the mental tightness of Professor Park's systematic theology, Emily released from father's customary control, both of them in a world much larger, much more diverse, than theology or even father permitted — yes, now the love-story is plausible. Under the Amherst elms love might live in the secret heart and the shy glance. In Philadelphia it could be declared.

George Gould's emotions tended to flow into his preaching. A friend wrote him after one sermon: " You are a master of assemblies." Another: " You are a true Christian orator! " " He had a wonderful power of imagination," says a third, " a face radiant at times."

The evidence first pointed to the likelihood that Emily heard her friend preach God's word for the first time at the First Presbyterian Church on Washington Square. It was the largest church in the city, five blocks away from the Coleman's place, on Tenth and Chestnut. How natural if the family went to hear a former Amherst student in his first pulpit! If he stood in that position, George Gould ceased to be a literary boy in a patched and darned jacket and became the power and authority as well as the poetry Emily adored.[1]

The story goes that Emily came home and that "the man" followed. He implored Emily to run away with him.

Emily would not. Of that interview, which remains dateless for us, we have many traces. Emily, in renouncing, was strong; the man, in pleading, was weak. She says: " I rose because he sank. I thought it would be opposite. But when his power bent, my soul stood straight."

If George Gould loved and pleaded and followed, the reason for Emily's renunciation was not, as Madame Bianchi asserts, because "the man" was married. Nothing so extraneous controlled Emily. Emily would never have allowed herself to fall more than a little in love with an already married man. Her spirit was fastidious; she was incapable of such treachery against the kind of love she was for ever glorifying for all her married friends. She loved the Brownings that they loved each other, and the Bowleses for the same reason, and the Hollands for the same, and the Higginsons for the same; and she saw something sacred in the formal and unromantic attachment between her father and mother.

Events are the results of character, of millions of rays of character, intermingled, playing upon a point the way a skyful of light-angles from a battery of search-lights flash and criss-cross. Emily's character was finished and

---

[1] I have no authority for this statement; records give 1853–5 as Dr. Gould's sojourn in the West; and a search of the files of the churches and synods in Philadelphia fail to locate Dr. Gould there at that time.

passionately exact. There were things she could do; there were other things she could not do. Added to her strength and her weakness were certain almost automatic ways of acting. She could not, she could not, she could not, leave her father.

The story goes that " the man " came back repeatedly. We have many evidences of letters exchanged with every precaution against discovery, over a period of years and years.

If this were all hallucination, if it were all pure fabrication, first invented in Emily's own mind, as some have said it was, could the story have been better contrived to fit all of Emily's primary needs and blank desires? Emily could not marry because her father had a habit of her. But she could not be deprived of the right to love, the right to renounce, the right to live. She took life " over her door-sill " to live with it on curious terms.

This love-story as told by Madame Bianchi, as told by anyone now, must be part legend. Emily would smile and say that a moment after it happened, it had already begun to grow legendary. But on the basis of the elements in Emily's mind, where this inquiry always begins and ends, where we find the symbols and obsessions, the conflicts and solutions of her life in small and allegorical form — and on the background of what Edward must have been to produce the Emily who should feel as she did about him — and with the meaning of these two fragile young men, Leonard Humphrey and George Gould, before us, this story is somehow true, even though part legend. Even if it took place as a pure hallucination, so perfectly fitted it seems to Emily's dilemmas, we should still say it was profoundly true.

". . . but at this period suffering much from ill health, from over study, and especially from lack of gymnastic training, now so happily enjoyed by students, he [George Gould] went West to engage with an old college friend in railroad engineering, with the hope of recovering his health; but instead contracted a malignant form of malaria in the swamps skirting the western shore of Lake Michigan, and this misfortune has been the one bane and misery of his whole subsequent physical life." [1]

The legend that tells of Vinnie's appeal to Sue: " Sue, come! That man is here! . . . and I am afraid Emily will go away with him! " reported by Madame Bianchi, would seem to belong to an even later period. Madame Bianchi finds it difficult to explain how Sue could be next door in 1854 when she was not even married or the house built until 1856. Shall we suppose that George Gould came once again when father and mother were away — to quote Vinnie — after his return from the West in 1856?

The possibilities stand in a variety of places. If we have placed him incorrectly in Philadelphia, or in Aunt L.'s garden, we apologize to his shade.

Emily's poem,[2] on the next page, indicates that on one occasion George Gould said he was going and never coming back. That would imply that he had gone and had

[1] *Worcester of Eighteen Hundred and Ninety-eight*, edited by Franklin P. Rice.
[2] From the Galatea Collection, Boston Public Library.

come back previously — weakly and importunately returned to renew the love if not to succeed in breaking the chain.

Because that you are going
And never coming back
And I, however absolute
May overlook your track

Because that breath is final,
However first it be
This instant be suspended
Above Mortality.

Significance that each has lived
The other to detect
Discovery not God himself
Could now annihilate.

Eternity, Presumption
The instant I perceive
That you, who were existence
Yourself forgot to live.

The " Life that is " will then have been
A thing I never knew,
As Paradise fictitious
Until the Realm of you.

The " Life that is to be," to me
A Residence too plain
Unless in my Redeemer's Face
I recognize your own.

⟩ EMILY DICKINSON ⟨

Of Immortality who doubts
He may exchange with me
Curtailed by your obscuring Face
Of Everything but He.

Of Heaven and Hell I also yield
The Right to reprehend
To whoso would commute this Face
For his less priceless Friend.

If " God is Love " as he admits
We think that he must be
Because he is a " jealous God "
He tells as certainly.

If " all is possible with " him
As he besides concedes
He will refund as finally
Our confiscated Gods.

CHAPTER VIII

BELLS FOR SUNSET

I N THE ENSUING SPACE OF YEARS PAIN IS OBSERVED
to have an element of blank. And the blank was literal, not merely real. Nothing seems to happen between this renunciation and the Civil War except a full
measure of pain, and, as Emily said, pain cannot recollect
when it began or if there were a time when it was not.

They went on, in a prolonged childhood, Edward's two
daughters, in the old house. They were back again in
the family mansion where Emily had been born, after fifteen years in the Deacon Mack house on Pleasant street.[1]
Emily had renounced life; Lavinia had never been allowed
quite enough to renounce. They would be spinsters together; and Lavinia would address Emily's letters, would
keep people away when Emily asked her to, would solace
mother and father and oversee Maggie's housekeeping.
Days went round and round in a routine anyone but a
recluse would find hard and sombre.

Austin got married. Edward's children were of course

---

[1] If the renunciation took place in her garden in Amherst, the very
spot is obliterated now, by a gasoline station, built in 1928.

his emotional property; Austin was all ready to go west with his bride when Edward offered to build the then fashionable Italian villa, on ground adjoining the sedate old mansion, if Austin would stay and live next door and go on in the family law-office. Austin stayed. Edward had faced two perils, Emily's attachments and Austin's marriage, but now both of them were well weathered. Lavinia offered no cause for anxiety. Emily was subdued, she read less, worked longer in the garden (would father ever grow jealous of her flowers?); sometimes she even excused herself to her dear friends when they came to call. Emily was suspended. She was practising slowly a new technique of living.

Eventually father grew jealous of her flowers. Emily records it jocularly, amused at the man. One morning Emily rose early and performed some service for her South Sea rose, before father came downstairs. The rose probably needed attending to, and Emily, tactful, thought not to irritate her father by wasting the middle hours of the day. " Father detecting me," she goes on, " advised wiser employment." At devotions he read the parable of the man with one talent, and, concludes Emily, " expected me to adjust the gender."

The contest over her reading was still going on. One day father burst into a denunciation of all Emily's reading, but especially *Uncle Tom's Cabin* and the works of Charles Dickens. " These modern literati," he called their authors and declared that " somebody's *rev-e-ries,*" [1] he couldn't remember whose, were ridiculous and not to be compared

---

[1] P. 122, 1894 *Letters*. Father pronounced it slowly.

with the literature that flourished when he was young. I paraphrase Emily. " I am in disgrace at present," she tells Austin. Dickens was bound up with *Indicator* associations.

Emily makes what sport she can of her state of mind. In a letter to the Hollands:

" Monday, I solemnly resolved to be *sensible,* so I wore thick shoes, and thought of Dr. H. ⊥ and the Moral Law. One glimpse of the *Republican* makes me break things again — I read in it every night."

Her laboratory note-book contains the following entry:

> *I never hear the word " escape "*
> *Without a quicker blood,*
> *A sudden expectation. . . .*

The stanzas conclude that she never hears of prison barriers falling:

> *But I tug childish at my bars, —*
> *Only to fail again!*

But Emily loved her jailer. The word " father " dots all her pages; he touches every circumstance of life. Her rebellion was the energy of living, covering her tacit love. Emily gives us many pictures of father — walking to the barn in dismay after his son leaves for Harvard, father putting out a fire as the head of the new insurance company, father struggling to get the railroad into Amherst, father going in his slippers, an old man, to get grains for the sparrows, walking through the snow to the barn and hiding when he scatters the wheat lest he embarrass the birds!

To Austin she wrote while he was away:

"He reads all the letters you write, as soon as he gets them, at the post-office, no matter to whom addressed; then he makes me read them aloud at the supper table again, and when he gets home in the evening, he cracks a few walnuts, puts his spectacles on, and with your last in his hand, sits down to enjoy the evening. . . ."

The best and strangest story about Edward takes us back to 1851, a year after his conversion. One Monday evening the whole town was startled to hear the wild clanging of the church-bell. People rushed to the streets, banging doors and overturning chairs, inquiring the nature of the disaster. Nothing was to be seen but an evening sky of crimson and gold, laced with rays of pink from the sun. It lasted for fifteen minutes, superb and peculiar. Then Edward sternly took his bareheaded daughters home.

Edward it was who rang the bell — he sped, when he happened to see the sunset first, to call out all his townsmen to look at nothing more alarming than the beauty of the sky. For fifty years he made a point of passing some of these very same townspeople face to face in the street without speaking.

"He was not severe, I should think, but remote," commented Mr. Higginson, for whom no one was severe.

And, to be sure, Edward was no more severe than other men; but in Amherst he was more of a man. His person reinforced severity. He was comparable with no other man, in Emily's eyes. He held a lever over Emily's soul which made him not several, but total. She thought of her father's lonely life and was struck to the heart; his very presence embarrassed her at times. His silence and his solitariness in the midst of affairs stood for ever before her eyes. Edward lived a life which he cared only now and then to express. Emily felt and to some extent accompanied that life. Father could rise at town meeting, where he was moderator, and say to his opponents, when discussing the place for a new road across the Notch: " If I was God Almighty, the road should go *there!* " — and get it there, despite murmurs. But he would also ring bells for sunset. He could ban witticisms and poetry and " rev-e-ries "; he would build insurance companies and railroads, and discipline ministers and decline to vote with his party, but he would not hesitate to alarm the whole town with the sound of persistent ringing if he liked and admired the colour of a particular sky. . . .

With Austin established with his wife next door, Emily had a new person — which sometimes for her amounted to a new universe — to explore and perchance to live in.

But Sue proved to be a blind alley.

She was an old Academy friend of Emily's and the kind of friend Emily seemed to be needing; that is, she had a point of view that was more worldly than that permitted a Dickinson. She shocked Amherst by hanging holly-wreaths in her windows at Christmas time; it was pagan of her. Sue came from a small town " up York state." She had an air of the incorrigible; but father was soon drinking an extra cup of coffee at Susan's breakfast-table, across the lawn on his way to the office, a cup not permitted the tyrant by his own mandates at home. She was as brilliant as Emily, with a heart less tender, and she seemed at first a heaven-sent accomplice against the rule of the noble tyrant.

> *One sister have I in our house,*
> *And one a hedge away,*

Emily wrote, in full swing of her rapture, at first.

But finally, for some reason not shown, in spite of affectionate notes and protestations to the end, Sue was simply not alive in Emily's heart when she was taken unaware and spoke of those she loved in emotional haste. We suspect that Sue shared to some extent the town view of Emily. Did Sue defy father? That is unlikely; Sue was clever. Perhaps she was a little hard, and what of worldly inclination appeared as a merit when she was young, became, when she grew older, not a merit, but for Emily, who was swinging far away from the world as she passed thirty, something of a defect. Magazines and books came to Sue's Italian villa that dared not put their noses inside the mansion-door. For Sue she wrote all her first gaieties, for even after the loss of Humphrey and the unnamed lover Emily's heart had less surrendered to bleakness than in the twilight years where life was seen to have been this thing and not another, and where, if there were no losses comparable, there were also no hopes. It is said that Emily told Sue the whole story of her second love, and Sue never betrayed her. Nevertheless she called her " my pseudo-sister." Scintillation was a sickness, in Sue. A few of Emily's best poems went to Sue by Maggie or by a niece or a nephew. Sue, with Lavinia and Mrs. Ford, was sure that in spite of Emily's avowals she wished at one time to see her poetry in print. And yet in the end, to quote Vinnie, Sue discouraged its publication.

For some reason, probably originating in temperament, Sue gave Emily no way of escape and very little nourishment in spite of the books she brought her; in spite of that faculty in Emily that could draw sweet from meagre soil, and flowers from static friendship. By being worldly in her particular way, she made Emily decline worldliness, turning her back again to tussle with the spirit.

There was Vinnie, pretty, pert little Vinnie, who began as a coquette and a mimic and ended as a little loyal drudge who never saw the bottom of her mending-basket. Vinnie's face in a picture we have of her wears the air of a rogue (all of Edward's children and even his wife and his daughter-in-law take on in time the look of amused, defiant, or guilty children). Vinnie's hair is dark, not red like Emily's; she is a Norcross and the younger child, whose life has been as much bounded by the older brother and sister as by her parents.

Vinnie, too, had a " lover "; but the feeling for him was never permitted to come to the point of renunciation. And Vinnie wrote poetry about stars and fire-flies.

Years wove Emily and Vinnie together very gently. Vinnie had no life whatever, and so Emily shared with Vinnie what little she had, and together the two of them made out. With flowers and witticisms they beguiled the years.

Symbols exist for the joining of these two lives. Vinnie's handwriting on the outside of the envelope tacitly assents to what is committed within. Emily was Emily for both; and Vinnie needed to be two Vinnies. Vinnie sews and Emily reads; Vinnie hastily hides the cakes that burned while Emily dreamed over little lines scribbled on the margin of the cook-book. . . . She had begun to aid and abet the small struggles of her sister while she was still so young that she did not even know the gravity of her treason.

Once, years later, when a fire rose up at night and tocsins rang to arouse the village, Vinnie came into Emily's room saying: " Don't be afraid, Emily, it is only the Fourth of July."

It was the Fourth, but the fire ignored the coincidence. It burned the Amherst House, the Post-office. . . . Emily in writing to her little cousins explains how she let Vinnie think she was deceived — since Vinnie has thought best to deceive her.

" She took hold of my hand and led me into Mother's room . . . and so much brighter than day was it, that I saw a caterpillar measure a leaf far down the orchard; and Vinnie kept saying bravely, ' It's only the Fourth of July.' . . . I think she will tell us so when we die, to keep us from being afraid."

Just to manage to live, that was the problem. Every year people starve to death of actual hunger in the world, and they know indeed what it is to be trying just to manage to live before they die. Emily never felt the faint sickness of real hunger. Still she wrote about it constantly, as if she had. She had absolutely no economic insecurities, no lack of plenty. Never for a moment did she face the miseries, the ungainly problems, that the struggle just to eat and sleep and keep warm entails for four-fifths of the world. She was fortunate. And yet . . . any life except this of security was utterly banned. Was not that something regrettable? And all the while that Emily, seemingly so fortunate in a world that had more pioneer women and hard-pressed farm wives and invalid wretches than it had gentlefolk, all the time Emily was starving.

What crumbs kept her alive! A boy passed her window frequently, absently whistling a peculiar cadence. His whistle furnished several poems and many reflections and letter-paragraphs. When someone brought the boy to meet Emily, Emily knew all about him, beginning with his whistle. Such trifles as the caterpillar on the leaf in the orchard prolonged life. And several times in her fifty-six years she had the great good fortune to hear a circus go by at night. " Friday I tasted life and it was a vast morsel. A circus passed the house." Years later she writes to her cousins: " They said hoy, hoy, to their horses."

Near-sighted eyes see with especial care, see with an urgent scrutiny. One Christmas the weather was so mild that the kitties could wash themselves out of doors without chilling their tongues. And a storm came close enough, Emily says, to untie her apron. When they moved from one house to another, Emily felt as if they were migrating to Kansas. . . . First Emily faced west — then the pole swung due east. She forgot Kansas — the Alps were before her eyes, blinding, in sunlight.

> On the bleakness of my lot
> Bloom I strove to raise.

The bloom was hers, summer and winter. And winter was clearly her season. She acknowledged it. Having done so, she gave herself little jaunts of the imagination into the tropics. There is a whole tropic vocabulary — its colours, sounds, scents, and textures — in what she has set down. The humming-bird comes from Tunis; she selects certain insects and flowers as tropic strays . . . cherishing in the greenhouse the South Sea rose and the *Daphne odora*, which belongs to the Riviera.

With two ghosts for company in her garden, Emily meditated in a kind of timeless ease — very gradually her thought was slipping over on the verge of verse. One ghost was restive; he became a black dot on a sheer white wall; he climbed, to Emily's despair, when she asked him to stay passive with the gentle dead youth in the garden. He would not; he was alive. Emily bent her head; after 1854 life seemed to have no major secrets to reveal to her in new events or surprises. Meditation was action.

> *My life closed twice before its close;*
>   *It yet remains to see*
> *If* Immortality *unveil*
>   *A third event to me,*
>
> *So huge, so hopeless to conceive,*
>   *As these that twice befel.*
> *Parting is all we know of heaven*
>   *And all we need of hell.*

Her garden, her ghosts, her deliberate father . . . with these Emily was willing to grow old — nay, anxious, since age was the vestibule to death, and death would bring the bright face of George Gould nearer than God's face. God could answer all the riddles, but no one could look directly at Him. George Gould's bright face now neared and dimmed. . . . People passed her by at a blind distance. . . .

Anyone who had ever come within shouting distance of Emily had soon, as in a spell, moved off again, had died or gone away past the range of eyes. She was a young blithe girl no longer, and now Emily in no way withstood or contradicted her father; no one contradicted him.

And yet one voice remained.

See her working in her garden under the shade of the great box-tree in early summer. The house-door is open and father and mother still sit at the table. Vinnie and Austin are away. Father has experienced political reverses — snowed under at the second election for Congress, combated on every hand; he is stiffer now, more conscious than ever that he has enemies and hostile neighbours. Father's voice is heard talking about something — the new railroad or the insurance company — no matter what; when father spoke, it was his *manner* of speaking that struck the nerves. Across the lawn Emily hears the babble of her young nephew. The sun opens a cloud and walks out into a stainless blue; changes his mind and goes back in again. The colours of the flower-bed have a new tone, a flatter variegation. But the voice that unsays father goes on and on steadily and monotonously saying *Noooooooooo* contentedly into a flower. Emily hears the obligato of the great wanton bee contradicting father word for word in a velvet voice . . . it is a very American bee, with a whole continent of pollen to plunder.

135

CHAPTER IX

UNDERGROUND

". . . so he left the land.

DEACON LUKE SWEETSER LOVED BRIGHT FLOWERED waistcoats and fast horses. Amherst knew very well the old jest about the Deacon and the Squire. When the Deacon bought a pair of new horses, Edward was not happy until he had outrun them on the road to Northampton — take a good stretch, a pretense at indifference on the part of the two gentlemen, and they invariably vied like two boys for the lead. When the Squire's horses succeeded in passing the Deacon's, the Deacon traded in his fast horses for faster horses. So it went.

The Deacon was a jovial man. A person still living remembers that, as a boy, " the Deacon let me ride his mare around a bit. Ed'ard's — certainly not! " Luke Sweetser had a general store on "Broadway." He was The Merchant of the little town, just as Edward was The Lawyer, and Hitchcock The Professor, and Colton The Minister. The Merchant employed boys about the store on odd jobs. George Gould worked his way through college and, ac-

136

cording to the story, knew The Merchant well enough to
entrust him with a secret after he left town.[1]

What was the Deacon doing crossing the wall and coming across the yard to accost Maggie, the Irish girl who
worked at the Squire's house? He had seen Maggie beating a rug outside the door, he made sure she was alone,
and then he came near and bowed. Emily was, of course,
nowhere to be seen. That she tended her flowers early in
the morning, and on quiet afternoons was evident from the
patch at the Deacon's feet. Maggie quit beating the rug as
the Deacon drew near. I quote again from my correspondent X:

". . . took off his hat with a sweeping movement of the
arm, making sure the letter would be in reach of Maggie's
hand. She would run up the back stairs, slip the precious
letter under Miss Emily's door, and give a certain little
'tap' three times on the door, the signal that ' the letter '
had arrived. Miss Vinnie knew nothing of this arrangement."

> *The way I read a letter's this:*
> *'Tis first I lock the door,*
> *And push it with my fingers next,*
> *For transport it be sure.*
>
> *And then I go the furthest off*
> *To counteract a knock;*
> *Then draw my little letter forth*
> *And softly pick its lock.*

[1] See reference to an advertisement for sarsaparilla, recorded by Obadiah
in the *Indicator*, which indicates that George Gould could repeat the entire ad and which would suggest that he worked where the ad stared him
in the face — i.e., Sweetser's store. Appendix IV.

Then, glancing narrow at the wall,
And narrow at the floor,
For firm conviction of a mouse
Nor exorcised before,

Peruse how infinite I am
To — no one that you know!
And sigh for lack of heaven, — but not
The heaven the creeds bestow.

The letters were postmarked Detroit, Benoit, Chicago, Waukegan, Kenosha. George Gould was helping to build a railroad. After a time they wore foreign stamps on their faces: London, Edinburgh, Paris, Geneva, Vevey. . . . They came in this manner for nearly ten years. They were Emily's underground connexion with — "Life."

If Vinnie "did not know of this arrangement," Vinnie did not post the replies, we may be sure. Did Maggie? Maggie came every evening to brush Emily's hair, and they talked softly to the caress of the brush. Emily gazed before her as at herself. But she saw like the Lady of Shalott — a figure of a young man clambering up the Alps, and wandering in museums, "for his health." This is how George Gould sailed away. We find the mere record in the autobiography of the friend with whom he sailed.

It is John B. Gough speaking:

"On Thursday, July 9th [1857], I gave a farewell address at Worcester, and on Tuesday the 14th proceeded to take the ship Niagara for Liverpool. Mrs. Knox and her daughter, her sister Mary Booth, and Rev. George Gould accompanied us, intending to remain with us — Mr. Gould

"MY FATHER'S HOUSE," AS IT LOOKED IN 1850
—From an OLD LITHOGRAPH

DEACON LUKE SWEETSER, WHO IS SAID TO
HAVE DELIVERED LETTERS IN HIS HAT
— *From an* OLD PHOTOGRAPH

proposing to travel in Europe for his health. Quite a number of friends were with us the next morning, and parted from us at the ship's side. The gun fired, the paddles moved, and we were away."

I envy seas whereon he rides,
I envy spokes of wheels. . . .

This gentleman records the friendship between himself and George Gould thus:

" Among the ministers who came to preach for us, was the Rev. George Gould, and from our first meeting we became friends — not in the ordinary acceptation of that term, but we loved each other at first sight. There was a rare tenderness in our friendship. Our souls were knit together; we were so drawn to each other, that we seemed to fuse into one, — it is a holiday when we meet; the grasp of his hand does me good 'like a medicine.' . . . We have been together in dark days, and sunny days, but neither clouds nor sunshine affect the stability of our love for each other."

Gough was a native of Sandgate, County of Kent, England, who had come to America as a boy of twelve, " bound over " for a period of years. Eventually he climbed to the temperance platform.

What drew John B. Gough towards the as yet unordained George Gould, sometimes civil engineer and evangelist? There is a hint in another bit of testimony — the older man was evidently fascinated by something emotional in the younger.

" In 1856 I first met Dr. Gould, and was fascinated by

his preaching. He is emotional with no sensationalism. He speaks with an earnestness that convinces you he be-lieves all he utters, with a deep pathos revealing the ten-derness of his own nature, an eloquence perfectly natural, a face radiant at times when he utters some lofty thought." Emily, too, had seen that radiance:

> ". . . *You saturated sight* "

> ". . . *your face*
> *Would put out Jesus*',"

" There is nothing stale or conventional in his preach-ing. He reaches the intellect and the heart, and were it not for his health he would have been one of the widely known, popular preachers of his day."

George Gould's taste in speech and in writing, which, I think we must admit, had something to do with the for-mation of Emily's style, is indicated by what he said of John B. Gough: " Some of his finest passages seem to be perfect gems of idiomatic English, lucid and flawless as a crystal. Not a word could be changed, added or taken away without marring or weakening the whole. Since John Bunyan no man has been the master of a more terse, mar-rowy, pat and vitalized Saxon style."

This, said the person who wrote of George Gould's own preaching after his death, applied as well to his style as to his friend's.

If Emily was George Gould's " scholar " and this was his literary taste, how natural that she should also finally perfect a style gem-like and idiomatic, lucid and flawless, terse, marrowy, pat, and vitalized.

Although it is nowhere stated, it seems likely that George Gould went as Gough's secretary on this trip. It is most unlikely that lecturing for the lyceum and supplying here and there in empty pulpits should have given him enough funds to go abroad for two and a half years. Gough was a very busy man; he was flooded with letters which he evidently thought it his duty to answer; he was involved in a bitter controversy in England with a Dr. Lees, who eventually was brought to trial for libel. Between 1843 and 1869 Gough mentions with pride that he delivered six thousand and sixty-four addresses. One of his books was dictated and taken down in shorthand. We are safe in assuming, I think, that George Gould accompanied Gough and paid his own way by secretarial labours. Later when a windfall came, he went to Italy alone.

The party, containing two unmarried young ladies, Miss Knox and Miss Booth, was entertained wherever John B. Gough took it.

"Friday evening, July 31st, we attended a soirée given by George Cruikshank, at his house in Morning Sun Place."

Dickens was away in the country, at work on *Little Dorrit*. There were still Pickwick chintzes at the linen-drapers, and Pickwick cigars at every tobacconist's. Gough records:

"On 12 August, we paid a visit to Houghton, and were entertained by Mr. George Brown, and Palto Brown, till the 25st, when I ran up to London for the first speech in Exeter Hall, returned next day to Houghton and remaining there till the 31st."

After four months in Edinburgh " they went to London in January 1858 into a furnished house at no. 4 South Parade, Trafalgar Square, Brompton."

These addresses became part of Emily's memory.

" 8 Edith Grove, Brompton," was another London address.

Finally, after lawsuits against, lectures by, and fêtes for John B. Gough, the party set out for Paris, on July 22 at noon, arriving there at eleven o'clock on the night of the same day.

George Gould was doubtless not quite, but still doubtless very nearly, as critical of London and Paris as his travelling companion, John Gough, who records himself as having been increasingly so. Where was the self-styled Nathaniel Winkle incognito in London? Did he ride on coach-tops, or talk to cabbies? Did he look in at pubs and recall the old quips and fables of the imagination, concocted in the *Indicator* room at Amherst?

His friend's autobiography is full of Dickensian jokes — too many perhaps; full too of a social fervour, fastened into the temperance rut, but having to do with the case of the working man, with the ferment in industrialized areas. Temperance was the great panacea.

Now the party was in Paris. How warily they looked about them, resolved ahead of time not to be pleased!

" We took rooms at the Hotel de Louvre . . . and ' did' the *Lions* as rapidly as one week would permit." Much of the space reserved for Paris is consumed by a eulogy for a Madame Busque who advertised " Specialté de Pumpkin Pie."

Nevertheless, there was a lesson to be learned from Paris; and in lectures to come, John B. Gough was going to be able to speak with authority upon the subject of the "wine-growing countries."

"I had heard so much of the sobriety of wine-growing countries, and so many propositions to introduce wine in this country as a cure for drunkenness, that I determined to make what personal observations I might be able, during a very brief sojourn on the continent. On the Boulevards and the Champs Élysees, we saw no more drunkenness than in Broadway or Fifth Avenue; but in the narrow by-streets, back of the main thoroughfares, I discovered as many evidences of gross dissipation, as in Baxter Street, New York, or Bedford Street, Philadelphia.

"I took a survey of several of the low cabarets, and found the same bloated or haggard faces, the same steaming rags, the same bleared and blood-shot eyes, the same evidence of drink-soaked humanity in its degradation, as in any of the grog-shops in the United States. In Geneva, — the same; we were kept awake by the bacchanalian revels of intoxicated men in the streets nearly all night. In Vevay, I saw more evidences of drunkenness than in any town of its population in our country. In Mayence, a fair was held while we were there, and I saw more drunken men on the street, and in the square, than I believe were to be seen on the streets, during the whole five days of the ' Peace Festival' in Boston. In Basle, and in Cologne, it was the same. . . .

"My friends told me I should be charmed with Paris;

but so far from that, I disliked it. . . . The city is beautiful, — yes, magnificent, and well worthy of all admiration for its architecture, its broad boulevards, its Madelaine, and its innumerable objects of interest. It is the delight of Americans. They never weary of ' Paris' — beautiful 'Paris' — and I have been criticised for want of taste; but the fact still remains — I do not like Paris."

At Geneva the party took rooms at the Hôtel de Metropoli and attended the English church. The Alps were near — the Alps should be approached with a feeling of reverence and awe. God was doubtless there. These mountains comforted the forlorn moral-minded American, confused and somewhat overwhelmed by the spectacle of old civilizations and man's blithe delinquency. The Alps, like nature back home, were eternal reminders of a greater Power, of purity, aspiration, holiness, magnificence, American ideals.

In lands I never saw, they say,
Immortal Alps *look down.* . . .

" Soon after noon, we arrived at Sallenche, and while waiting for dinner, and a change of our voiture, I strolled out with our two friends; my wife, being weary, remained in the hotel. Standing together on the bridge, I said: ' How new all this is to me — the mountains, valleys, waterfalls, picturesque villages, chalets — all new and strange; the sky so clear and blue, the clouds so pure, — it is all glorious. What a peculiar cloud that is behind those hills! so white, so clearly cut, it appears almost like — why, it is — yes — no — George — that *is* the *mountain* — that *is*

Mont Blanc! I *know* it! And as I caught the first view of the monarch of the Alps, I trembled with excitement. With tears in my eyes, and my heart full, I turned away to hurry Mary out to enjoy it with us."

They were happy, with the Alps to verify their religion, to withstand wicked old Europe. They stayed four days at the " Hotel d'Angleterre " and made " excursions familiar to every tourist " — the first day to Montanvert, the next to the summit of the Brévent.

" We started on this excursion with a guide, two mules, and our alpenstocks — more ornamental than useful, like the dandy's walking-stick — but very pleasant souvenirs. At the Chalet de Planpras, we left our mules, and after a lunch of bread and milk, ascended by the 'chimney,' and climbing over rocks, and wading through snow, reached the summit, at an altitude of eight thousand feet. That was the grandest view my eyes ever rested on. Behind us, Salenche, with its bridge, far away the white ridges of the Vaudois, and Bernese Alps, were plainly seen; below us, Chamounix, like a nest of ant-hills; the glacier de Bossons; the glaciers d'Argenterre and Taconay; the river Arverion, rushing from its source at the foot of the Mer de Glace, and joining the Arve near the village, then like a stream of silver flowing through the valley; and before us, the Grand Mulets; and higher up, the snow-capped king of the Alps, with the Dome de Goute, and the Aiguilles, silent in their grandeur. The stillness, so profound, was only broken by the crack of the ice in some glacier miles away. As we stood there, we could only say with David, as he surveyed the glory of the heavens — ' What is man, that Thou art mindful of him?' and, feeling our own insignificance, amid these stupendous works of creation, could but utter thanksgiving, that the Creator of these wonders, the Framer of this Universe is God — and 'God is love'; and we, who are lost in wonder and awe at His works, may come to Him and say, 'Our Father which art in Heaven.'"

Everything else was false and debauched. The shrewd, knowing American eye could detect the falsities in European religion. Cathedrals drew the little party, but it came out petulant and overawed, in two contrary states of mind which could not easily be fused. The party, very much alone, except for the mountains, had endless encounters with papist guides, people very nearly heathen:

"In Cologne, we purchased — as every one does, or should do — some veritable 'Eau de Cologne,' and visited the Cathedral. We saw the skulls of ten thousand virgins — that is, we saw *some* skulls. The attendant showed us a small cracked jar, carefully enclosed in a case, lined with crimson velvet, and told us that was one of the jars the Savior filled with wine at the marriage of Cana. My wife turned away, and he said, with a shrug, 'Americaine — hah! not moosh like relique.'"

Emily followed the travellers by an act of the imagination.

> *Our lives are Swiss, —*
> *So still, so cool,*
> *Till, some odd afternoon,*
> *The Alps neglect their curtains,*
> *And we look farther on.*

Italy stands the other side,
While, like a guard between,
The solemn Alps,
The siren Alps,
Forever intervene.

Gough says:

" We visited the glacier de Bossons the next day . . .
left for Martigny by the ' Tete Noir.'

" On Saturday the 6th, we left for Vevay; arriving there,
we took rooms at the Hotel du Lac, and remained four
days. We visited the Castle of Chillon and standing in the
dungeon, by the pillars, we were reminded of Byron's
'Prisoner of Chillon.' At Vevay Mr. Gould left us
for a pedestrian tour, and we proceeded to Basle; then
to Mayence, down the Rhine to Cologne, where I
became weary of sightseeing, and proposed our return
home."

Elsewhere we find that George Gould spent two summers, not one, in Switzerland; the second time he went
alone, tramping about by himself. What letters he wrote
back to Emily on the coigns of little cliffs above Swiss
towns, we shall never know. But the inns, the road dust,
the bright overhanging masses, were surely mingled, as
he walked, with the thought of her, the troublesome, the
only person, the incomparable, the desperately loved. It
was eight or nine years after the spring of 1850; and
George Gould had toiled through malarial marshes in
Michigan, and lectured on literature in the Western towns
where the Indians were still on the war-path. How odd,
to be in company with the Alps and to find it as necessary

as ever to write Emily that he loved her and would always love her!

Then he went over the Alps, into Italy, by degrees, to Nice and Rome. At about this time Emily discovered the existence of the Brownings.

Of course she needed only to read the *Springfield Republican* and the *Atlantic* to know all she needed to know of them. Nevertheless, it is significant that George Gould's trip into Italy should come at about the time that Emily should begin to speak of them as if they were friends, people, not merely poets. The intense flake cast by the mirror in the sun ran down the Apennines and hovered over Rome; and everyone there interested her.

In February 1854 Mr. Higginson's Journal records:

" We have just been reading a nice letter from Barbara [Mrs. Higginson's sister] . . . . She is having a superb time with St. Peter, Martin Van Buren, Mrs. Browning and other Roman notabilities. She and Sully walk on the Campagna as if it were the Cambridge Common; little Lizzie plays with young Brownings and Crawfords; and Bab [Barbara] lends my ' Woman and Her Wishes ' to Fanny Kemble and Harriet Hosmer."

In September, when Barbara came home " with an atmosphere of art and wonder about her; and Brownings and Kembles as familiar household words in her speech . . ." Mr. Higginson recorded: " Barbara seems on the whole to have loved her [E. B. B.] very much and found her more attractive than him; he is very bright and talkative, observing everything and attentive to everybody; she, dark, little, quiet, and reserved, with black ringlets around her face, but not becoming to her; looks older than she is and invalid-like; shows traces of her sufferings and has a subdued intensity of manner. . . . She is very modest and even timid when her own poems are spoken of; whereas R. B. talked very coolly of his and defended the alternatives in the last edition; not that he was egotistical; but perfectly childlike and free. His male friends say that he seems more American than English; but she is more *interesting*."

William Wetmore Story was in Rome, writing his friends in Boston of all the joys of his warm life; Charles Eliot Norton and Charles Sumner were either just leaving or just entering Italy and the Story's place; American news, American gossip, went to Story in letters from James Russell Lowell. The Storys kept open house for attractive young Americans at 43 Via Sant' Isadore. Story knew Ripley, and Ripley knew Gough; a letter may have guided George Gould up the stairs, straight to Story's handclasp, and thence to Browning's.

Of course it was not necessary for George Gould to take Elizabeth Barrett's " spirit-small hand " and Robert Browning's hearty one in order to admire their poetry or to send it to Emily. Even if he spent days in Rome, conscious of their presences, listening for chance news of them, haunting the lonely museums with other visitors, a little hungry, feeling quite foolishly out of place, his nearness to tangible greatness counted with Emily. " Italy," " Rome," these were words to conjure with; and she was often home-sick for lands she had never seen.

Aurora Leigh had come out in 1856. Emily makes no

149

mention of it till the sixties. She loved the poem for many reasons. Bad as it is, prosy and preachy, it still boils with metaphor here and there; any reader will note, as he reads, that the metaphor is the poetry of the poem; and the stretches of hundreds of lines between, mere writing. Emily loved this metaphor; and it is uncommon good. Besides, she liked the story; it remarkably resembles her own in certain respects. The repressed Aurora, pictured as living a double life — one life of the mind, and the other of the prickly petty world — the Aurora who tried in secret to be a poet, the Aurora burdened with household routine, the Aurora who loved her father and parted with a cousin — all these Emily may have cherished to break down her feeling of isolation and bring her into the company she so desired. There was even a Susannah in *Aurora Leigh* who brushed the heroine's hair, as Maggie did Emily's own. And when she came on lines like:

> *I was not, therefore, sad.*
> *My soul was singing at a work apart*
> *Behind the wall of sense, as safe from harm*
> *As sings the lark when sucked up out of sight*
> *In vortices of glory and blue air . . .*

she found a description for her own inner life. Such passages as these — and there are many of them in *Aurora Leigh* — she undoubtedly marked — that is, if they were not already marked by George Gould's pencil, before he packed them to be delivered to Emily by Deacon Sweetser.

Hundreds of parallels lie in this poem.

> *I would rather take my part*
> *With God's Dead, who afford to walk in white . . .*

found response, and later expression, in Emily:

A death-heat is
The same as life-heat. . . .

And again:

I retain
The very last word that I said that day
As you, the creaking of the door.

These clearly bore fruit in Amherst. Elizabeth Barrett's reference to Mount Chimborazo and Teneriffe crops up in Emily's poetry. Every reader knows the lines; he may not know that the proper names came from *Aurora Leigh* and not from the atlas; and he will be surprised, perhaps, to know that Chimbarazu is to be found in the note-books of the Reverend George Gould. How easy it had been for Emily to be there, beside George Gould, on that lawn in Siena described by Story in a letter to Charles Eliot Norton from the Villa Belvedere, on the 6th of August 1859:

" Browning too is at a stone's throw from us and every evening we sit on our lawn under the ilexes and cypresses and take our tea and talk until the moon has made the circuit of the quarter of the sky."

If Mrs. Browning was often convulsed with laughter at Landor's " scorching invective, perpetual God-bless-my-souls, etc.! " how Emily might have enjoyed them! How she might have talked to Ba! And the big man with the direct glance!

Instead, Emily was using a few of the words on the backs of envelopes sent from foreign places:

⤷ EMILY DICKINSON ⤶

Pigmy seraphs gone astray,
Velvet people from Vevay.[1] . . .

Paris could not lay the fold
Belted down with emerald. . . .

Venice could not show a cheek
Of a tint so lustrous meek. . . .

Frugal Emily!

[1] George Gould, who mis-spelled Vevey in taking notes for Gough's book, evidently passed his spelling on to Emily.

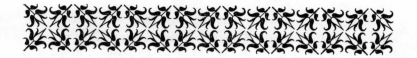

CHAPTER X

A MARRIAGE IN WORCESTER

GEORGE GOULD CAME BACK ON THE S.S. *ARABIA*, arriving on August 11, 1860. They were singing that camp-meeting song *John Brown's Body*.

How should he live, and what should he do?

Would Emily relent and marry him? Answered by a sigh — the Squire's face behind Emily's was sufficient answer to that question.

Would he, George Gould, once so high of heart, be able to do a man's work in the world — that is, God's world? Or would he continue to be a weakling, always, as he had been ever since Edward Dickinson had said him nay — an invalid with a broken heart, too eloquent and emotional for a regular pastorate, too literary for plain ministerial labour in the little town that stood in its thousand varieties dotted over New England.

War-talk filled the air. A war had been coming for a long time — Obadiah's references, back in 1850, to George Gould's orations, foretold the very war that stood like a cloud over America now. Politicians had arranged a war satisfactory to the people. Politicians like the Squire. The fuse was set. Knowing that the fuse was set, waiting for the first rocket, induced a state of mind inimical to dream.

And so George Gould decided to be ordained, to get into harness — there was no other balm in any Gilead but work for the Lord. Perhaps his health and his spirits would improve. Too long he had tarried; God's voice, in a clamorous land, gave instructions for a new, a dedicated life. The sound of the war-thunder increased, and it was necessary to take sides. Far back in his mind he remembered Patrick Henry and was sorry. And he could wish for a spiritual, not a temporal, solution.

New Englanders ran true to form. Wendell Phillips and Emerson were speaking at the Music Hall in Boston, to insulting throngs; Mr. Higginson was speaking in Worcester. When the first shot went off, Mr. Higginson proposed getting Captain James Montgomery and fourteen men into the mountains of Virginia " to divert the attention of the Confederacy from the national Capitol."

Sometimes the war seemed like a toy. This insurrection, as they called it, agitated old men on street-corners standing crooked over their canes, under the town elms. In Amherst the students led a patriotic demonstration across Main Street and the Common when they heard of Fort Sumter. The next day the Honourable Edward Dickinson addressed a citizens' mass meeting. By October a boy named Francis Dickinson, a far-off cousin of Emily's, was killed in the Battle of Ball's Bluff — both legs shot away — the first Amherst boy to fall.

Voices in the pulpits shook; the *Springfield Republican* used larger type and redder adjectives.

COLONEL THOMAS WENTWORTH HIGGINSON
THE OUTLOOK, 1898

PHOTOSTAT OF EMILY DICKINSON'S SECOND
LETTER TO MR. HIGGINSON, WHEREIN SHE
DESCRIBED HER TEACHER AND HER LOVER.
SHE ADDRESSED THE ENVELOPE HERSELF
— *From the* GALATEA COLLECTION *in the* BOSTON
PUBLIC LIBRARY

"You will never take a hopeful view of anything, I see, till you give up reading that unfortunate 'Springfield Republican,'" wrote Mr. Higginson to his mother, November 1, 1861, before he himself went to war. ". . . It is a singular fact that the war is said not to have raised the price of gunpowder because the amount does not exceed the amount ordinarily expended in field sports. . . ."

Emily was in an agony of suspense. She later wrote:

> *The only news I know*
> *Is bulletins all day*
> *From Immortality.*

But she wanted other news. Perhaps she feared that George Gould would go to war and be shot. He had rambled so, and grasped at straws, had knocked about the West as an engineer; she may have feared that war would touch his gallantry, appeal to his unsettled mind. He was as yet without a profession. That bare-headed life under the grass worried her like a wasp, she told Samuel Bowles.

Elizabeth Barrett Browning died. Whether or not George Gould had seen or spoken to the Brownings on his trip into Italy, the two poets who had done, despite a father, what Emily and George Gould had not done were something deified for Emily. In many ways she tried to mark the event of Elizabeth Barrett's death with a great black mark. She was astonished that Robert Browning could go on making poems — until, she says, she realized that she, too, in her small way, sang on " charnel steps." The momentum of events was changed and the world unnatural. A boy-child was born into the Bowles family, and

Emily wrote Mary and Samuel requesting them to call him
Robert (Browning) for her. And she added: "He is the
bravest man alive, but his boy has no Mama. That makes
us all weep, don't it? "

John B. Gough came to lecture in the College Hall at
Amherst. How did Emily contain herself when Vinnie put
on her merino shawl, and father his beaver, and the whole
town turned out for Gough?

Gough and Higginson, both associated with Worcester,
both now lecturing for temperance and abolition and women's suffrage, doubtless knew each other. They had, at
least, certain mutual friends — George Ripley, among
others. Despite differences of opinion and differences of
class, men like Higginson and Gough would hit it off very
agreeably; they had points in common. George Gould,
Gough's dear younger friend, may easily have joined the
lecturer's group. Except for his theology, he, too, would
be welcome among Higginson's hosts of friends — he who
had once admired Emerson to a fault.

Of this possible connexion between George Gould and
the sending of Emily's poems Higginson makes no reference in his account of how they came to him. His only
knowledge of Emily, he says, until he went to see her in
Amherst in 1870, was from her Uncle William, Edward's
younger brother, "a prominent citizen of Worcester . . .
a man of integrity and character, who shared her abrupt-
ness and impulsiveness, but certainly not her poetic temperament. . . . He could tell little of her, she was
evidently an enigma to him as to me." This sounds as if
George Gould refrained from mentioning his knowledge

of Emily's poetry, even if he did know Higginson, and even if, as it is possible and I believe, he urged her to send Higginson her poems.

What George Gould's hopes may have been in such a case cannot but interest us. Was he attempting to get Emily into the " real " world? He had failed to get her to run away with him; that he loved her still seems inescapable. Would the literary Mr. Higginson do something for Emily and check the introversion which was growing so desperate in her words? If Emily were hailed as a poet of importance, would she come gradually out of her shell?

In his sermons we find the Reverend George Gould saying: " I have no gospel of asceticism to preach to you." And again he says: " The Bible, my friends, is not a morbid book. You will find morbidness in plenty, in human writings, in religious memoirs and in devotional diaries, but never in the Word of God. The Bible is never misanthropic, is never ascetic, is never hypochondriacal."

Meanwhile Emily found sleeping difficult and thinking difficult; the pressure in the pulse too great. An impending sense of things about to happen all about her. Several fixed ideas overcame her. In three months she wrote Samuel Bowles again to query: " Can I rely on your ' Name ' ? " In January 1862 she asked Mr. Bowles: " Did you vote on Robert? " Samuel and Mary, with their fourth child in their arms, embarrassed by all this entreaty, announced that they had named the new child Charley.

Emily began to jot down mystic sentences for Mr. Bowles; what she wrote to George Gould we shall never know. The sentences whipped like little snakes on the page, bending this way and that, rearranging themselves in verses. Emily jotted and stared as if she were going mad. In her letters of 1862 she kept talking of going mad: " Insanity, for the sane, seems so unreasonable — but I am only one and they are four and forty . . ." and from an edited passage: " Think Emily lost her wits . . . but she found 'em, likely."

Either George Gould had stopped writing from Worcester, or he was allowing Emily to know too well what he was about to do.

She refused to busy herself with preserves for the soldiers. The good housewives of the south and west parishes criticized her bitterly. Some hideous violence in the nerves that surround the deepest self shook her mind. She looked to someone for relief. The measured tread of home was driving her mad. There was no relief. Only more headlines in the *Springfield Republican,* and young men brought home after battles, unrecognizable. No one had been allowed to see Frazer Stearns, for instance; and Emily called it murder. Frazer was killed on the 14th of March. On the 14th of April the Honourable Edward Dickinson presided at a meeting which accepted from his regiment " a six-pound brass gun taken in the battery where Adjutant Stearns, of the 21st Massachusetts Volunteers met his death while gallantly fighting." Austin went about in a daze, saying of his best friend: " Frazer's killed." Austin did not enlist. Father went on offering bonuses from his own pocket to farm-boys who would shoulder muskets. The town murmured a little against the Squire, whose son was too good to fight in the same line with their own.

During a winter of such conflicts and dissonances Emily began to write poetry. The new life began; the old one had been spirited away. A long-delayed power broke Emily's passivity to bits. Up rose a giant under the guise of a small woman. She worked. She wrote as if to dictation. And so one April Emily composed a note and put four poems into an envelope for Mr. Higginson, while the spring campaign was starting on the Shenandoah.

And that fall, while Emily was still fearing perhaps lest a Minieball shoot George Gould's heart out, she got the news that he was about to be married.

CHAPTER XI

THE MAN AT THE POST-OFFICE

M R. HIGGINSON WAS A GENIAL MAN, BUT HE DIDN'T have any Yankee horse sense. He made a good Abolitionist. He arranged to have some rifles, which had been sent west for guerrilla war in Kansas, transferred to John Brown, and the rifles went off at Harper's Ferry. In his genial way Mr. Higginson had a good deal to do with precipitating the war.

And he was never sorry. Every May since, the South is sheeted with the pink bloom of the peach-trees, he tells us in *Cheerful Yesterdays,* which sprang up where the Union Soldiers marched below the Potomac, throwing away the stones of northern peaches as they ate them on the march. A clumsy way of getting peach-trees planted, to be sure, but Mr. Higginson seems anxious to reconcile us with the world on such disproportionate grounds. He points out another example of the charmed working of events: the modern whitewing is a direct if somewhat costly result of the same war, first organized to sweep New York clean, and drilled in white uniform by an ex-Colonel whom Higginson knew and admired. When the world was tipped off its plumb (not to speak of being turned entirely upside-down) Mr. Higginson obligingly stood on his head — like a Lewis Carroll character — before giving anyone his conclusions. . . . On a trip far out west when he was lecturing for a lyceum circuit, Mr. Higginson discovered nineteen people in that frontier wilderness who regularly subscribed to the *Atlantic Monthly*. Nothing that ever happened in his lifetime — which covered a good deal of bitterness and slaughter and the spectacle, for those able to see, of a society laid out as on an operating-table — ever seems to have offset the clear gain of those nineteen subscribers.

Facile and prematurely mellow, Mr. Higginson began as a minister of the gospel and ended, partly by a sheer ability for longevity, in admiring Theodore Roosevelt; he loved to tell a good story; he was a personality and a scholar with a fine relish for both the active present and the passive past; he knew everybody, he moved about very much at home in the world; no victorian theory frightened, no genius overawed, him. It must be added that he was evidently brave, alert, and humane. He was a temperance man, but he guarded the rights of the individual and, in spite of his zest for reform, did not go the whole hog with extremists who agitated for prohibition. He loved reform:

"Living in a university city, I am occasionally asked by students how they can best train themselves for public speaking; and I always begin with one bit of counsel, based on half-a-century's experience: 'Enlist in a reform.'"

Reforms were dirt-cheap.

He helped the feminists — was he not a humanitarian all round? Having quit the ministry, Mr. Higginson meddled a good deal with social matters — thus enlarging the sphere of his influence for good. New England made causes, and the country tried them on its piano. Fanatics, like Garrison and John Brown, came from the common people; in order to be heard they needed the supplement of a reformer. All the best Boston reformers, like Howe and Wendell Phillips, were aristocrats — people, we might say, who hadn't had much to do with reality. The Wentworths of New Hampshire, who contributed our very considerable reformer's middle name, were such unmitigated snobs (and this Higginson records with amusement) that someone spitefully said that they always spoke of Queen Elizabeth as " Cousin Betsy Tudor."

Liberal ministers and India merchants made up his paternal line, and Thomas's father was steward or treasurer to Harvard College. Thomas himself lived to a sweet old age, to write many memoirs, while admiring Tennyson and corresponding with Darwin and Carlyle; he knew " the best " Matthew Arnold called " culture," and lived to put most of the great Victorians and the Transcendentalists to bed — by way of an article.

Cheerful Yesterdays is a charming book, full of *bons mots*. The *bon mot* itself was something to have brought in. Higginson recalls, when he writes his last memoir in 1905, the intense gloom of the early Americans, and their wrong-headed disbelief in democracy, repeating some of the period's criticisms of the Constitution — and very apt criticisms they are, too:

" It must always be borne in mind that the whole period I have been describing is a profoundly serious one and that the buoyant element, which in these days relieves itself in a *bon-mot*. . . ."

A saltier soul might have got more substance and fewer Victorian witticisms out of his numerous experiences; but only Mr. Higginson, as he was, could have written anything so persuasive as his account of the time. He tells us, for instance, how he broke down the Court House door in Boston, before hostilities, in an attempt to rescue a fugitive slave who was being returned by the law to his master. A scuffle resulted, in which the police clubbed him while someone knifed a marshal's deputy — and Mr. Higginson came down the steps to hear an old fellow say to him: " Mister, I guess you've left your rumberill." The young reformer (he called himself a revolutionist) took his umbrella and went to get his face washed.

The narrative gives us confidence in Mr. Higginson. He was nothing compared with Thoreau and Emerson and Hawthorne, his friends and fellow-beings; but we can be sure that he genuinely likes the Negro when he says he does, and we remember how Emerson, after a mental identification with the cause of the slave, confessed that he couldn't bear to have a black man in the house. What Mr. Higginson lacked as a philosopher, he made up by a natural warmth, a tenderness unfeigned.

Fields liked Higginson's urbanity and wanted him to give the *Atlantic* everything he wrote. That spring, in the midst of other things, he contributed two articles which interest us: " Snow," in February, and another which evoked a small deluge of amateur poetry.

" Since that Letter to a Young Contributor," he writes Mr. Fields in April, about the time Emily's letter arrived, " I have more wonderful effusions than ever sent to me to read with requests for advice, which is hard to give. . . . One begins:

> *Summer is come*
> *Winter is gone*
> *Oh! the brier*
> *And prickly thorn*

and ends:

> *My little home*
> *Is safe and sound*
> *And I'm a til-*
> *Ler of the ground*

And again a few days later, during which time Emily's poems arrived:

" I foresee that ' young contributors ' will send me worse things than ever now. Two such specimens of verse as came yesterday and the day before — fortunately not to be forwarded for publication! "

Three years before, Mr. Higginson had discovered a very satisfactory young lady of talent. When the *At-lantic* editors accepted a story of Miss Harriet Prescott's, Mr. Higginson, who loved to write his mother in a slightly boastful vein, recounts his part in the affair:

" Do you remember a Newport girl named Harriet Prescott [Mrs. Spofford], who writes me immense letters and whom I think a wonderful genius? She has just sent to the *Atlantic* a story, under an assumed name, which is so brilliant and shows such an extraordinary intimacy with European life, that the editors seriously suspected it of being a translation from some first-class Frenchman, as Balzac or Dumas, and I had to be called in to satisfy them that a demure little Yankee girl could have written it; which as you may imagine, has delighted me much. It is called ' In a Cellar,' and will appear in December."

Later in the same year:

" Emerson says: ' To-day is a king in disguise ': and it is sometimes odd to think that these men and women of the ' Atlantic Monthly,' mere mortals to me, will one day be regarded as demi-gods, perhaps, and that it would seem as strange to another generation for me to have sat at the same table with Longfellow or Emerson as it now seems that men should have sat at table with Wordsworth or with Milton. So I may as well tell you all about my inducting little Harriet Prescott into that high company.

" She met me at twelve in Boston at Ticknor's and we spent a few hours seeing pictures at the Aquaria gardens. . . . Duly at three we appeared at the Revere House. . . . Harriet was whirled away into some unknown dressing-room, and I found in another parlour, Holmes, Lowell, Longfellow, Whipple, Edmund Quincy, Professor Stowe, Stillman, the artist, Whittier . . . Woodman, John Wyman and Underwood. . . .

" Down we went: Dr. Holmes met us at the entry; each bowed lower than the other, and we all marched in together . . . at the Autocrat's right . . . think of the ordeal for a humble maiden at her first dinner-party. Little Dr. Holmes came down on her instantly with her laurels."

1862 was as busy a year for Mr. Higginson as it had been morbid and reflective for Emily. He was taking fencing-lessons. And besides he had meetings to organize and little quarrels between factions of the Boston movement to smooth and patch over — the gentle Whittier wouldn't co-operate with Garrison and Mrs. Chapman; the non-resistants wouldn't fight; the pure abolitionists didn't care about the Union, that new ideology which had supplanted slavery. They wanted to be sure that Mr. Lincoln, who wasn't an aristocrat, could be trusted to remember the slaves. It wasn't Mr. Higginson's war any longer; nor Garrison's, nor even radical Boston's; it was, by sleight of hand, Mr. Lincoln's, and he, a plainsman politician, had grown mystical about the Union. Mr. Higginson was trying to form a regiment, keeping one eye on the policy of White House; he delayed to be sure of Lincoln. Strangely enough, the abolition of slavery, which on the platform of Faneuil Hall had been a very exalted emotional axiom, with a moral halo around it, now seemed to be mixed up to some extent with economics. Mr. Higginson didn't want to fight a base economic war. He was in a sort of moral dilemma.

Someone wrote:

> *There was a young curate of Worcester,*
> *Who could have a command if he'd choose 'ter,*
> > *But he said each recruit*
> > *Must be blacker than soot,*
> *Or else he'd go preach where he uster.*

This was prophetic. Mr. Higginson hadn't said anything of the sort. In August 1862, however, he joined the
51st Massachusetts and was given a company and re-
cruiting office in Worcester; and then Brigadier-General
Saxton, of the Department of the South, wrote saying that
he had received authority to recruit a regiment of freed
slaves and asked Higginson to be its colonel.

Being colonel in a black regiment was going to be an
adventure; life had often been an adventure. He had
befriended runaway slaves and plotted the escape of others; he had gone to Kansas with thousands of dollars in a
money-belt around his waist and a pistol in his hip-pocket;
he had taken John Brown's wife on a futile errand to see
her husband before he was executed. He had performed
Lucy Stone's wedding ceremony, and some day he would
describe it; and he had written a memoir of Margaret
Fuller Ossoli after she was drowned with her husband
and child off Fire Island. Thomas's invalid wife watched
these exploits from her sick-room.

And he, in the happy hurly-burly, lived and wrote
without pause poems, essays, letters, prefaces, lectures.
A bibliography of his writings covers twenty-five small-
print pages. He recorded for his mother a continual narrative of the men and women he met, writing down the
anecdotes he overheard in trains, telling her with gusto
the little events of his busy circle; and still, even with war
sputtering between two lines of muskets south of the
White House, he went on writing his lucid and amiable
essays for the *Atlantic* and played near the centre of the
literary life of the time.

167

Let us never forget that Mr. Higginson had an aptitude for people. Four years before, he had written in his
private diary a series of little jottings on his contemporaries which make clear his abilities. Literary values and literary personalities are easily confused, and
Mr. Higginson in a literary world could not always
tell a hawk from a handsaw, but he was able to note
that:

"Mr. Emerson is bounteous and gracious, but thin,
dry, angular, in intercourse as in person. Garrison is the
only solid moral reality I have ever seen incarnate, the
only man who *would do to tie to,* as they say out West;
and he is fresher and firmer every day, but wanting in
intellectual culture and variety. Wendell Phillips is always
graceful and gay, but inwardly sad, under that bright
surface. Whittier is the simplest and truest of men, beautiful at home, without fluency of expression and with
rather an excess of restraint. Thoreau is pure and wonderfully learned in nature's things and deeply wise, and
yet tedious in his monologues and cross-questionings.
Theodore Parker is as wonderfully learned in books, is as
much given to monologue, although very agreeable and
various it is, still egotistical, dogmatic, bitter often, and
showing marked intellectual limitations. Mr. Alcott is an
innocent charlatan . . . maunders about nature and when
outdoors has neither eyes, ears nor limbs. Lowell is in-
finitely entertaining, but childishly egotistical and mo-
nopolizing."

What would he say, if he had the chance, about Emily
Dickinson?

For this is the man Emily Dickinson chose to decide whether she was worth rescuing from isolation.

Emily, who had practised for some years in her inner life an utter self-reliance, could not climb out of her isolation by herself. She was walled into a very high tower; her virginity, her genius, certain terrors and reflexes over which she had no control, and her mirror-bright, many-faceted mind made her dwelling as impenetrable as glass, as invisible as glass; and, like glass when she gazed through her wall at the world outside, it magnified many times normal size.

An old fairy-tale repeated itself symbolically that April, while the temperature hung about 72° in the shade. The tower and the bad enchantment naturally required a knight-errant. We have seen the nature of the spell in which Emily moved, although she knew its power well enough to wish it broken. She had had the equivalent of a hundred years' sleep after pricking her finger on a thorn. She was awake now, watching out of the tower for a rescue, and she had signalled to one exceedingly chivalrous knight who seemed to be looking for adventure.

But people in a fairy-tale are not prepared for the accidents and irregularities, the dissonances and the marginal mischances which distort the events of the real world. They have not yet cultivated a taste for accident and imperfection, the wry and undertoned. A pure diagram suffices, and pure colour paints a picture; if there are hags and wizards, they must be killed; if there are maidens in distress, they will be rescued. In a fairy-tale it is possible to demand of life a flawless love and a fleckless sky.

How deeply Emily had inured herself to bitter-sweet reality we can tell by the dissonance in her verse, by its thoughtful irregularity, its delight in acknowledging the sovereignty of discipline. But deeper still were the dreams and stubborn hopes of a child. Emily, like most diffident adults, had, by torment and ridicule, slain and buried the child in herself. But her adult life had so little substance and satisfaction, so small a means for growth, that the child kept returning to dictate motives and fantasies, resurrecting itself imperiously to insist that it was a more real Emily than any other. Mr. Higginson beautifully sufficed: he was a child's knight-errant; in him knighthood was in flower. Jonathan Edwards had thundered the conviction of infant damnation; Higginson, a sort of antibody in the Puritan blood-stream, was one of the first inventors of the literary cult of the child, for the same reason that he contributed to the cult of the Negro. Emily who had felt the singeing wind from the sermons of old Edwards, devoutly expected this contemporary gentleman to be what he looked to be through the lens of her isolation.

Certainly no appeal beginning in such tender and sensitive hidden dreams could have touched mild Mr. Emerson, or egotistical, sagacious Mr. Thoreau, or incurious Mr. Hawthorne. They would never have done anything so romantic, so rash, or so humane as rescue a person like Emily. They were content and needed no exploits to please themselves with themselves. Emerson might have pointed out in an aphorism the compensations of solitude; Thoreau perhaps, if compelled to pay any attention, would have offered Emily an apple to eat off a wild apple-tree, the tree of self-knowledge — he died a month later, having himself taken one bite of the apple; and Hawthorne, if he had known who it was he had before him, would have thought of his mother, who lived in a darkened room for forty years. He would have said nothing.

The little note, written after a morbid winter, betrayed hardly a sign of any agitation. Unless we read between the lines. It is a bare, queer little note, demure and careful; as unlikely to send Mr. Higginson flying to Emily's rescue as anything he ever received. He received so many. The tiny envelope containing her pencilled name was not enough to interest him; and the poems were, temporarily at least, just words on paper. Mr. Higginson took twenty years to do what Emily supposed he would do with one motion of his thumb and finger when he looked in the little envelope for her name. Her official announcement of herself as a poet meant nothing to her chosen critic — at least nothing comparable to her excitement. Very slowly Mr. Higginson admitted the discovery that had been forced upon him.

But now he wrote, as he always did, when he had time, a kindly reply.

His letter is destroyed. Emily destroyed it before she died. She had been writing:

> *And if I gain, — oh, gun at sea,*
> *Oh, bells that in the steeples be,*
> *At first repeat it slow!*

Will my reader turn to poem IV ("Life") in *Collected Poems* and examine the graphic suspense based on the little gamble?

When the letter came, she was prepared, her nerves were steeled for the sort of answer we get after sending up our sums in arithmetic to be corrected, not by our teacher — a person of limitations, obviously — but, rather, by the Spirit of Arithmetic. Hers was an exact mind and she customarily took up into her hand only such amounts of anything as she could perfectly assay. Either yes or no, plus or minus, would have been sufficient, she wanted no mitigations. Neither did she want that dim word from a dim world where we all live in ordinary circumstance.

(Late in life, writing in response to some query from her sister-in-law, Emily says exactly what she wished said to her in this, one of her moments of greatest suspense: " The answer is an unmitigated *Yes*, Sue.")

Her poetry was either extraordinary or entirely mad; it could occupy no middle position. That she knew, on that basis she awaited an answer. But Emily was wrong in requiring clairvoyance of Mr. Higginson, hero of a hundred *Atlantic* paragraphs, just about to go to war in high feather. It never occurred to her that she would get back an indeterminate reply in which the critic was either playing for time or playing safe, because she had never before tried gambling with the imperfect roulette-wheel of a wobbly world. She was in consequence keyed a little too high to make human allowances; while Mr. Higginson could make no judgment whatever without personality to guide him.

The superb certainty was too much to require; Emily nevertheless required it. Roulette made a good symbol for certainty; men have always loved the wheel, cruel as it is, for the definiteness of its decisions. If there had been a little machine to test poetry and record its degree by a percentage or a pillar of mercury, Emily would have preferred it to Mr. Higginson. The only important person extant in her world — her father — could be counted on to be as constant and as true as mercury, or as mathematics. We understand that she hoped for a like reaction from Mr. Higginson because she had had it since she was a child in her father.

Extremes were Emily's accustomed climate: the first chapter ended on the note of June, but during these pages it must have swung back into the cold it had not really escaped; June couldn't last in the middle of April. Back it came before or after Mr. Higginson's reply, freezing and spreading a flurry of snow before it, to say: "Oh, no, no, no. *What a mistake you made, Miss Emily!* "

She answered him ten days after her note, which arrived on April 16, apologizing for the delay, saying that she had been ill and must write from her pillow. The compromise scathed her; to break a proud isolation only to be patted on the head! Her second letter permits us to reconstruct what Mr. Higginson said in his first. He seems to have inquired her age, what books she read, what companions she had . . . these facts were material evidence to an estimate of her worth. He even wanted to know a little about her family. In his second letter he urged her — doubtless with some crumb of praise for further verses

— to mend her rhymes, give over the uncontrolled, the *spasmodic*, he called it; and he nettled Emily a little by advising her to delay publishing. In fact, Mr. Higginson botched things badly.

Emily was so unreal to him. To have been once so ungraceful himself must have bothered his further grace. He had started off on the wrong foot and he always remained awkward and ill at ease with his protégé. This was unusual for the kindly man who knew how to use his charm, who rarely offended people, who kept even his anti-abolitionist friends during the war bitterness with a *bon mot* or two — he who had no timidity with Browning or even with that god among men Tennyson, when he found him grouchy on a visit; he who could tell his fellow New Englanders their faults without discomfiture. Emily felt in him a constraint that amounted almost to embarrassment. Her letters grow stiff and self-conscious. They had struck an impasse of temperament.

Life was rewriting the drama. Emily's dreams had sketched a different script.

Mr. Higginson, who knew how to treat Victorians when he caught them, those fine bright moths who dried their wings very vigorously and prettily while he stalked them with his butterfly-net (he really did hunt butterflies — this is not a metaphor without background), had caught a new specimen and a rare one.

He had found in the flood of amateur poetry that came just before he went to war a poet who was both a Puritan and a modern, without Victorian stain. How queer she looked! Emily felt she looked queer. In one letter she explains that while he seems to think her dissimilarity superficial, she feels alone and *gauche:*

" Myself the only kangaroo among the beauty, sir, if you please, it afflicts me. . . ."

The gamble had failed, how gloriously Emily was not to know. In a dream, as we all wish in dreams, Emily had had the absurd wish to hear someone with a face like God's say naïvely, but with authority: " You are a great poet, Emily Dickinson."

This verdict is addressed to a mortal now and then, and sometimes it is true. Emily hoped, although she could not quite know she hoped, for such language. She had Elizabeth Barrett and Emily Brontë in a far corner of her mind. Destinies persuaded her. Her name was Emily Elizabeth. She lived in solitude, her father " had a habit of her," as Elizabeth Barrett's had had. It all seemed plausible, as things will seem, in dreams.

The gamble had failed. But even Mr. Higginson's luke-warm response saved Emily's life. She says so.

Her extremity must have been great to make his vague help a boon. She explains that his meagre praise would have made her tipsy, except that " I had tasted rum before." He got the full credit for a kind of rescue. . . . But was it not rather the decision to gamble that had saved Emily's life, since somehow it was saved?

She had taken one chance with life, and one chance, fully taken, is enough. She had begun to live, after twelve years' preparation, in a new and tragic limitation. The letter to Mr. Higginson broke some spell, and the letter to Mr. Higginson came in round-about fashion from a war which Mr. Higginson had helped prepare. The importance of the ultimate reality, the hurly-burly, the struggle — it was that that roused Emily.

She is always cryptic and grateful, humble and flirtatious in her letters (accepting the role of eccentric she put off when she still hoped not to have to play it with him), writing discreet, self-conscious sentences to cover her silly disappointment. Higginson preferred the eccentric Emily, it helped her case in his eyes, for he did not realize as Emily did how undistinguished and uninteresting a queer woman can be in the backwoods. For him it helped her case and coloured the picture; it had an extraneous value. And least of all did he take note of the anonymous mind — the anonymous mind dazzled his eyes a little painfully, so he shut them. Harriet Prescott, who wrote *In a Cellar*, had been more tangible and more entertaining.

Now, with seven hundred and fifty poems and her letters before us, we are impatient and feel rightly enough that if the values of great writing had had any reality for her critic, he could not so have failed her. Still, we cannot blame the good man. He had not seven hundred and fifty poems, but four. In the imperious manner of a little girl Emily demanded, under the demure disguise of her letter, to be told her writing was alive — not that she was a young lady of talent and sensibility who might some day publish in the *Atlantic* with Mr. Higginson for sponsor.

Four poems cannot stand as index. Seven hundred and

fifty poems under the subdivisions "Life," "Love," "Nature," "Time and Eternity," "The Single Hound," and the poems since published, must be read as one poem. Her units of thought are part of a cosmology, the highly organized statement of an invulnerable attitude. She wrote, not seven hundred and fifty terse verses, but one long dissertation on one theme in as many units of sense. Her point of view need only revolve on its own axis to turn us in the direction of any conclusion she ever set down. The texture is exact, however the units may vary; and only by knowing how they interlock and accent one another do we perceive the greatness of the mind that made them. But in her childish, regal way Emily required an answer on insufficient evidence, being too proud to give Mr. Higginson more than a hint, and expecting on that basis some miracle of recognition.

The winter before, two editors — probably Samuel Bowles and J. G. Holland — came to visit her father and called Emily penurious when she refused to give them a poem for publication. Like the true miser she was, Emily doled out her fragments to her friends, she allowed no one the privilege of herself entire as long as she lived. There was a store of riches in that old dresser where she kept her manuscripts, each rolled like a parchment and tied with a single thread; not so niggardly was she that only a small number saw the light before she died, and, dying, she left word that the little rolls were personal papers and should be burned.

Mr. Higginson took them as personal papers; he was inclined to be literal; it made Emily uncomfortable.

177

"When I state myself, as the representative of the verse, it does not mean me, but a supposed person."

Mild reproof. And she did not tell her age. He should not have asked.

She pretends to have misunderstood his question, and answers that she " made no verse, but one or two, until this winter, sir."

The correspondence went on all summer. It went on for years. So did the poetry.

Hope that " opens and shuts like the eye of a doll " can set one insane. " Hope is a subtle glutton." Like all the good similes about her life, these are Emily's own. She wore hope through while Mr. Higginson temporized. In the microscopic carved handwriting that announced a new state of mind before she had had time to become acquainted with it, she wrote one day this answer, designed, it would seem, for Mr. Higginson, Helen Hunt Jackson, Samuel Bowles, J. G. Holland, and all others who had lovingly encouraged her to write and publish or discouraged her from it. The poem makes Emily's ambitions clear by a negative and scornful statement of them.

("Dr. Holland once said to me: 'Her poems are too ethereal for publication,'" writes Mrs. Gordon L. Ford, in the first collection of *Letters*.)

And if not always too ethereal, sometimes too rugged, and obviously too impudent:

> *I'm nobody. Who are you?*
> *Are you nobody, too?*

Here is the recoil from Mr. Higginson; although how long the recoil took, coming back on the delicate spring

178

of Emily's temperament, is not possible to say with
exactitude.

> *How dreary to be somebody!*
> *How public, like a frog*
> *To tell your name the livelong day*
> *To an admiring bog!*

The Boston, the *Atlantic Monthly,* bog croaked monotonously on for the rest of Emily's life, but she did not
hear it. In such an absolute fashion may a recluse continue
to live.

CHAPTER XII

CHEQUER-BOARD

STILL WE CAN SEE WHAT ROLE POOR MR. HIGGINSON was required to play.

It was not much to ask him to do — to be the passive representative of several diverse people, to be father and Humphrey and the denied lover all in one; but at a great distance, and in entire innocence.

As so often happens when we find an image for something secret, Emily's secret faded from around the image, and the features of the substituted face came too distinctly through. Higginson had not the pure and terrible quality Emily saw in her father, although she tried to give his face a touch of arrogance it did not have, saying in a letter that a photograph he sends lacks it, and for that reason she finds the picture at fault. The poor camera could not photograph what was not there. Nor was Higginson Humphrey. Humphrey believed in Emily and gave her understanding evidently, even before she showed herself clearly. Higginson could not be the lover denied, because Higginson was not in love with Emily.

But he focused what otherwise would have remained

180

deranged: Emily's picture of father and teacher and lover.
Otherwise she would have had only God, as she foresees
at twenty. Higginson, with his bright brisk nebula of
affairs, emphasizing the things of this world as opposed to
eternity, stood, until he was worn to shreds, between
Emily and the great sun of heaven, the intolerable signet
of authority — to which the soul, which had seceded from
the universe, must in the end return.

One metaphor clarifies the pattern unnaturally; another, printed over the first, will serve to blur it back to
life again. A squint at the sun, and the eyeball retains the
red pattern after the eye is shut. We can see Emily revolv-
ing round the sun in a mute and uninhabited universe; one
glimpse reveals the motions of a lifetime. But read her
letters and her poetry and complicate the picture; follow
the scallops of design in this life or any other and behold
the fine writhings at the centre and then the oblique stif-
fening outward, or a folding and an unfolding, in contradiction. And so the reader will get many metaphors to
describe Emily's mind, as he reads what she has written.
At times her mind will look like a flat steel engraving in
intermingled millions of strokes, and then it will be a
paragraph printed over a paragraph in a book of only one
page; and then it will seem an opaque single film on which
exposures have been multiplied. This intricacy and com-
plication end only in a primary intricacy, which is, after all,
both the centre and the outside circle of the design, and its
whole simplicity. For while Emily was choosing people
so that she might escape from God through them,
she was unwittingly searching in them for Him;

and while she was requiring that they give her God's opposite, she was also preventing them from doing so, by acting towards them as one would act only towards God.

The beloved teacher was one aspect of God; father was another. But often Emily did not stop with either of these partial attitudes. And when she came blinking out of her dream in 1862 to write Mr. Higginson a note to ask for criticism on four poems, she quite forgot what she knew of the finite world, and really wrote the letter to a temporary indwelling of the spirit in Worcester, Massachusetts.

The supposition held until she got a reply. A few minutes, and Emily saw her mistake. For her correspondent proved to be only an ex-minister,[1] a New England provincial, a likable and fallible man. Novelists would show a person like Emily in collapse at such a sudden drop; people are supposed to crumble, or turn to another god, or retire embittered, when they have so fooled themselves in secret. Emily shifted gears promptly. About ten days after her first note, she wrote again, this time from her pillow, ill for her own reasons, but able to answer like anyone else in the new tone of voice, quietly abandoning her first impulse. Still, throughout the letter and all the letters to follow, the discarded desire keeps emerging from the lower voice in the fugue that will not be entirely woven out of sound. When she tries to explain how she began as a poet, she must tell her own version of the truth:

" When a little girl, I had a friend who taught me Im-

---

[1] " I was told you were once a clergyman." Galatea Collection.

mortality; but venturing too near, himself, he never returned. Soon after my tutor died . . ."

Could Mr. Higginson "teach Immortality"? That was the real question. She desired approval — to have him kindly nod to her was sweet; it was needed, but it was not what she craved. Later, once or twice, she could not help asking again the same first question. One letter wonders: "Or is it unconveyed, like melody or witchcraft?"

The letters begin: "Dear Friend," and are signed in shadowy memory: "Your Scholar."

Now and then the signatures vary, and once, for no reason pertinent at all, Mr. Higginson got a note ending: "Your Gnome." It was a little unfair to puzzle her teacher so, but pupils often fall into such habits, and to puzzle Mr. Higginson was Emily's only revenge.

Indeed, until much later, when Emily was safely dead and unepigrammatical in her grave, it was all too tense, too cryptic and feminine, for Mr. Higginson, who thought he knew all about women. After she died, her bad grammar did not matter and her jests stood nobly on the page, in a little heaven of their own making. But while she was alive, Emily was too disquieting, and Mr. Higginson — like nearly everyone else when faced with disturbing values — preferred the firm peace of things not so vibrantly living.

Did he sense that a game was being played and that his part was blindfold? Mr. Higginson looked all his life long for adventures and ran from one corner to another in pursuit of them; but the most fascinating gambit he might have ever found was repeatedly offered him and repeatedly declined. Did he ever sit at his desk and ponder Emily's sentences? It is probable that he did not; he could see no oblique gossamer; her mystery baffled him, and so he called her queer and shut up his desk. He even probably had a little pigeon-hole marked *Correspondence with E. D.* Only very late in life did he explore the pigeon-hole; and he seems never to have supposed that Emily's poetry was anything in final estimate but amateurish eccentricity.[1]

But even a human piece in a chequer-game knows something about his movements to and fro on the board, and so Mr. Higginson may have faintly suspected at times that he stood in various black and white squares and fought mimic battles. Emily herself only dimly knew of the way in which her hands moved, taking the one pawn from the square that belonged to father and setting it down for experiment in the square reserved for lover, and then, as if her hands were hypnotized and could not resist, trying to see Mr. Higginson in " God."

" Are you perfectly powerful? " one letter is compelled to question.

See Mr. Higginson retiring to his study and the shut desk, politely excusing himself to Mary, his invalid wife, with the explanation: " I've just got another from my eccentric poetess." A step or two, a quietly closed door. Mary wearied of people very certainly; especially these women, writing Thomas packets of letters stuffed with

[1] See the proposal by Higginson to write an article " The Female Poets of America," in a letter in the Manuscript Division, New York Public Library.

poems; women were a pack of imbeciles writing packets of letters . . . they were all the same: Anne Whitney and Harriet Prescott, who wrote *In a Cellar,* and now this new one up in Amherst . . . women with meagre talent, all entreating a man for his help. Meanwhile Thomas, who seldom could spend much time on literary matters now that the war claimed so much of his attention, had caught himself on one of Emily's sentences. Did she mean the *Atlantic,* he wondered. She protested that fame was not her primary concern and said: " My barefoot rank is better "; but still she might be meaning the *Atlantic* when she asked if he were perfectly powerful. If he wrote a little introduction, he might get a few of the least odd of these taken; but she really should wait and not hasten to publish; she should read the best poets and set herself technical tasks and learn syntax and, above all, try for melody.

If she would try for melody . . . Emily knew a scale with microscopic intervals; Mr. Higginson heard the standard seven and no more. That left gaps, and he urged melody. Emily, who could not hope now, she thought, to get God to listen, or anyone so well endowed for perfect response, found that she must write for herself, her most conscious self . . . for the anonymous mind.

Meanwhile Mr. Higginson thought the little literary flirtation charming, and when he didn't understand, he simply left off writing; while Emily, much preoccupied with her secrets and her slow art, still had time to mourn his silence. When he ceased to play, she pursued him with the gentle petition:

" Speak, if but to blame your obedient child."

Father, like an archaic Calvinist, had disliked poetry, with compressed lips; Humphrey had made poetry a very large breach. Others prevailed — George Gould, and the Reverend Charles Wadsworth, men of God, who permitted poetry. Father still indicated that he preferred Emily not to meddle with poetry. But time passed; and Emily renounced many things — her gaiety in the world, and a man, and feminine foibles. Father liked and trusted such a daughter; father found a sternness in his child he had not known she had; it kindled him, for he saw that she was his own; he could condone small irregularities; she, of his three children, was the real Dickinson after all, and poetry only an innocent pastime. She should have her books, her greenhouse, her dog Carlo, and her correspondence with this Boston critic, unsound as his politics were; father did not mind now; Emily, who for so many years had led him a merry chase, was now quite herself, and father rapped on her door every morning to wake her and warned her at night not to work by candlelight lest she ruin her eyes. And the evening and the morning was the only day.

Emily did not allow her poetry to take place next the family lamp on the reading-table, under her father's eyes . . . he probably never saw a line that she wrote, and if she desired to keep her poetry from the world's eyes, she learned the impulse first in hiding it from her father's. Emily knew that a fast horse or a well-argued case at court would always stand higher in her father's opinion. And since her father despised soft and voluminous or what he would call poetic speech, Emily inevitably sharpened

186

hers, and all the time his legal phrases were creeping into
her poetry, transformed there, just as she herself was her
father transformed.

The overstrain, the guttering candle, wore out the poor
eyes and shut one more line of communication with the
world. Emily went to 86 Austin Street, Cambridgeport,
to stay with her cousins Fanny and Louisa Norcross, to
submit to the Arlington Street doctor, who took away all
her books, *and* her pencil. This was in 1864, and again in
1865. During these two years she spent almost six months
on each visit; and the days were difficult, the nights hot
and sleepless; objects blurred, beyond the window; re-
covery was slow — nerves and eyes were both gone. Only
her cousins made the experience bearable; Emily loved
them with an especial gaiety and fondness.

Emily's letters to these cousins imply that they knew
all her secrets. " That old nail in my breast pricked me,
that was all," she says, once; often she makes clear their
intimacy. Fanny and Louisa may have known, not only
Emily's secret, but George Gould as well; their mother
came from Monson; for several years George Gould
supplied pulpits in and near Boston. During 1864 and
'65 he was in Springfield and Hartford, vainly attempting
to address his congregation at least once on every Sunday.
By 1870, he ceased the struggle and retired from an
active pastorate. He had managed to maintain a pulpit,
despite his tremendous popularity and applause, for only
eight years.

Six years after, Mr. Higginson may (or may not) have
been startled to find himself standing on the father square

of the chequer-board. Emily began to hint that she was writing — not for Mr. Higginson after all — but for God Himself. Mr. Higginson was dull, Humphrey was dead, father was indifferent, and the lover denied was not an audience any longer and may have felt some hurt at Emily's devotion to her destiny when he brought her his own instead. After 1862 Emily, loving him still and knowing he loved her, seems to have broken up her love into fractions for Higginson, for Bowles, for Wadsworth. George Gould had broken it up by breaking a certain fidelity in marrying after twelve ascetic years. In 1876 Emily sent Mr. Higginson a poem entitled *Immortality*, which without deviation remained the old and only theme. Immortality, besides, being the very subject she had asked him to teach her. He had not been able to teach her, but he did like the poem and wrote to say so. She replied:

"I am glad *Immortality* pleased you. I believed it would. I suppose God Himself could not withhold that now."

Which is the only openly bitter sentence Emily ever put down.

In the mean while she combed the ranks of acquaintances for friends. None of Emily's women friends are required to wear God's very heavy, clanking character. The world was divided between authority and creation, and the authority in Emily's society was chiefly or wholly masculine; the creation almost wholly feminine. Creation entailed a contradiction of authority, Emily thought; creation was usually heterodox, but hidden; women were in the secret; women were the sly or merry subjects under a very alien rule. Only in one fashion could a woman change the fixed scheme of things and break her antithetical position. If she fell in love, a woman achieved something outside the usual destiny. It must be the Victorian passion, the mystic union; something to set aside the rules of both earth and heaven. Emily was allowed this life in her imagination, and she had no opportunity to test actual love between herself and her lover. . . . She had, therefore, three rooms in which she might live: one in authority, the second in the room of her love, and the third with women, where she faced against authority. Emily assumed with Helen Hunt Jackson and Maria Whitney, the agnostic, with Vinnie and sister Sue, and Mrs. Bowles and Mrs. Holland, " the sister," and, most happily of all, with her little cousins Fanny and Louisa Norcross, that she need never interpret feminine signs, and she gestured her dumb show before the blind gaze of teachers, father, and God.

But a masculine friend always turned out to be a foil for Edward, as if Emily must test his opposite and find, if possible, the better clime of another person to which she might migrate. Emily did not know that she was attracted to these genial liberal men of the world because they were not only her father's opposite, but her own; but whenever she tried (and she was always trying) to pack up and start a residence in a warmer world, it became clear that she had a nostalgia for home. " Home," she said almost too aptly, " is the definition of God." " To see you " [Mr. Higginson] " seems improbable, but the clergyman say I shall see my Father. The subterranean stays."

She chose J. G. Holland, a joyous, pious person, who

wrote under the pseudonym of Timothy Titcomb, and who later edited *Scribner's* and made it a forum for the best of the moderns. Bowles and Holland and, when summoned, Higginson, all combined to lift the archaic sadness Edward cast before him. They all were, to some extent, disciples of the doctrine of newness, and their instigator, Emerson, instructed them in a glow of benignity. Emily follows their lead, saying: " I believe the love of God may be taught not to seem like bears," and " It is a godless thing to be a boy in a New England town." She, with the rest of them, watched to discover the Satan Jonathan Edwards had made so personal to her forbears, and, not seeing him, concluded: " He must be making war on some other nation."

She took Judge Lord, a rare old soul, for her own. He came to visit father and remained to adore Emily. He sent her notes and quips from the Salem Court House, where Hawthorne had suffered the stigma of a removal from office and local persecution. With him she exchanged a *badinage* designated as the " Judge Lord brand." He was higher in the legal hierarchy than father; he was more human, more literary, and less gaunt within.

These liberals, these humanitarians, Higginson, Holland, and Bowles, satisfied something that could not be withstood. Between them they disagreed — Bowles thought Higginson a heretic, and Holland too pious; Bowles and Holland joined in opposing all Higginson's reforms, woman suffrage, temperance, and transcendentalism. The two editors thought of themselves as the two blades of a pair of shears. They snipped many a fine-spun thread in their editorial columns. But taken together, they were nevertheless liberals, in one sense or another, and fully opposed to the old school which Edward represented. They were editors and lecturers and men of affairs, believers in the people. Father was only a very much respected local lawyer, a friend of Daniel Webster; father was a small politician, sometime Congressman and hereditary trustee and treasurer of Amherst College. He moved against the current. Higginson's father had had the same position of treasurer, care-taker of higher education at Harvard, and when some Hebrew Bibles arrived with a bill for payment, he protested that he should send them back because they were bound at the wrong end. Higginson studied the Bible his father had declared mismade, but he found texts in it to confute old Jonathan Edwards, who still stalked in the Puritan unconscious; he remembered Cotton Mather and perforce Calvin and did his best to find reforms to distract the introvert from the tenets of his ancestors. Sweetness and light were two words uttered seven years later by Matthew Arnold, but the Disciples of Newness had been smiling a determined smile for years, convinced that any progress, however flimsy, away from Calvin and Edwards and Mather was progress indeed. Edward Dickinson must have found Higginson's cheerfulness intemperate, a sort of fanaticism, and what Edward felt clearly, Emily always felt moving in her mind, like a cloud. Everybody agreed that Edward had a remarkable character; but, like his greatcoat, he did not have it cut over to suit the times. When he joined the church rather later in life than was customary, he

contented himself by saying simply that he only wished to
" be a better man." That restraint curled at the root of
Emily's religious glee. Edward, who embodied a sense
of property and the integrity of the Puritan as identical,
distrusted those romantic states of mind which had brought
the first religious settlements to the new country; he
distrusted the ideals of democracy, rabble movements
and Jeffersonian individualism — his temperament could
make a constitution, but never a revolution. Romantic
politics and a sense of property are antithetical. He was
a Whig — but call him a Tory Whig. The liberals, the
humanitarians and reformers, of which number Mr. Higginson will do for an example, offended him as a matter
of taste, just as he mistrusted the fanatic religious convul-
sions that were sweeping the country; just as he felt angry
and hot under the collar at Jenny Lind's concert, partly
because that Swedish lady extracted four thousand dollars
above costs from Northampton alone. America, like an
animal that is injected full of virus — the experiments
first conceived in Europe — had its Shakers, its Fourier
Communists, its Adventists, its Carmelites, its Mormons,
and its Brook Farm. It had also social agitations attached
to its liberal pulpits. It was a mad continent, seemingly,
attacked by every conceivable theory-germ isolated in the
old world, and its madness was held in check only by the
discipline of hardship. As soon as the hardship abated,
the isms multiplied. America had been more or less discovered in order to give the sick world a place in which to
carry on experiments. Edward did not know this. Democracy, if Edward had had his way, would have extended

as far as his class, and there would have established its high watermark. He was stricken to death as an old man making a speech in the legislature, arguing against the spring thunder of a new age, although they called it a speech for the Hoosac Tunnel.

In consequence the old and the new battled for the upper hand in Emily. She makes avowals on both sides. Father called Theodore Parker poison, for Theodore Parker was wrecking father's world entirely, in his eloquent Boston pulpit. Theodore Parker and Higginson and Emerson anathematized Daniel Webster, called him a traitor and a politician; ah, alas, everything father had embodied with such probity for so many just and beautiful years in Amherst was now being put to scorn, and in 1861 one of the common people with hay-seed still in his hair, and not Daniel Webster, had just been elected President. Perverse Emily could be expected to be on the other side, if only to plague her father — so Edward would doubtless put it. She began to read abolitionist tracts, and all the time the mobs in Boston were dragging abolitionists off by their heels and tarring and feathering them and riding them out of town on a rail.

The battle went on and on in Emily, all during the war. It is hard to place her, and because she did not show a violent preference for any one of the current points of view, she is supposed to have been uninterested. Not a word about the slave escapes her. And when Mr. Higginson opened a letter from her in South Carolina, he found no patriotic little sentences, but only a request that he avoid death for her sake if he could do so with honour.

Mr. Higginson came back from the war Colonel Higginson and took up his old life, shook it, and put it back on like a comfortable coat. Peace hath its victories no less than war. He must write about the Negro for the *Atlantic*.

Emily had gone to war too, but not in the body. Emily had gone early with the first sign of war; she went the first winter, and when she wrote: " I had a terror since September I could tell to none; and so I sing, as the boy does, of the burying-ground, because I am afraid," she was trying to tell him about it. This is the way she went to war. After the train whistled in the evening, Emily waited for the step on the path that meant that someone was bringing the *Springfield Republican*. When it came, after father and mother had read it, Emily read it, every evening, devouring every crumb of detail. We have seen that Emily disbelieved in evil and that she disposed of the reality of Satan, so far as she was concerned, by saying that he must be making war on some other nation. But Emily was treating with Boston radicals in her mind. And the Boston radical had found evil in the form of slavery; from this discovery soon proceeded war, and few would maintain that, even for holy ends, war was not evil. Emily's good world crashed.

Austin's dearest friend, Frazer, had gone. Austin did not go. Emily held her breath, and then Frazer was killed on the first of April, "his big heart shot away by a Minie ball." Indeed death, which had come in 1850 to take Leonard Humphrey, had come again with a battalion of aids, and the young were falling like ripe wheat before a wide scythe.

The winter of 1861 and '62 had made soldiers of clerks and farm-boys; for them it had multiplied death; death was simultaneous now, *en masse,* the possession of regiments and battalions — a mass affair, multiplied and common, but remarkably diminished in scale. When death came singly to Amherst, it came to play a formal drama, dignified and heroic, with the leading role cut and fashioned carefully by God for the individual soul. Now a nation, split in two, was making the experience wholesale.

Emily had learned to manage her life by renouncing it. That the clerks and farm-boys were in the act of renouncing life, too, made her no ideal recompense. In spite of her environment, which abounded in the rhetoric of nobility, Emily lacked the fervour to co-ordinate battlefields with a just world. The war put an end to her first reliance in a just world, and it cut across her emotions and her mind at the precise juncture of a governing obsession.

She had been hovering over battlefields all winter. The war was a profound shock. Her letters show it and she says so. Still the degree of her agitation went beyond the sentences written down in letters. We know now how habitually and instinctively she hid the source of any mortal trouble until she had used it for a victory. But we can tell how the war altered her mind by finding it embedded deep and hidden very often from view, a fact over which many anxious queries swarm in the poems and letters.

She was thirty-two years old and she had renounced life — that is, personal life, the life of Emily Dickinson. Another life, the life of the anonymous mind, engrossed her. She could not renounce the life that remained with her; nothing could keep the anonymous mind from what required to be scrutinized and understood. When the war upset her, Emily grew aware that she was housing something avid, wilful, and possessed of a wild vitality — something that wanted a great deal of sustenance to appease its appetite — that had the intenser need for living on one plane because it had forgone life on another.

No wonder 1862 had been a morbid winter. Emily, like a delicate barometer, felt the pressure of a cloudy and destructive century to come. The chaos she witnessed and deplored in the conflict and saw on the horizon, which many would argue was only the temporary accompaniment of war, has extended and enlarged down to our own day. It has become so much the necessary condition of growth to our way of thinking, so necessary to " life," as we term it, that it is hard for us to believe in a *living order* of any kind. Chaos and life have become murderously synonymous.

She saw the mercury falling; already things were shattering. She was the fastidious spiritual inhabitant of a lawful, functioning universe, and she set about to clear away the wreckage as best she might, rearranging the great tenets of an ancient theology, not as theology now, but as profound poetic truth, startled and challenged by the way the old world crashed before the new. Emerson and Higginson and Garrison, and even Thoreau, invited the new in, and hurried the old out of the back door.

While Mr. Higginson was at camp, she wrote to him

repeating the old fact, which may seem very clear to us now that we have traced the line, but which, when the phrase stands alone, seems like undifferentiated experience: " Perhaps death gave me awe for friends, striking sharp and early, for I held them since in a brittle love, of more alarm than peace." Death and war, as stages of the soul, never the ethical points of slavery or secession, became Emily's preoccupation.

And the war, which first broke up years of self-sufficiency, which appalled Emily by its chaos, its accidental and therefore immoral processes, which turned her to poetry and then to that representative of the world she professed to renounce, finally ended by walling Emily back into an even completer isolation. The war woke the poet and sealed up the recluse. The recluse ceased to expect to find God by letter.

Often Emily identifies or compares herself to the good soldier in her poems. One beginning " Success is counted sweetest by those who ne'er succeed," published by Helen Hunt Jackson in a *Masque of Poets*, opens the first volume of the *Collected Poems* and stood first in the 1890 edition of *Poems: First Series*. It is three stanzas long, and ends on the battlefield. Another has also three stanzas, wherein she dared to affirm a bravery greater than any hero's — a belief shattered when the war first came, now emerging in clear syllables:

> *To fight aloud is very brave,*
> *But gallanter, I know,*
> *Who charge within the bosom*
> *The cavalry of woe.*

197

Who win, and nations do not see,
Who fall, and none observe,
Whose dying eyes no country
Regards with patriot love.

Here, as always in her work, is a genius for dramatizing the self, giving it heroic tests and combats, keeping it lithe, making it live in a stoic universe, in as definite and lawful a pattern as the mind of man has been able to invent. The Puritan soul, which had a very dull time of it with the Puritans of small imagination, found in Emily Dickinson a poet capable of assigning it a resplendent role, as strenuous as the clash of life and death.

The *Springfield Republican* of October 3, 1863, told of the death of Major Hunt, killed accidentally while experimenting with his invention, " the sea miner." Emily had liked Helen's husband tremendously. She was stricken for her friend.

The draft of 1863 was as unpopular as a rattlesnake. Amherst resented conscription — she had filled her quota loyally with brave young men; the draft was an insult; an infringement of private privileges. This draft aimed at men between twenty and forty-five. Many men bought substitutes. To cry it on, the Honourable Edward Dickinson spoke at every meeting held to canvass and assist in securing volunteers. Where was Austin? Had Frazer's death chilled, not fired him? The draft officer found 567 males in Amherst, of which number 156 were already at the front. Seventy-nine were either coloured or foreign and were thus exempted. The town must deliver impartially of its 332 remaining. We are forced to conclude that

Austin's name was either not drawn, or that he purchased exemption, or that he was exempted after physical examination. Bonuses beginning at five dollars and running as high as one hundred dollars were offered by patriotic citizens for volunteers.

Nevertheless, the Dickinson name went to the front in somewhat less favoured persons. Francis H. Dickinson died in battle. David L. and John W. Dickinson died of wounds and from disease, respectively, and (Corporal) Chester Dickinson, junior, and (Sergeant) E. Baxter Dickinson were wounded. Thirteen Dickinsons from Amherst enlisted. Austin lived for four years in the darkness of some shame. Emily lived beside him. Traces of jests at Austin's expense are still to be found.

It was a pitiful mess, this Republican war. All its actual motives were disguised with oratorical phrases and unreal idealisms. An age was passing in America, as Edward knew; as Higginson knew; indeed, as everybody knew. The clutter was swept past on a tide as natural as a flood. Aristocracy, both North and South, was doomed; the North was dying in the act of killing its cousin the South. And the industrial, the bourgeois class of the North bided its time, employed the noble excuses for war invented by the cerebral New Englanders, preparing under cover for the next period, its own.

An oblique place Emily called war. Whitman was nursing in the hospitals, closing the eyes of the dead. Emily was doing something similar. In death the soul came close to the surface, like a dim shape held just under water. Scrutinizing the dying with the eyes of a scientist, Emily hoped to catch some glimpse of the soul in the moment of its escape. All her life long she wrote almost greedily to ask for details of the behaviour of the dying, and in her poetry the exact glaze of the eyes, gesture of the hand, shade of the countenance are over and over fixed unforgettably. If possible, Emily was going to see the soul naked. The soul, the single premiss of her arduous philosophy, should be studied in the holocaust. A curious mixture of scientific coldness and mystic rapture always directs the research:

> *Faith is a fine invention*
> *For gentlemen who see;*
> *But microscopes are prudent*
> *In an emergency!*

Emily had looked at death very closely ever since 1850. Death had not degraded Humphrey. But now the war degraded dying and ignored the soul; and because it could manufacture death without reference to the soul, Emily finally rejected the war.

Mr. Higginson came back from the war and found Emily still sitting up for him, ready to start where they had left off. But by the time he was almost converted to her genius (finding it exceedingly durable), she no longer needed him — except as one more letter-writing friend. She had coolly embalmed the incident of the roulette game (which took place, alas, like so many other things, only in Emily's mind), and she managed of her frugal relationship with Mr. Higginson all that was needed.

Now she might have a little amusement out of the figures it afforded:

> *I bet with every* wind *that blew, till Nature in chagrin*
> *Employed a* Fact *to visit me and scuttle my Balloon!*

Indeed, the relationship, if fully dissected, furnished endless parable:

> *I took my power in my hand*
> *And went against the world;*
> *'Twas not so much as David had,*
> *But I was twice as bold.*
>
> *I aimed my pebble, but myself*
> *Was all the one that fell.*
> *Was it Goliath was too large*
> *Or only I so small?*

One tiny double-edged verse in *Poems: First Series*, has baffled all our critics. It is in someone's phrase the Dada of the late Victorian period, and one line has been quoted until it has become a household phrase; but no one has attempted to say that it connotes more than a delicate nonsense. Let my reader turn to poem XII of the collected volume and decide whether or not at this juncture Mr. Higginson and the Mighty Merchant are not the same person. Emily had asked for no other thing than simple recognition. Higginson was willing to give her almost anything else — fatherly advice, invitations to become a part of his literary coterie; he offered a charming correspondence and really good guidance on how gradually to make her mark and win a *petit* fame. Brazil? He twirled a button. . . .

Rouge et Noir and *Rouge Gagne,* which have little threads of evidence to connect them with her first note to Mr. Higginson, may have been suggested by a poem Julia Ward Howe contributed to the *Atlantic.* Mr. Higginson knew Mrs. Howe well; she belonged to his set; his set was clearly appointed to write all or, if not all, nearly all the important American masterpieces. " They created American literature, and freed millions of the slaves," he says. He continues:

" I never encountered, at home or abroad, a group of people so cultivated and agreeable as existed for a few years in Newport in the summers. There were present as intellectual and social forces, not merely the Howes, but such families as the Bancrofts, the Warings, the Partons, the Potters, the Woolseys, the Hunts, the Rogerses, the Hartes, the Hollands, the Goodwins, Kate Field, and others beside. . . . "

Mrs. Howe, the centre of this cultivated group, wrote first the *Battle Hymn of the Republic,* and then many sentimental pieces about her children. Of all her poetry, however, Mr. Higginson liked *Rouge Gagne* best:

The wheel is turned, the cards are laid;
The circle's drawn, the bets are paid:
I stake my life upon the red.

The rubies of the bosom nine,
The river of life, so swift divine,
In red all radiantly shine.

Upon the cards, like gouts of blood,
Lie dinted hearts, and diamonds good,
The red for faith and hardihood.

In red the sacred blushes start
On errand from a virgin heart,
To win its glorious counterpart.

The rose that makes the summer fair,
The velvet rose that sovereigns wear
The red revealment could not spare.

And men who conquer deadly odds
By fields of ice and raging floods,
Take the red passion of the gods.

Now Love is red, and Wisdom pale,
But human hearts are faint and frail
Till Love meets Love and bids it hail.

I see the chasm, yawning dread;
I see the flaming arch o'erhead:
I stake my life upon the red.

In this affirmative mood much poetry was being written; Emily's shreds, glints, jewels, and cryptic profundities could not talk to Mrs. Howe's hearty bravado; two little trifles in the poem, however, are kin to Emily's manner and they are no more out of place in the poem than all the other mixed germs of style: rhyming " red " with " paid " and " laid " is Emily's habit, and the word " errand " is the kind of terse actual word she loves for sound, for strangeness, and for metaphor.

Helen Hunt Jackson lived at Newport, too, after her husband died, in the same boarding-house with the Higginsons. She was very modern for her contemporaries. When she travelled, she carried fine stuffs from the Orient and her own collection of Japanese prints and transformed her hotel rooms always into suitable quarters. And, almost, Mr. Higginson persuaded her to become a feminist. Helen had two griefs, for she had lost her little boy as well as her husband. She began to write because she needed money. Later she remarked: " I do not write for money, but I *print* for money." If these women were anything like graces competing in literature for the palm from the hand of the arbiter, it was Mrs. Jackson who received it:

" The poetry of Mrs. Jackson unquestionably takes rank above that of any American woman, and its only rival would be found, curiously enough, in that of her early schoolmate, Emily Dickinson. Emerson, as is well known, rated it above that of almost all American men. Her words include, first, the simple poetry of domestic life; secondly, love poems of extraordinary intensity and imaginative fullness; thirdly, verses showing most intimate sympathy with external nature; and lastly, a few poems of the highest dignity and melody in the nature of odes, such as ' A Christmas Symphony ' and ' A Funeral March.' "

Some time between Major Hunt's death and her marriage to Mr. William Jackson of Colorado, Helen Hunt visited Emily for two weeks and spent hours upstairs preparing manuscript. Vinnie supposed that Emily joined with her and allowed some of her poetry to be sent to editors here and there. It may have all been Helen's. But rumours have always persisted that Emily had some part in certain of Helen Hunt's literary efforts; and we have letters showing that Helen Hunt went on begging for poems under different pretexts for years — as if she had some reason to suppose that Emily might relent and publish some. This visit of Helen Hunt's is significant for two reasons: it probably accounts for the story that Emily was to have joined in the writing of *Mercy Philbrick's Choice;* and it strengthens the very grave doubt that anything concerning the fidelity of Major Hunt could have been in Helen Hunt's mind, if she came to stay with Emily for a fortnight, during which time she thought of little else but her literary career!

Another visitor was the Reverend Charles Wadsworth. He came twice, both times on religious business, before he died in 1882. His personality must have been magnetic, since Emily so cherished his friendship — for his sermons are ordinary, dull, and opinionated, without the slightest distinction. He was seventeen years older than Emily and very respectable, although he enjoyed the reputation of being heterodox and against the majority. His only other real link with her, at this distance, seems to have been the fact that his eyes were very bad.

In 1868 Mr. Higginson was suggesting gently that Emily become part of his group. Emily was very slow to understand; she seemed only to be interested in writing her poetry, in snaring a sentence or two about " Life," and in getting Mr. Higginson to say now and then that as poetry it would do. She showed no contemporary interest if it had not already appealed to her. If the horizon was narrow, it suited all other narrow circumstances to which she was already accustomed. Mr. Higginson, who was a true provincial, watchful, was much worried that his pupil cared less about proper "centres" and new movements and what was being said at Mrs. Sargent's.

Still he had several indomitable spinsters to handle; he went to see them, they talked, he recorded. He writes in his diary of his meeting with Anne Whitney, who was a poet and a sculptor outside the pale:

" Here I am in a farmhouse next to Miss Anne Whitney's. . . . After my nap this afternoon, as I was beginning to write you . . . up came a message that Miss A. W. was below, so down I went. White dress and cape bonnet; face between Elizabeth Whittier and Susan Higginson: looking older than I expected. Her brother was with her, which made it less remarkable for her to call on me. She and I agreed on a walk which we later took — a lovely walk through green lanes fringed with barberries to a beautiful great elm tree and some superb oaks. A. W. is like her poems, in a less degree — spirited and decided and a little abrupt and odd, sometimes saying very condensed and graphic things, but with no grace, herein being unlike her poems. I don't know how she liked me; she said I was entirely unlike her expectations which I believe is uncommon for people to say, isn't it? She did not repel me, neither did she charm me. . . ."

But still with all these other "talents" he was trying to do his duty by Emily. . . .

He wrote her of Whitman.

Emily replied that she had been told that his book was disgraceful.

He tried to get her to read Miss Harriet Prescott's works.

Emily declined.

During the war Mr. Hawthorne had died, Emily's eyes had failed, and Colonel Higginson had been wounded. Emily went to Boston for treatment; she wrote Higginson briefly to inquire for his well-being. When he came back, Emily was again in need of a physician for her eyes, and Higginson was writing to her, begging her to come to Boston that he might meet her. This is her reply:

"I had promised to visit my physician for a few days in May, but Father objects because he is in habit of me."

Father's habits put before everything, as a matter of course, even before Emily's eyes! Perhaps father knew that Mr. Higginson was in Boston! It is also possible that Emily and her father were both in the "habit" of each other, and that Emily did not want to go to have either her eyes or her idea of Mr. Higginson tampered with.

Now, good as Mr. Higginson was, we have seen that he could be boastful; and without doubt one or two sentences establish the fact that he could also be patronizing. He went to see Emily in 1870, nine years after she had first written him, when his war was over, but hers still being waged, and Emily forty-three years old. She had kept her sanity, her wit, and her integrity, had included Mr. Higginson in the intimate circle of her friends, had borne his rather pedantic reproof and only mildly explained in her letters to him how his apologetic pedagogy was missing the point. She merited a cordiality in the private of Mr. Higginson's mind, beyond the easy judgments of stupidity. But, characterizing her to his mother, he calls her *his,* which was not true, and applies the usual word " eccentric."

". . . I saw my eccentric poetess, Miss Emily Dickinson who *never* goes outside her father's grounds and sees only me and a few others. She says ' there is always one thing to be grateful for — that one is oneself and not somebody else.' But Mary thinks this is singularly out of place in E. D.'s case. She (E. D.) glided in, in white, bearing a Daphne odora for me, and said, under her breath, ' How long are you going to stay? ' "

Later, in 1890, in the inevitable *Atlantic,* Higginson described the meeting, but for the public this time — for a public more sure of Emily's greatness than Higginson had been. He revises the whole account, trying to tell the truth, to be sure, but often sliding off into nervous ambiguity. Nevertheless, as we have seen, Higginson had an aptitude for people and he gets something from having seen Emily:

" After a little delay I heard an extremely faint and pattering footstep like that of a child, in the hall, and in glided, almost noiselessly, a plain, shy little person, the face without a single good feature, but with eyes, as she herself said, ' like the sherry the guest leaves in the glass,' and with smooth bands of reddish chestnut hair. . . . She told me of her household occupations, that she made all their bread, because her father liked only hers; then saying shyly, ' And people must have puddings — ' this very timidly and suggestively, as if they were meteors or comets. . . . The impression," concludes Mr. Higginson, still ill at ease, "undoubtedly made on me was that of an excess of tension, and of something abnormal."

"And even at this day," he says, trying to describe how she made him feel, "I still stand somewhat bewildered, like a boy."

A letter to Mary,[1] written a few hours after the meeting, with its candid conclusion, is better biography:

Aug. 16, 1870 at Amherst
Tuesday 10 P.M.

I shan't sit up tonight to write you all about E.D. dearest but if you had read Mrs. Stoddard's novels you could understand a house where each member runs [?] his or her own server [?]. Yet I only saw her.

A large country lawyer's house, brown brick, with great trees & a garden — I sent up my card. A parlor dark & cool & stiffish, a few books & engravings & an open piano. Melbone & O. D. Papers among other books.

A step like a faltering child's in entry & in glided a little plain woman with two smooth bands of reddish hair & a face a little like Belle Dove's; not plainer — with no good feature — in a very plain & exquisitely clean white piqué & a blue net worsted shawl. She came to me with two day lilies which she put in a sort of childish way into my hand & said " These are my introduction " in a soft frightened breathless childlike voice [2] — & added under her breath Forgive me if I am frightened; I never see strangers & hardly know what I say

[1] Galatea Collection, Boston Public Library.
[2] One person still living told me that Emily had a "*high surprised voice*" all the time.

—but she talked soon & thenceforward continuously —
& deferentially — sometimes stopping to ask me to talk
instead of her — but readily recommencing. Manner between Angie Tilton & Mr. Alcott — but thoroughly in-
genuous & simple which they are not *saying many things
which you would have thought foolish & I wise — &
some things you wd. hv. liked.*[1] I add a few over the
page.

This is a lovely place, at least the view. Hills everywhere, hardly mountains. I saw Dr. Stevens the Pres't
of College — but the janitor cd. not be found to show
me into the building. I may try again tomorrow. I called
on Mrs. Banfield & saw her fine children — she looks
much like H. H. *when ill* & was very cordial & friendly.
Goodnight darling. I am very sleepy and *so* good to
write you this much. Thine own

T

E. D. again

" Could you tell me what home is "

" I never had a mother. I suppose a mother is one to
whom you hurry when you are troubled.

" I never knew how to tell time by the clock till I was
15. My father thought he had taught me but I did not
understand & I was afraid to say I did not & afraid to
ask any one else lest he should know.

[Her father was not severe I shld. think but remote.
He did not wish them to read anything but the Bible.
One day her brother brought home Kavanagh hid it

---

[1] Italics mine.

under the piano cover & made signs to her & they read it. Her father at last found it & was displeased. Perhaps it was before this that a student of his was amazed that they had never heard of Mrs. Child & used to bring them books & hide in a bush by the door. They were then little things in short dresses with their feet on the rungs of the chair. After the first book she thought in ecstacy " This then is a book! And there are more of them! "

" Is it oblivion or absorption when things pass from our minds? "

[Major Hunt interested her more than any man she ever saw. She remembered two things he said — that her great dog " understood gravitation " & when he said he should come again " in a year. If I say a shorter time it will be longer."

[When I said I would come again *sometime* she said " Say in a long time, that will be nearer. Sometime is nothing."

After long disuse of her eyes she read Shakespeare and thought why is any other book needed.

[*I never was with any one who drained my nerve power so much. Without touching her, she drew from me. I am glad not to live near her. She often thought me tired & seemed very thoughtful of others.*] [1]

" Women talk: men are silent! That is why I dread women.

My father only reads on Sunday — he reads *lonely* and *rigorous* books.

[1] Italics mine.

If I read a book & it makes my whole body so cold no fire ever can warm me I know *that* is poetry. If I feel physically as if the top of my head was taken off, I know *that* is poetry. These are the only ways I know it. Is there any other way?

How do most people live without any thoughts. There are many people in the world (you must have noticed them in the streets). How do they live. How do they get the strength to put on their clothes in the morning.

" When I lost the use of my eyes it was a comfort to think there were so few real *books* that I could easily find some one to read me all of them."

" Truth is such a rare thing it is delightful to tell it."

" I find ecstacy in living — the mere sense of living is joy enough."

I asked if she never felt want of employment, never going off the place & never seeing any visitor. " I never thought of conceiving that I could ever have the slightest approach to such a want in all future time." [& added] I feel that I have not expressed myself strongly enough.

[She makes all the bread for her father only likes hers & says " & people must have puddings " this *very* dreamily, as if they were [carrots or comets, probably the latter] — so she makes them.

Before the meeting in Amherst, however, Mr. Higginson had tried his best to induce Emily to come to Boston. " You must come down to Boston sometimes. All ladies do. . . . I wonder if it would be possible to lure you to the meetings on the thirtieth of every month at Mrs. Sargent's, 13 Chestnut Street, at ten A.M. where somebody reads a paper and others talk or listen. Next Monday Mrs. Emerson reads and then at three and a half P.M. there is a meeting of the Woman's Club at 3, Tremont Place, where I will read a paper on the Greek goddesses. That would be a good time for you to come. . . ."

This is a comic passage, but it was not comic when it was written down. There was no reason why Emily should not conform (all ladies did), why she should not listen while others talked (it was not so where she was better known), why she should not patiently sit through a whole session in one of the drawing-rooms of the Athens of America while one of its liberal scholars read a long paper on the Greek goddesses.

Mr. Higginson concludes in a postscript, to encourage one he knows to be timid, never having quite realized the extent of her arrogance: " I have a right to invite you, and you can merely ring and walk in."

But Mr. Higginson was abundantly right in seeing that her poems would bring her nothing but criticism if published, in telling her (on the assumption that she wanted what his other protégées wanted) to mend her original ways. Emily's poetry could have hardly found an audience while she was alive, in the sweet regularity of Longfellow's circle, or even on its fringe. Emerson's was much less irregular than Emily's; he was more famous than Longfellow, and still his verse was heavily criticized for being too homely and lacking in poetic elegance. Her only chance for a small group of tolerant admirers (since she was a Puritan and, unlike Poe or Whitman, concerned with the realities of the Puritan mind) was to conform and make herself friends and connexions within the Boston group. Higginson was surprised at her stubbornness. It was not modesty, it was an outrageous self-sufficiency.

In the same letter which gives the invitation to take part in the literary rites at Boston, Higginson fully and very beautifully makes his peace with posterity. He begins in complete, if somewhat clumsy, humility, troubled that he can do no more for her than he does, assuring her of his abiding interest. " I feel always timid lest what I write should be badly aimed and miss that fine edge of thought which you bear."

Then he writes the only sentence that can be applied to Emily's true situation, with an insight that justifies Emily's having chosen him in the beginning:

" It is hard for me to understand how you can live so alone — with thoughts of such a rarity coming up in you and even the companionship of your dog withdrawn. *Yet it isolates one anywhere to think beyond a certain point, or have such flashes as come to you. . . .*"

From which single sentence we must admit that Mr. Higginson knew his America, his literary *milieu*, and, to some extent, " his " Emily Dickinson.

CHAPTER XIII

MR. BOWLES

LIFE KEPT SLIPPING UNDER THE FENCE IN VARIOUS disguises to tempt Emily. Mr. Samuel Bowles was Austin's dear friend, and Austin's children called him Uncle Sam. When Mr. Bowles came visiting from Springfield, he would run in for a minute to see Vinnie and Emily, just down the path, before he went home to read the *Republican* in proof, on his way to bed. A plate of cookies and a glass of ruddy wine, some little roots wrapped in moss for Mary Bowles's garden, and Mr. Bowles would take his hat and go.

Once Mr. Bowles brought Emily a jasmine plant.

This was the same world that held the boy's whistle, the caterpillar on the leaf far down the orchard, and the clocks that ticked like an insanity, to tell Emily the story of time. Before the face of Mr. Bowles another face flickered, faded a little, and then merged. He reminded her of George Gould. Emily saw a similarity that brought the two faces together at once, and soon Mr. Bowles was being a temporary representative of the man who could not come in the flesh, and soon he was being a troublesome person in himself, and Emily began to be in love, almost, with Mr. Bowles.

215

When George Gould lived in Worcester, she first wrote
to Mr. Higginson. Now George Gould was pastor of the
Olivet Church in Springfield — and so now Emily could
not help thinking about and dwelling upon and hoping for
news from — Mr. Bowles. Everybody called Mr. Bowles
magnetic. "You have the most triumphant face outside
Paradise," Emily wrote her friend.

Mr. Bowles was accustomed to adoration; it rippled
around him wherever he went. He took Emily's. He was
handsome, merry, melancholy, irresistible. Emily wanted
to be Mary Bowles's friend, too. That was more difficult;
Mary effaced herself. First Emily wrote a silly poem entitled by herself *Baby*, when she requested the new child
to be named Robert, for her. That failed. Then she wrote
Mary Bowles, anxious to communicate her joint love, and
enclosed a little poem to explain how fond she was of her
two friends. The note was too fond and almost annoyed;
Emily had once before known the perils of her affection.
She said: "My cheek is red with shame because I write so
often." This little letter in rhyme to Mary Bowles got no
reply:

> *My river runs to thee:*
> *Blue sea, wilt welcome me?*
>
> *My river waits reply.*
> *Oh sea, look graciously.*
>
> *I'll fetch thee brooks*
> *From spotted nooks, —*
>
> *Say, sea,*
> *Take me!*

Once, when in the family group someone spoke impatiently of Emily's tiresome oddities, Mary Bowles is said to have defended her: "Poor Emily! She is her own worst enemy."

One autumn Mr. Bowles came over to call on Emily herself; and the wine was ready, and a flower, and a trembling woman. But at the last moment she would not see him, and wrote: "Shall I keep the wine till you come again, or send it by Dick? It is now behind the door in the library, also an unclaimed flower. . . ."

Farther down the page: "I write you frequently, and am much ashamed."

One poem gives the pleading of a small child for the zenith of some desire. Indeed, to come upon it, under the general title "Love," where it undoubtedly belongs, is to think its language laden with poignant feeling. It is merely Emily asking Mr. Bowles to accept a barrel of apples from the Dickinson cellar.

"Mother never asked a favor of Mr. Bowles before . . . that he accept from her the little barrel of apples. 'Sweet apples,' she exhorts me, with an occasional Baldwin for Mary and the squirrels. —

> *Just once — oh! least request!*
> *Could adamant refuse*
> *So small a grace,*
> *So scanty put,*
> *Such agonizing terms?*
>
> *Would not a God of flint*
> *Be conscious of a sigh,*
> *As down his heaven dropt remote,*
> *'Just once, sweet Deity?'*

Around the supper-table in Springfield they couldn't see why Emily should make such a fuss over a barrel of apples.

Her letters thereafter contain many cryptic sentences.

"Don't you think you and I should be shrewder to take the mountain road?" she queries, out of a clear sky.

Both Mr. Bowles and Mary suffered from ill health; and now Mr. Bowles fell very ill, and Emily inquired in alarm about his "Darkness."

Another visit, when Mr. Bowles grew better, and another apology: "Perhaps you thought I didn't care — because I stayed out yesterday. I *did* care, Mr. Bowles. I pray for your sweet health to Allah every morning, but something troubled me, and I knew you needed light and air, so I didn't come. Nor have I the conceit that you *noticed* me. . . ."

Mr. Bowles sailed, the summer of 1862, for Europe, there to try to regain his health. The gossips had it that Mr. Bowles was planning to spend much of his time with a brilliant woman who was known to be his friend. Emily consoled Mary.

"When the best is gone, I know the other things are not of consequence. The heart wants what it wants, or else it does not care.

"You wonder why I write so. Because I cannot help. I like to have you know some care — so when your life gets faint for its other life, you can lean on us. We won't break, Mary."

At the same time she wrote Mr. Bowles, to assure him that nothing shook at his departure. Although she did not go to Italy herself, she begrudged no one else the going.

"We did not change. We have the same guests we did — except yourself — and the roses hang on the same stems as before you went. . . . I had one letter from Mary. I think she tries to be patient — but you wouldn't want her to succeed, would you, Mr. Bowles? . . . Should anybody, where you go, talk of Mrs. Browning, you must hear for us, and if you touch her grave . . ."

Mrs. Browning's grave was a solemn symbol.

Nearly every letter prays for the time when Mr. Bowles will come to Amherst, and nearly all the others explain that Emily could not come down. An undated note reiterates: " Dear Friend: I cannot see you . . ."

Mr. Bowles came back to America and went on a tour of the continent in 1865, and wrote about it. He took Mary with him. Emily hoped for his improved health, and then said: " I hope we may all behave so as to reach Jerusalem." She was as little sincere as she ever was when mentioning good behaviour. The letter concludes:

" Take

Emelie! "

This is the chronicle of a genuine friendship.

But Emily, although central, was only one of several of Mr. Bowles's friends. His biographer says: [1]

" His closest intimacies were with women of a characteristic New England type. There is in that section a class of such who inherit a fine intellect, an unsparing conscience, and a sensitive nervous organization; whose minds have a

[1] George S. Merriam, *The Life and Times of Samuel Bowles*, I, 217.

natural bent toward the problems of the soul and the universe; whose energies, lacking the outlet which business and public affairs give to their brothers, are constantly turned back upon the interior life, and who are at once stimulated and limited by a social environment which is serious, virtuous, and deficient of amusement. There is naturally developed in them high mental power, and almost morbid consciousness, while, especially in the many cases where they remain unmarried, the fervor and charm of womanhood are refined and sublimated from personal objects and devoted to abstractions and ideals. They are platonic in their attachments, and speculative in their religion; intense rather than tender, and not so much soothing as stimulating. By the influence of such women Mr. Bowles' later life was colored — his views were broadened, his thoughts refined, his friendships exercised in offices of helpfulness and sympathy."

It must have been a relief to spring from this fastidious feminine introversion into the vulgarity of the man's world.

Mr. Bowles was popped into jail on arriving in New York in December 1868 and stayed there one night. Emily read the papers. The *Springfield Republican* was involved in a fifty-thousand-dollar libel suit for having outspokenly called Jim Fisk and Jay Gould " audacious swindlers," and Mr. Bowles in his editorial columns, with the *Nation*, flayed the Tammany Hall tiger. Like Mr. Higginson, Mr. Bowles was eternally in the thick of things, but never too busy for friendship. . . . He could not give as much in return as Emily endlessly gave; Emily's was an excruciating, embarrassing love. Emily was supposedly idle, engaging in neither war nor reform. She ignored red petticoats, the badge of the emancipated woman; she ignored Margaret Fuller and the other feminists; and she had refused to spend her hot summer afternoons in the kitchen putting up extra preserves for the soldiers. People said Emily was a selfish, spoiled, unnatural creature, and appended: " Poor Vinnie! "

Then Mr. Bowles fell ill again, and Emily rushed to his comfort, in her letters. During his convalescence he came to Amherst, and evidently, at last, Emily found it possible to talk and to be answered; she felt happy. She wrote:

" I went to the room as soon as you left, to confirm your presence, recalling the Psalmist's sonnet to God, beginning

I have no life to live but this —
To lead it here,
Nor any death but lest
Dispelled from there.
Nor tie to earths to come,
Nor action new,
Except through this extent —
The love of you."

Only once is there any hint that Mr. Bowles had an interest in Emily's poetry. His taste seems to have been in a quite contrary direction. " Now I call that a poem," he once exclaimed, after reading Bret Harte's *Conchita* aloud. Of Disraeli's *Lothair*, which sold eighty thousand copies in a year or two, Mr. Bowles remarked emphatically: " It is the best book I ever read! " Once, perhaps, when he visited Emily's father with Mr. Holland in 1861, he did apply to Emily for a poem to be printed in the *Republican*. Father doubtless lifted his very stern eyes and looked for just a glancing moment at Emily before she replied. Emily said the editors thought her penurious when she refused " her mind." For twenty-five of Emily's strenuous writing years she corresponded with Mr. Bowles and sent him trifles. It is evident that Mr. Bowles valued her poetry less than did Higginson. His family agreed that Emily's writing, like all her action, was sententious. Mr. Bowles seldom sat down in any group of friends without the familiar gesture of drawing a manuscript of some literary discovery from an inner pocket; he was always reading, quoting, passing things on — some choice phrase or fortunate line. In the memory of one who saw him almost daily for years at this time, he never read or praised a word of Emily's verse.

But perhaps Mr. Bowles liked Emily's brevity. He himself introduced the short crisp paragraph on the editorial page of his paper, and many other editors imitated. It took a great knack, and Mr. Bowles had it. Emily read the *Republican* every night. It was like a letter from the great world outside.

With time the friendship equalized a little. Mr. Bowles found perhaps that he even needed to talk with Emily for the good of his own soul. He called her his " rascal." She signs herself so. Did he criticize a stray verse? It would be interesting to know. In a postscript Emily added — we trust not mysteriously to him: " I washed the adjective."

Did anything happen? Did Mr. Bowles, in the two

years during which George Gould preached in Springfield, carry a letter inside his breast-pocket when he drove away? Love by this time was less single — Emily needed to express a love for her friends that was intense and startling. It was not " untrue " any longer to love other than George Gould.

" Of your exquisite act there can be no acknowledgement but the ignominy that grace gives."

" The last day that I saw you was the newest and the oldest of my life."

" It was so delicious to see you," she wrote in 1873. ". . . We, who arraign the *Arabian Nights* for their understatement, escape the stale sagacity of supposing them sham."

" Your coming welds anew that strange trinket of life which each of us wears and none of us own; and the phosphorescence of yours startles us for its permanence."

In 1878 Mr. Bowles died.

". . . the look of Arabia in the eyes, is like Mr. Samuel."

" Was not his countenance on earth graphic as a spirit's? "

This is what remains of Emily's difficult love for Mr. Bowles.

CHAPTER XIV

HOW TO BE LONELY — WITH EXAMPLES

Oh, God! I could be bounded in a nutshell and count myself a king of infinite space, were it not that I have bad dreams.

— Hamlet

EMERSON CALLED THOREAU, OR, RATHER, A SELECtion of his letters, a perfect piece of stoicism. The theme of the solitary, which Thoreau had from Emerson, which he carried under his coat next his vitals, foraging for it as he went, and then in 1862 dropped, Emily had already undertaken, and by Thoreau's death she was an adept and knew the technic of loneliness. Thoreau lived of his own free will in solitude for two years by Walden Pond, where he built himself part of a house with his own hands and raised and prepared much of his food, baking unleavened bread and throwing the nasty yeast-bottle out of the window. The symbol of yeast was lost on him, it implied only a necessity to return to the humiliation of civilization and grocery stores. The immortal yeast spore, member of a vast branching and subdividing community carried in a seething bottle from England to Plymouth, was not a part of nature in Thoreau's eyes.

"I am no more lonely than a single mullein or a dandelion in a pasture, or a beanleaf, or sorrel, or a horse-fly, or a bumble-bee. I am no more lonely than the Mill Brook, or a weather-cock, or the North Star or the south wind, or an April shower, or a January thaw, or the first spider in a new house."

But he was. True, he was no more lonely in Walden than he had been trying to talk to Emerson, losing his time — nay, almost his identity. In nature he did not feel that subtle lessening of himself. The first entry in his Journal says:

"To be alone I find it necessary to escape the present, — I avoid myself." This at twenty. At twenty-two: "How shall I help myself? By withdrawing into the garret, and associating with spiders and mice, determining to meet myself sooner or later." At thirty-seven: "'Walden published.' Elder-berries. Waxwork yellowing. . . . Society seems to have invaded and overrun me. I have drunk tea and coffee and made myself cheap and vulgar. . . . It is with infinite yearning and aspiration that I seek solitude, more and more resolved and strong; but with a certain genial weakness that I seek society ever."

Thoreau missed the final stage of the experience by a flaw in character; he was not a perfect piece of stoicism. The world made a rage thicken in his throat; he was never solitary, because he was always worrying about the world . . . its mistaken economics, its bad education, its immoral gold-mines, its absurd telegraph-wires, its improper food, its divorce from nature. He ended by coming out of a solitude which did not solace him, to speak for John Brown. In 1862 he died.

In 1862 Emily began to live. She had become a solitary like the little snail that glides, withdraws a waving horn, curls the crinkled edge of its travelling skirt inward instead of out, and comes to a stop near a rubble of stone which it resembles in texture and colour, in order to be let alone. Without a scratch on nature she took what she needed from it and maintained an impervious existence which lasted about thirty years in extent of time. No measurements exist for other kinds of estimate.

She had no taboos and no panaceas; coffee and tea and society and yeast-bottles were not moral abominations. She became a recluse without either violence, extreme diligence, or backsliding. Her life was a matter of taste, the expression of a preference; and she did not need to alter anything in her surroundings or in her neighbours in order to live. To live was to use completely the fate that had befallen her. In short, the world might be this or that, but making it over was not her business. " My business," she says to assist us at this point, " is circumference."

After 1854 she ceased to rebel childishly; life need not be changed, it need only be comprehended. Emily's solitude went inward into regions of polar cold; her solitude expanded and solidified, becoming a vast place, a frozen waste, a zone where the white lights of ordinary living could be broken up into brilliant colour: Emily's solitude became an extremely barren zone finally, into which she could introduce and in which she could examine, analyse, and dissect life in quantities minute enough to be properly handled.

To begin with, her father wanted her at home. " I must omit Boston. Father prefers so. He likes me to travel with him, but objects that I visit." Emily was not indifferent to her father. She stayed at home. She had no place else to go except to George Gould, who was poor and sick — and married. She feared the world that demanded arts and crafts in which she was not skilled. Her only craft was that of dutiful daughter. At home, aside from her day-labour, she could treat shreds of the world's material with her own dyes. She could be ignored.

One man who might have married her died when she was twenty. Another fell in love with her and renewed by a millionfold the design of renunciation. George Gould was reckless; he doubtless read Browning's *The Statue and the Bust;* he wanted Emily to face life with him. Emily shook her head; she went back to her business. That and the ensuing years were the perfect piece of stoicism.

When George Gould married Nellie M. Grout of Worcester, the gigantic edifice of chastity and immortal love had come down about her ears. George Gould had needed a wife, even with her immortal love. Emily learned something by that discovery. It disciplined her romanticism.

And add that her father had a habit of her, and of Vinnie. "When Father lived I remained with him because he would miss me." [1] Vinnie was withering into a little spinster; Vinnie had been pretty, dark like a tropic flower

[1] Galatea Collection.

that puckers before noon; Vinnie had had many beaux. But beaux ceased at last, just as butterflies do after the full of June; father had not been able to relinquish either of his girls; he kept them both snug and safe in the old brick mansion, immured, to be sure, but in a perpetual youth — his children until both they and he were old, never seeing what the world saw: a pair of twittering little ladies. And while her sister was being awarded a fate identical with her own, Emily was transforming her destiny, so that while Vinnie was a spinster, Emily became a recluse. The same stream went over both lives, but the tints that came out after the "treatment" were almost antithetical.

Father kept Emily's shell.

The great powers come resembling miracles; when the body is caught in a trap, it will invent an untrappable identity for itself and name it spirit, and the spirit's freedom will become the body's power. For some the spirit is a good fiction only; for others it is triumph. Emily first admitted that she was caught; her verse states captivity over and over. Did her father know that she obeyed and escaped him both at the same time? She obeyed him in so far as he had a right to demand that a child obey; but she obeyed him most easily after she had discovered how to escape. She used her right to privacy and the wall of her mind against him when he came too far, as he, for all his reserves and repressions, wished to come. He had prohibited the world; very well, she could forgo the world. But she would not forgo her idea of the world, and there her father found the battle lost. Emily would not call the world evil. She went inward and away from the world, not because she called it evil, but because she required room and privacy. Either Emily would have the world or she would have herself. . . . Herself she had. Every external prohibition deepened the underground self. Father could keep her a dutiful but not an empty daughter.

Partly to escape her father, and partly to obey him, since obey she must, Emily became a recluse. Force controlled her very little, but enough to make her emphasize the fact that it should not domineer her spirit. " No rack can torture me," she says, and: " Captivity's consciousness, so's liberty." She reiterated the principle as if it were an axiom to be proved. It proved.

And yet, beneath will, or spirit, or desire, or her conscious self, Emily was her father's prisoner. Otherwise she should never have employed the axiom.

Thoreau had an opposite emotional problem. When he made the gesture towards the world which Emily made as a young girl, his mother — who of course was the one to bind him down — said briskly: " You can buckle on your knapsack, dear, and roam abroad to seek your fortune."

The thought of leaving home, says one writer, made the tears roll down his cheeks.

Death, God's messenger, first turned Emily towards solitude in 1850. Solitude is only a sad chilly negative zone, not the frozen absolute of the recluse. It had touched Thoreau on the shoulder when his brother died; to both Thoreau and Emily death implied the mood of the years to come. Writing to her dear A. in 1853 Emily said, as if everything was settled for ever:

"I thank you, A., but I don't go from home, unless emergency leads me by the hand, and then I do it obstinately and draw back if I can. Should I ever leave home, which is improbable, I will, with much delight, accept your invitation. . . ."

Which, written at the age of twenty-three, sounds like the quiet resolve of a woman twice that age.

By 1854 Emily was deep in the business of suffering; her second love concentrated all the pain of her life into one point. Life at last had sent her what she prayed for; but in such way that her only choice was to renounce it. By 1862 she was alone in spirit as well as in fact. Thoreau neither loved nor renounced a person, as Emily in her barren world loved and renounced; in consequence, he neither valued nor renounced the world, as she did. It is easy to forgo what one does not love; no one calls attempting to turn one's back on an irritating spectacle renunciation. Thoreau had no lever of power over the world, to lift it and use it at will, as Emily had; apparently, to love if only to renounce is to have power; and to fail to love is to fail.

Thoreau's mother had the impulse to push him out of the nest like a wise mother bird who has one fledgling that will not try to fly. Thoreau wanted the nest; he finds life too heterogeneous; a nest is a simple place. He sees no point in most of man's activity; Nature became his only friend. His loves towards people — that is, towards the world — were never clear-cut enough to focus any passion in him and, being without embodiment, could never suffer the dazzling pain we find correctly appraised in Emily. Emily grew great and profound by means of a pain which spared nothing. Thoreau grew wistful, restless, hurt, and exceedingly indefinite as regards his personal failure. This is the mythical record of his disappointments, as he called it:

"I long ago lost a hound, a bay horse, and a turtle-dove, and am still on their trail. Many are the travellers I have spoken concerning them, describing their tracks and what calls they answered to. I have met one or two who had heard the hound, and the tramp of the horse, and even seen the dove disappear behind a cloud, and they seemed as anxious to recover them as if they had lost them themselves."

Emily's records are not myths, but crystals of existence. They stir no musky odour of literary memory, but seem instead as emerald-clean as the ice-chunks Thoreau wrote about, cut from Walden Pond and left lying like large precious stones in the village street.

> *I reason, earth is short,*
> *And anguish absolute.*
> *And many hurt;*
> *But what of that?*

Nature, which stood all about Thoreau, was invited by him to flow in and inhabit the vacancy at the centre of himself. But Nature would not. And then Thoreau practised "infinite expansion," spreading himself as wide as the known world, in order to enclose Nature by such means, at the centre of his heart. But Nature, after all Thoreau's trying, turned out to be discontinuous with the self, and Thoreau abandoned the wooing at last and died.

While Thoreau was carrying on this curious courtship, Emily was inspecting the heart. She found that the heart acted with diminishing values and she found a way of writing that would parallel the process; no one had ever before made such a bare graph. Only John Donne, two hundred years before, had suggested multitudinous possibilities in line after line of rapid sketch. Emily set one plane of requirement sharply on the plane above and the last she arranged to cut as the apex of the whole:

> *The heart asks pleasure first,*
> *And then, excuse from pain;*
> *And then, those little anodynes*
> *That deaden suffering;*
>
> *And then, to go to sleep;*
> *And then, if it should be*
> *The will of its Inquisitor,*
> *The liberty to die.*

Ten years after her letter to her dear A., Emily brought the fruits of her solitude to Mr. Higginson. She had renounced life — that is, the life of Emily Dickinson. Another life, the life of the anonymous mind, engrossed her. She could not renounce the life that remained with her — where is the point for severing existence from speculation? Nothing could keep the anonymous mind from what required to be scrutinized and understood. Mr. Higginson took no notice of the anonymous mind; it dazzled his eyes a little painfully, so he shut them. He offered Emily a literary personality. She declined, and returned to her business. After that she made Higginson and Helen Hunt

Jackson come to her; she three times refused to see Mr. Bowles, when he had come miles to see her, on the bare explanation she *couldn't*. With pride she announces to Higginson: "I do not cross my father's ground to any house or town," as if it were the accomplishment of a lifetime. In a sense it was.

Thoreau may have been a strong stimulant. She would not mind his crankiness, she would not criticize him, but inspect his clever simplicity like a little girl visiting and admiring her big brother who has made himself a shack in the woods and who dares to sleep out all night by himself. With nightfall, Emily would put on her shoes and stockings and go home, leaving her brother to his weekend. *Walden* and *The Week* were published while Emily was still a novice. If she read them before Thoreau died, she must have absorbed him to the point of saturation, for she is not very conscious of his influence and only refers to him in 1881 when she says: "The fire bells are oftener now, almost, than the church-bells. Thoreau would wonder which did the most harm."

Her admiration was elsewhere, and with women, chiefly.

From the first the Brontës had had the central position, and George Eliot, George Sand, and Elizabeth Barrett Browning lived with their several meanings for her. Of Sand and Mrs. Browning she exclaimed: "Women now, queens now!" And writing to her little cousins in Boston, of George Eliot, she said: "What do I think of 'Middlemarch'? What do I think of glory . . . the mysteries of human nature surpass the 'mysteries of redemption.'"

Emily must have known that she bore a striking

resemblance to Charlotte Brontë — she knew the Brontës
so well that she could describe a kitten as being the "color
of Branwell Brontë's hair." Emily was infinitesimal in person, as was Charlotte; they were both plain, with reddish-
brown hair and the pallor that matches such hair; their eyes
were remarkably fascinating — in both "their only good
feature " — and near-sighted.

It was untamed Emily Brontë, only twelve years older,
but "gigantic," in her mind, who attracted Emily Dickinson. It was not the attraction of similarity; Emily Dickinson could no more resemble massive Emily Brontë than
the wild Haworth moor and its savage people could be
put into Emily Dickinson's neat garden of larkspur and
Canterbury bells. Charlotte, in her mitts, adoring Professor Heger, her "teacher," had more points of resemblance
in common. Charlotte sent a short story to Wordsworth
before she was famous, and he, like Higginson, replied
without committing himself. Charlotte's father, Mr. Patrick Brontë made a terrible scene when she proposed marrying Mr. Nichols, the curate. Still, it was Emily Brontë
who had been the true solitary and poet. Emily Brontë,
too, toiled at her irksome housework — the "prickly art,"
Emily Dickinson called it — and one servant, Maggie in
the American household and Tabby in the Yorkshire, over-
saw and annulled errors. Carlo and Keeper were alike essential to their mistresses. Emily Brontë had gone to school
at Roe Head, but stayed only a short time, being dread-
fully home-sick and returning in poor health. Clocks terrified them both. Emily Brontë lived in the vicarage and
on the moors, away from people, with the exception of a

single half-year — the Brussels half-year — to which Emily Dickinson's Washington spring corresponds. Emily Brontë's poetry was written in microscopic characters; Emily Dickinson's began minute and shy, almost microscopic, but grew bold, as her power grew with the years. Emily Brontë lamented the death of a much-loved person — *Cold in the grave,* a theme Emily Dickinson could almost repeat word for word remembering Humphrey. Emily Brontë's poetry is chiefly concerned with God, death, and the soul. So is Emily Dickinson's, and she first read Emily Brontë's poetry after Leonard Humphrey's death in 1850. . . . Emily Brontë died in 1848. . . . Charlotte destroyed all her sister's remains and manuscripts except *Wuthering Heights,* which had been published two years before, and the poems, from which she made a very sparse selection. . . . Emily Dickinson left some kind of word that her sister Lavinia was to destroy her manuscript. She did not herself destroy it. . . .

Whether or not she knew that her ancestors had lived for five centuries in and about Leeds, not far from the Haworth moors of Yorkshire, the Brontës' world, we do not know; but evidently a feeling of kinship was deep and instinctive. Yorkshire was still in some ways more rugged than Emily's prim New England; and Emily Brontë, sitting before the fire, on the point of death, with her comb in her hand, and her long black hair on either side of her face like an Indian, embodied the Yorkshire source of something elemental that had come to Hadley in the early days, with the Dickinsons.

At nineteen Emily Dickinson read *Jane Eyre,* and she

wrote at some time or other a poem to Currer Bell. The Brontës were as familiar as neighbours, and yet in time they may have palled a little, as neighbours do, and especially for their lack of humour. Emily Dickinson could not but admire what was hewn in a wild workshop with simple tools out of homely materials, and she had that granite poem *No coward soul is mine* set up over her by letting Vinnie know she wished Mr. Higginson to read it at her grave when she died; but Emily Dickinson's labour was not, after all, on granite or even on marble. She employed gem-tactics; her poetry had flash, had facet.

So long as Emerson dreamily confiscated the stamps enclosed in letters requesting his autograph, he made no literary mistakes. But in 1855 he wrote Whitman:

"I am not blind to the worth of the wonderful gift of *Leaves of Grass*. I find it the most extraordinary piece of wit and wisdom that America has yet produced. . . ."

"Wit and wisdom" are hardly the words for *Leaves of Grass*. The book has no wit whatsoever; wisdom is too quiet a word for a dithyramb. Certainly it was an aberration for Emerson to champion Whitman's mind; he later felt so when he sent Carlyle the book.

But Emerson had had traffic with Rousseau, and Carlyle stuffed the German poets into Emerson's portmanteau. That confusion in Emerson, which everyone remarks, accounted for the fact that he did not see immediately that Whitman's unity, his equality, his largeness, his expansive halloo, all derived from one central attitude which directly contradicted what Emerson was for ever saying.

Only when Emerson ran away from the American scene and became an Oriental sage did he admit unity. Whitman admitted it in America and obliterated all values, all gradations, by calling everything " good." Life was good, and death was heavenly death, and the common prostitute was the equal of anyone under heaven, and the pismire is no less perfect than the grain of sand or the egg of a wren or the journey work of the stars. This will to see life without distinctions made Whitman's poetry very nearly into formlessness — the vague, the indefinite, the large were ideals in life and art both. We find, since he cannot construct, since he cannot make form, that his chief method when he is not using language for these effects of formlessness is the making of a catalogue; simply a list of things — all equal, none inevitable.

Emily says:

> *The soul* selects *her own society,*
> *Then shuts the door.*
> *Behold the atom I* preferred. . . .

Preference, choice, rejection, *valuation*, are her whole art. Not only is one thing good and another bad, one thing chosen and another rejected; but one thing is chosen as fitting for a special instance, and another retained for its proper time. We thus see that Emily made in life and in art an infinite number of judgments. Her aristocratic nature failed to see any fault in such behaviour — vulgarity consisted in the inability to discriminate. Whitman's democratic soul longed to erase even the differences of personality and temperament; *I, Walt Whitman,* is to signify

anyone, everyone, the mass. Strangely enough, Whitman
has a poem called *The Base of All Metaphysics*. Now, here
we should hope to have something to fasten to. This is the
conclusion of the poem:

*The dear love of man for his comrade — the attraction of friend to
friend,
Of the well-married husband and wife — of children and parents,
Of city for city, and land for land.*

As soon as life is robbed of all difference, it vanishes and
leaves merely the *élan vital*! Only the embryo is permitted such allness as we find desired in Whitman's caressing croon.

Emily voices, for America, an art of choice which it has
not yet learned or begun to practise. She pictures life in scale
and in value, in choice and rejection, in form and design
— not in mere quantity, mere bulk, mere amorphous
welter. Rejection is one means of defining vital impulse
— what the sculptor chips off is not to be deplored. Small-
ness is as acceptable as largeness to her, since all size is relative; grains of sand are as structural as mountains. Limitation, in other words, cannot greatly worry her power to
live; life in one particle, if properly treated and understood, will contain enough scale to make the exercise of
the soul possible. This power to choose, to say no as well
as yes, which was native with Emily, happened to assist
her in her central renunciation. She knew how to renounce
— that is, she knew how to renounce and still not be defeated. For although the renunciation cheated her of life
and love and caused her great grief and almost cost her

sanity, and although it did not need to be, coming as it did from the imposed tyrannical nature of her father, Emily proved that renunciation in itself could be made to yield riches; that in her seeming defeat she was simply arranging to fight life in another trench and in better circumstances.

Emily felt a quiet will to triumph, a will towards immortality. But her beginnings were all fragile and human and, in the world's phrase, queer. No poet ever came so close to failure; no one ever walked so near insanity and yet remained sane, or held in so desperate a war such contending obsessions, vanities, aversions, shames, or fierce desires for splendour and applause.

To trace Emily's nature in her poems is like tracing a pattern in mottled foam, or in the lines on a tree's trunk, or in lichen on a rock. If you draw a small square, you get one outline predominant; if you enlarge by the fraction of an inch and allow another element to enter, you will find the growth in all directions almost too rapid for your frame. Emily wrote many lines to stand as texts for this chapter; they follow one another with endless traceries: "The soul unto itself is an imperial friend," which is balanced by: "Or the most agonizing spy an enemy could send." . . . She could reveal the preoccupations of the acute recluse in writing:

> *The brain within its groove*
> *Runs evenly and true;*
> *But let a splinter swerve . . .*

and then indicate the catastrophe. She noted: "Much madness is divinest sense," and "Faith is a fine invention,"

239

and still admitted microscopes in the very next line. And
then suddenly, shrewdly, says:

> *Experiment to me*
> *Is everyone I meet . . .*

picking the kernel out of a man as a squirrel does from
a nut.

But follow the life behind the sentences and see the
woman who made them, and of what they are made. Under this sanity, this shrewdness, goodness, wisdom, and
merriment, was a vain, strange, unnatural woman, half
child, morbid, eccentric, superstitious, primitive as a wild
bee or a moth, and often undoubtedly and to her own
knowledge on the verge of going mad. The doctor found
her just before she died still on the verge and called it
"revenge of the nerves." Amherst called Emily queer
and let it go at that.

Amherst was right, she was queer. But many people
were queer who could not define queerness quite so
forcibly:

> *'Tis the majority*
> *In this, as all, prevails.*
> *Assent, and you are sane;*
> *Demur, — you're straightway dangerous,*
> *And handled with a chain.*

Queerness, we can see, centres on something that con-
tests the majority vote. Majority's opponent was what
Emily called the self — *herself*. She had a terror of being
in any way coerced, forced, or handled by this majority.
It became a mild mania; she could not bear to be in any

way possessed by it. Self-possession denied such violence. But the cause was subtle, lying beneath an obvious explanation, like a snake coiled under a bright flower. As she retreated step by step from the world, Emily seemed to be backing into the arms of her father, and the terror of being possessed by her father drove her into darkness on the edge of which the world and father both lurked, ready to drag her out of herself. Emily's motive grows intensified and displaced; the world could never have made the complete introvert she became, for the world, as we have seen, did not threaten Emily's purity, and it could not reach out, past her father's garden, to seize her. Emily's formal father, with whom when she was fifty she could feel embarrassment because he asked her to sit with him for an afternoon, embodied an enduring menace. She dwelt in his house and ate his bread (besides baking it) and loved and tended him; and all the while she was undergoing desire and revulsion and fear until she was forced to invent inaccessibility.

In the steady flood of sanity from her poetry Emily's morbidity shrinks to the darkness housed under a pebble. And many of the constant and trifling signs of morbidity can be explained in natural causes. Emily was myopic — her eyes had to come very close to an object before they could focus, and so, in consequence, her handwriting was bold and queer, and it was not unnatural of her to resist changing it, even when postmasters could not read it. But it is also true that she was superstitious about her handwriting; it was her style; her style was herself, and her self was pretty well ignored and undervalued. No wonder that she cherished it with a stubborn tenderness. Once only, Emily mentions in her letters this habit of hers, and then when she is in Boston for her eyes; the physician has taken away her writing-materials and forbidden her little notes. She explains to Higginson, who has been wounded in South Carolina and to whom she writes compelled by concern for him, that she may only write the merest line and " I enclose the address from a letter lest my figures fail." Since in this case Emily is only enclosing her own address, the aversion for writing on the outside of an envelope remains unexplained by her. But her first editor, Mrs. Mabel Todd, says that the addressing difficulty became a habit and explains, undoubtedly with much evidence in mind: ". . . it seemed as if her sensitive nature shrank from the publicity which even her handwriting would undergo, in the observation of indifferent eyes . . . the actual strokes of her own pencil were, so far as possible, reserved exclusively for friendly eyes."

But even with her friends Emily was as miserly at times with her poetry as she was at other times prodigal. She was only prodigal, after all, with shreds. Her friends folded up Emily's letters, exclaiming that she was a rare soul; but nobody quite called her, freely and without reserve, a poet. And so she cherished what was not cherished by others. And she was also a natural miser. . . .

It was not all pride or protest against neglect. Emily refused to have her poetry published even when she most pathetically desired the contact of readers; she requested her friends to burn her letters lest foreign eyes see them;

Mrs. Todd's phrase "friendly eyes" has more meanings than one.

For vanity, turned into humility and shame, coursed in Emily's blood; she was prodigiously vain. She wore spotless white, she imitated many of the virtues of the saints by instinct, and, like a saint who is God-intoxicated, Emily was vain. A saint's progress is usually from himself to God, whereas Emily seems to have built on a rudimentary vanity a deliberate celebration of herself in order to conceal her attachment to God. Almost daily her self-love collapsed; father and God returned, as men do, to their homes after the day's work. . . . The saint's love for God, which seems unnecessary, difficult, and abnormal to the rest of the world which dwells in an easier egotism, is for him his only salvation; otherwise he should only love himself, which would be an abomination. It was a difficult life, so passionate and so repressed. Emily the poet was sane with a laborious sanity, created from its opposite. Emily the person walked from light to darkness and then, with pupils distended, back to light again. She was both natural and unnatural; and she lived under enormous pressure.

Part of the pressure was her virginity. And expending little, refusing much, hoarding all, Emily lived. It looked like negation. But late at night, or at noon, rushing up to her little bedroom, Emily reversed the process and let the words fall on paper without reserve, stint, or restraint. She observed no taboos, and God did not stand, censoring, at her elbow. When she wrote, Emily cared nothing for God or his universe, being very much absorbed in her own.

243

In other words, the anonymous mind saved her and saved her almost daily. Vanity compressed her and made her self-conscious; her vanity refused to be photographed and, after the age of eight, refused to be painted into family portraits, for Emily's features were not considered flowery enough for beauty by the tastes of her time. Vanity urged her to conserve all fragments of herself, her handwriting, stray stanzas of her poetry, and the myth of her mannerisms. She preserved all that might be considered characteristic with an almost superstitious self-valuation. It was a kind of atrophied self. This same blind awe for the self, this feeling of tender self-conservation, a child displays when first someone pares his little finger-nails. He looks on the process with alarm, he watches the little crescent nails fall, and if no one sees them, he will furtively pick them up and hoard them in a match-box — he may even eat them for safe-keeping. So barbaric kings have acted and they have trembled like children when a trusted holy man buries the clippings from the holy beard and the parings from the holy hand, even with protective ceremony, lest an enemy find the poor self, in one of its fragments, and so be powerful to work on it a bad magic. And mothers weep over the first curls from the heads of their first-born, and poets, being as wise and as silly as mothers, never cease to remember the tresses of the beloved, fringes of a mystery. . . .

Emily would not traffic with cameras. She felt a distrust of the magic in the photographer's little black box that resembles the savage's who feels that if his picture is taken, he will surely die. Indeed to be *taken* was what Emily certainly felt that she could not possibly endure. She had no photograph for Mr. Higginson, and when trying to explain why, she explains that her father urges her and that she resists. She gave her teacher instead a very self-conscious word-picture: ". . . [I] am small, like the wren; and my hair is bold, like a chestnut burr. . . ." "Small" and "bold"—could a camera catch both "small" and "bold"? [1]

And she disliked the symbol of putting herself on the back of an envelope; Emily, who had a great deal of time for working out symbols and aversions, and who had no hostages in the world beyond to lead her to compromise with it, objected to being scrutinized, smirched, handled, and stamped with the everyday ink of the world's post-marks, tossed into a mail-sack, treated like other people, disregarded, and so indiscriminately *touched.* And what does this mean? Emily meant to say that she was not an ordinary person; in others words, that she was a genius. In such a fantastic manner she asserted herself.

The unnatural Emily grew as she grew older; but only in the letters. For an instant or two, turning the pages that record her, nearest to her daily struggles, we come face to face with a person we do not know . . . eyes shut in upon themselves, and sentences all awry, said only for her own ears. The old New England figure who dwelt in so many upper chambers on so many farms and in so many cottages under elms stands there in Emily's place, and Miss Dickinson, who had had an unhappy love-affair, seems to

[1] A daguerreotype has recently been discovered taken about the age of twenty. The owner of this picture would not permit a copy of it to be made for this book.

be just another one of the weary gibbering throng. If we had only her letters, even with their supreme passages of letter-writing, we might conclude that from day to day life was too much for her, and that she, like so many others, failed after a little set-to with something too grim, lurking under the elms and over the tops of the orchards.

But it is not true. The verges of insanity are never crossed quite, and Emily lasted out her days untaken by the spectre. The very words that show her so unstrung and tangled in her letters will fight their way eventually into her poetry, and the ideas, which sound for cryptic effect written to her friends, come out whole, as bodily perfect as only long sanity can make them. She is so fond of phrases that certain ones went into five or six letters. Friends felt when the phrases were published that they were simply being used for the practice of an art, which was partly true. The poems and letters stand side by side to testify to Emily's enduring labour. Emily's poems about the mind and its minute peculiarities have been carried out of crying darkness, every one of them to the safe distance where we may reach them for ourselves. At last, after wishing to do nothing else in the world, Emily succeeded in objectifying her mind and giving it reality in poetry. All other ways of being real had been tried and had been found to fail.

Was Thoreau doing anything like this at Walden Pond? No, for although he had a Puritan mind, he did not approve of it. He watched nature instead, to find, if possible, a message. Thoreau was never either so courageous or so cowardly as Emily; he did not choose to live with himself, or with any other self; selves were horrors. Thoreau is a great writer, but a writer without a focus, and he became a solitary without a focus. Nature is no focus. When he lay dying, he wished that his sister could place his bed and its covers in the form of a shell so that he might curl up in it. That was his last attempt to make a nest of life. There is no created system in Walden. " I went to the woods," he says, " because I wished to live deliberately . . . to drive life into a corner and reduce it to its lowest terms." And what, after he had lived in the woods, had Thoreau to say? Read the *Journal*, read *Walden*, read every line he wrote . . . he has nothing to say. The pretence of having something to say, of being that specious New England thing the philosopher-reformer-clergyman on paper, kept Thoreau from uttering his sensuous joy. Poets are permitted what Thoreau only partially permitted himself; he is nearer Keats than Emerson, but still, because Emerson got in the way, he did not focus as Keats did. Thoreau laboured against his time, against the conventions of prose-writing, against Emerson. In his prose-writing, where he preached enough to placate his conscience, he is much more abandoned to his rich sense of life, as a poet should be, than he is in his poetry. Writing poetry for its own sake was still almost sinful in New England. In his prose, not letting his right hand know what his left was doing, he could turn colour and sound and detail into literary perfection. However, every page implies, for all his literary joy; " Because I have undergone solitude, I am better than you are, sinful world, and I despise you because you cannot do what I have done." That is the obvious flaw in Thoreau, and many have detected it. He kept three chairs in his shack at Walden: one for Solitude, one for Friendship and one for Society. Solitude did not work beyond the point of writing *Walden*. Friendship failed, and, as he said, he hated Society.

Emerson had instigated solitude, had embodied friendship, and had lived in society without friction. Thoreau was emotionally attached to Emerson and so found it necessary to quarrel a little with him. Thoreau's emotion forced him to exaggerate the Emersonian doctrine — as if to say: " See here, I can go you one better." Ludicrously enough, even Thoreau's " huge Emersonian nose " was longer and uglier than Emerson's. Thoreau's nose was longer, and his prose must be better, and he must be the true solitary, about whom Emerson was only a voice crying in the wilderness. Some of it was forced, in consequence. A little sadly Emerson observed that Thoreau in conversation " only felt himself in opposition." Aside from the world, which was a burr in the armpit, Thoreau had nature and literature. What is all this talk of idleness in nature? Thoreau worked like a beaver; he worked all day long, industriously plotting in his mind what he should compose at night in his shack. Emerson might be a tired pioneer; Thoreau had an " aboriginal vigour." At forty-five he had written twelve volumes of *Journal* in addition to all his other writings; it is significant to note that he compressed the bulk of the *Journal* into a small *Walden*. His classic prose is no by-product.

Watch him kneeling on the ice to peer down through the hole he has broken to see his ax where he has dropped it by accident, rocking upright, gently waving in the water on the bottom of the pond. Kneeling there, he composes two pages about his ax. . . . Later, that night in his cabin he will enjoy the scrupulous act of writing. So he accepted, with gratitude and alacrity, everything Nature gave him, the heroism of the musk-rat, the lost kitten, Bill Wheeler fancied as Diogenes, and the Great Elm. The noises of wood-birds on the Musketaquid are like stains of colour on pure glass. Can you see Thoreau turning away from the river to go home, absorbed in working that sensation into language? When he chased his father's pig, he would have been put out at the loss of time had he not known that every waddle of it was getting him closer to something he might record. Spanking the woodchuck is half in the spank and half in the telling.

As Thoreau said, nature was the hone to the knife.

And as for neighbours, " I hate them commonly, when I am near them."

Solitary animals come face to face at times, on secret paths that intersect in the deep woods. If you read Emily's poetry and Thoreau's prose, remembering New England, remembering the America that toiled in dogmatic gloom for two centuries, you will see a deep wood, since cut down, then inhabited by his mind and hers. In that wilderness of speculation a sentence from Emily's writing sometimes confronts a sentence from Thoreau. Emily says as if she were motionlessly regarding Thoreau's *Nature* all the while:

> *But nature is a stranger yet;*
> *The ones that cite her most*
> *Have never passed her haunted house,*
> *Nor simplified her ghost.*

The wilderness had its traps, and Thoreau fell into one
of them. Like the fox who gnaws its foot free, he limped
off, leaving part of himself behind. Romantics in Europe
behaved in a less desperate fashion. Solitaries dotted the
landscape like buck-shot spattering the ground from the
blunderbusses of Jean Paul Richter, Chateaubriand, and
Jean Jacques Rousseau. Byron and Emily Brontë and
Coleridge were literary solitaries — miles apart as they
were, they were still miles further from Emily Dickinson
and Thoreau. Something wild and pungent kept Emily and
Thoreau from the elaborations of the European cult. They
were touched by the colours of 1798, but they avoided its
softness and its theatricality. Pioneer stock had made
them; their natures were still close to a life once expressed
in implements, in labour, in limitation, where the hand
and the mind grew proportionately in skill. Thoreau wrote
of axes and bread-making as easily as he did of the cries
of the birds and the Iliad. Emily's poetry chose instinctively the homely image, and only rarely the flimsy sentiment. With the serious care of the pioneer, both kept a
religious memory which turned them from the romantic
extravagances of their time. For, however they might
dramatize the soul, or the self, they had at heart the gravity of God.

In August 1862 Emily undoubtedly read Emerson's
biographical sketch of Thoreau, in the *Atlantic*.
In enumerating certain qualities peculiar to the dead
Thoreau he happened to hit on others that were to be the
genius of Emily, who, while she must have read the article,
saw nothing to remark in it.

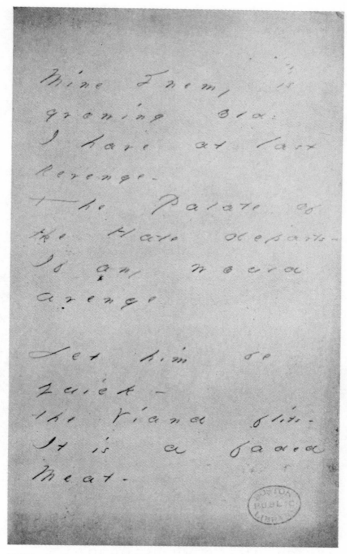

THE "BOLD" HANDWRITING OF THE MATURE
POET   *— Courtesy of the* BOSTON PUBLIC LIBRARY
GALATEA COLLECTION

HELEN HUNT JACKSON, WHO IS SAID TO HAVE
WRITTEN THE STORY OF EMILY DICKINSON'S
LIFE IN "MERCY PHILBRICK'S CHOICE"
— *From an* OLD PHOTOGRAPH

CHAPTER XV

EVENTS IN A VACUUM

ESOTERIC TIME — SCHEDULES FOR THE ARRIVAL OF humming-birds from Tunis, calendars of days for the opening and shutting of flowers, the brightening or the darkening of the sun, taut on the grass-sheen inside a high hedge, clocks to tick off the day-labour of the mind, measure in minutes a mediation which is neither slow, as is sunlight, nor fast, like lightning; sun-dials of angles on the gravel path that distort the travelling shadow — these ignore our human time docket; there is order and measurement for these things, and punctual coming and going, but the record is best kept in poetry. Month-lengths can be wound inside a day like a spring inside a watch-case; a cube of celestial sunlight, set in thin air, has for some a solidity around which whole seasons may buzz and bustle like ants around an apple-core — at last to be moved off, with infinite collective push, out of the path of days, still passive to the ticks of time. There are, for some, holes and pockets in time like the holes in the air an aviator avoids. Emily Dickinson inhabited one of these vacuums, and in it she was superbly alive . . . the years slid in a single wave over her head as she sat motionless and alert in a timeless garden. "Two lengths has every day," " Dawn and meridian are one."

Emily lived a double life: one life to the tune of Amherst's clocks; the other by an esoteric chart. One life was meagre, nervous, and sterile; the other abounded in peace and realization. She was born, she lived, in rectitude; she pursued the occupations of a gentlewoman, sewing, reading, tending the sick, embroidering a garden with a trowel on Amherst soil . . . she travelled in little journeys to Boston, to Springfield, and at length to Washington and Philadelphia; and she fell in love and renounced a man after a few kisses. As fact it is meagre. The clocks everywhere told her so perpetually.

What shall genius do, born into the body of a woman christened Emily Elizabeth, small, timid, near-sighted, the second child of Edward and Emily Norcross Dickinson? How shall genius live? For genius, even more than the mortal body, hates to die. Vacuum was the answer.

Emily was nicely fitted for an onslaught on time. Her religious background furnished her with the conception of eternity. She needed no physicist to call it the fourth dimension. Little Mary Lyon, standing on a chair beside the mantel, watching an hour-glass run, announced to her mother that she had " found a way to make more time." More sand was Mary Lyon's remedy. No poet would make such a mistake.

The monotony of her world, the static power of father and society and religion, set her contending upon the other extreme. Genius, even more than the mortal body, hates to die. Emily's reaction is described very fittingly, in general, by a contemporary mathematician and philosopher, Alfred North Whitehead, as a deep instinct for self-preservation:

"A static value, however serious and important, becomes unendurable by its appalling monotony of endurance. The soul cries aloud for release into change. It suffers the agonies of claustrophobia. The transitions of humour, wit, irreverence, play, sleep and — above all — of art, necessary for it."

This world outside time, " *exterior to time,*" as Emily put it, was an individual re-creation of something common enough in the thirteenth century. Before clocks were invented to tick and bells to toll and campaniles to remind and remind of time, the soul dwelt in eternity. After the thirteenth century the concept shrank into a mere word — after having been, not a mere word, but a world. A dry, a seldom watered word, it came down in a mummy-case from the ages, wrapped into the body of Christian theology. It was often brought out for inspection; the curious handled it, but few watered it or wanted it to grow. Emily watered it, and it grew. She neither believed in time, except as one believes in a shadow, nor allowed herself to do very much living in time. She hated clocks and all ticking paraphernalia.

And so she differed. Behold how she differed from the muslin souls around her! Consider her rebound — given a sheet of white paper — from the role of devoted daughter and dainty original saint! On paper Emily tasted rum and knew "a bliss like murder." Outside was defeat. For genius, it was bells within, as Emily put it. Briefly it was "bells," because she was writing poetry. She wrote of both selves: one defeated and one victorious. Side by side with the melodrama of a mind that did as it pleased, Emily put the record of that pained prisoner the modest chirruping bird, forbidden life in any raw quantity, living on crumbs from father's deliberate hand and infinitesimal sips of dew. The poor bird symbolized the little child caught in a mesh of time, Emily's earthly aggravating self, a self hard to shake, impossible to murder. Emily could not kill that self — she could only slip out of it. And by some click of secret machinery it was often left lying limp on the ground, while the disembodied Emily, the anonymous mind, rose and exulted over all the small patterns of the earth, high on a precipice of air.

This midge, on the current of self-important brisk little Amherst, committed no greater sin, in Amherst's eyes, than refusing to go to church. But the poems record, to name a few: *drunkenness*, often repeated; *gluttony*, often repeated; the sensations of *starvation*, a central theme; the pretence to the experience of *imprisonment*, *blindness*, *beggary*, *torture on the rack*, *larceny*, *gambling*, *miserliness*, *martyrdom*, *vagabondage*, and the practice of *witchcraft*.

Is it any wonder that Emily declined Mr. Higginson's Greek goddesses, no matter how hard Mr. Higginson tried to lure her to Boston? How prosaic the afternoon: Cambridge mitigations, the decorous limbs of a museum piece, with amended tales of jealousy, lust, and cunning on

Mount Olympus! No levity, no light — dear God, the solemnity!

Between 1862 and 1886 Emily's life was busy; indeed, it was distracted with an invisible toil. In that time she wrote at least twelve hundred poems, probably several hundred more, poems in numerous versions, minutely corrected, recast, enlarged, compressed, transformed for the sake of a word, usually framed with foot-notes, synonyms, antonyms, variant readings, choices of words — experiments of which number many failed, some lived to fail again, and others became accomplished facts. At the age of fifty-six, worn out by her explorations, adventures, and accomplishments, she died.

> *On the bleakness of my lot*
> *Bloom I strove to raise.*

Emily's Amherst garden was her comfort and her salvation in the lean years before she became an active poet. Neighbours peeping over the hedge doubtless said to each other that Miss Emily's garden pretty nearly kept her going, didn't it? A good thing she had something to fuss with, to take her mind off herself. Miss Emily knew as much. But what a pleasure to cultivate another garden nobody knew about, whose crimson and lavender no neighbour could glimpse, and walk down paths and gloat over midnight flowers too exotic for New England! It took an esoteric chemistry to get flowers from such soil as hers, Emily felt; but the fact that she could bring odd bloom from familiar clay verified the dogma of her life. Poetry, appraised at a greater value than even a place in heaven, was the result of a studious miracle. Nothing can keep the soul from its *consolation upside-down:* even odd Emily Dickinson could by these special powers become a poet.

She began to write, and Amherst began bringing her its shreds and trifles. A dog's feet went by at night *like intermittent plush.* For joy of that Emily perhaps spent a week perfecting the phrase. Soon a snake divided the grass *as with a comb.* Her garden teemed with subjects, so long as she cared to look; when she went in to her mind, she could look about herself there with equal simplicity, and God was no more veiled than the railroad train that lapped the miles and licked the valleys up.

What long experience lay behind this effortless power? Remember Emily, as taciturn at times as her father, working for the summers of twelve years out of ear-shot of mother and father and Vinnie and Austin and Sue, talking — when she talked at all — with two ghosts: one ghost of a living man, one of a dead. Death and Life, in other words, had a dialogue which Emily frequently interrupted; they were both pretty thoroughly cross-questioned before she got through with them. And at length, when she wrote poetry, she had much to report. By the time that she was ready to declare: "*The Soul selects her own society,*" or "*The heart asks pleasure first,*" for instance, their meanings were as assumed, by her, as the colours of the earth, or the routine of the seasons. Her theme was truth; her expression had been so long reined in against a full gallop in the direction of her beliefs that when she at last began to write, her first line took the bit into its teeth and ran by the shortest cut at top speed to its conclusion. Emily wrote as she had always talked, headlong, deliriously, using the concise enchanted word, and with that brevity that all clever talkers use. But the phrase was no longer merely on the tongue; it was written down and had new possibilities. What to do with it? Turn it, not once, but a hundred times, link it subtly with a family of phrases, repeat it, dwell on it, put it away and let it season like a bit of wood, live for nothing else but to see it perfected, and you will grow old in a trance and die busy.

The dull days, established like noiseless machinery, had little to manufacture except what Emily fed them.

" I rise because the sun shines and sleep has done with me. I brush my hair and dress and wonder what I am and who made me so . . . and then I help wash the breakfast-cups, and anon wash them again, and then 'tis afternoon and ladies call, and evening and some members of another line come in to spend the hours, and then the day is done. And prithee, what is life . . . ? "

The very dullness induced dream, and the dream became a species of energy purer than action. Prithee, what is life, and who made me? Ask the jocund birds and they simply fly elsewhere, bored by introspection. Brushing her hair, and very sleepily and still fixedly facing her image in the mirror, Emily went on looking for an answer. If it was a matter of peering into herself, that self the mirror mirrored, she looked long, persistently, as if hypnotized by the act.

Sometimes the self-encounter was pleasant; sometimes it was not. Sometimes Emily faced herself in a fond

reverie; more often it was as if she were outwaiting something exceedingly shy that would come out from hiding
if she waited long enough, to be most quietly seen. Emily
waited for it as Thoreau had, when he sat still whole
mornings while the woodchuck ventured closer.

Amherst was as good as any place, the time was better
than most times, for the making of an American poet.
The Indian summer of the Puritan code gilded the mind's
landscape; clouds threatened to make sunset stormy. All
that was about to die, that had never been expressed, was in
the air. But the other poets were busy with lesser matters;
they were emotionally elsewhere, not in New England.

Emily's life was like a clean and polished cup, ready for
filling, waiting on the shelf; on old wine was ready to be
poured.

She had long been passive — at the disposal of truth,
or life, or beauty, meaningless abstractions on paper, but
powerful in use. She had waited for something, she did not
know what; she had been both introspective and sane; she
had loved Life more than her life, and she had wished so
passionately to see some reality of which all things visible
are but the cloud that at length it happened; she saw and
heard.

Henry James knew, although he deplored, the inclination to spend a lifetime in this fashion. In his eyes, Emily's
interest in " Eternities " only served to pass the stupid
days. Obsessions he revered in the art of Europe were
simply social diseases at home.

" The doctrine of the supremacy of the individual to
himself, of his originality and, as regards his own char-

acter, *unique* quality, must have had a great charm for people living in a society in which introspection, thanks to the want of other entertainment, played almost the part of a social resource. . . . There was much relish for the utterances of a writer who would help to take a picturesque view of one's internal possibilities, and to find in the landscape of the soul all sorts of fine sunrise and moonlight effects."

James's own generation, which went pathetically about Europe's art galleries and cathedrals, looking at everything and anything except its own soul, came home again at length, to shudder and stare at itself and grow old and queer, with nothing to be seen in its own eyes, when it peered in on itself, but a blur of fine old kaleidoscopic cathedrals.

Emily's Amherst life penetrated into her inner life at a few points; her inner life came out in action rarely. We saw her renouncing a ride in the spring woods at twenty. Shortly after, the person with whom she shared her mind in secret, died. Before twenty-four she fell in love. At thirty-two she began to write, and continued to do so until her death, averaging fifty poems a year for twenty-five years.

Any day of her domestic life might have been expanded to cover the detail of a whole lifetime. In 1880, at fifty, Emily was nursing her mother, just as she describes doing at the age of twenty when she renounced the spring ride. No matter how people or their actions added or subtracted themselves to or from her surroundings, her life held the usual objects and the same tasks, and the days that cut little segments in an arch over her, with larger marks for years, had very little to do with what was happening in another dimension, in her mind and under her hand.

To live so made her an artist; poems live in this manner. These seven hundred and fifty poems, so angular, so structural, lacking gloss, vanishing hues, and decorative curves, are alive because of some activity at the centre; their sound is their sense, and when the mind touches them, they are flint to steel; they are entities, they are events.

It is impossible to date many of them. They began in a vacuum: external life stained them very little — often not at all. It is important, however, to peg them to earth wherever possible. Time did not interest Emily, but time and Emily interest us, and we will reject no method, however humble, of making a chart on which to place them as events.

Several methods serve to bring the poems into successive order. The most obviously interesting, an examination of the manuscript and a comparison of the handwriting of the different periods, cannot be employed until Madame Bianchi allows someone to study all the manuscript in her possession. The task of dating twelve hundred poems on the basis of handwriting is in itself a project on which a poet or a scholar may spend years of labour.

But we have a rough idea of the order in which the poems were written, through Mrs. Todd, the first editor, who inspected much, if not quite all, of the manuscript and chose from the various versions, and edited (how much we cannot know) and copied the poems off for the printer, in 1890. This covers the work published in *Poems: First, Second,* and *Third Series,* four hundred and forty-six in number. The poems in these three volumes, arranged under the headings: " Life," " Nature," " Love," " Time and Eternity," begin each division, in each volume, with the supposedly earliest written. Mrs. Todd says in her preface to *Poems: Second Series* (1891): " Although there is nowhere a date, the handwriting makes it possible to arrange the poems with general chronological accuracy."

Mrs. Todd had had much practice in judging this hand. In her edition of the *Letters* (1894) she explains that many letters had also needed an expert eye, since they often bore no date and contained no incident by which to place them. The handwriting in the early period is exceedingly small and clear, averaging twenty words to the line, and then by 1853 " quite different from the earlier letters, more resembling the middle period." The writing of the middle period was a rapid sort of print, very beautiful and carved, with gaps between strokes, many characters standing alone, and no punctuation except dashes. The date for the later period is not given by Mrs. Todd, although the facsimile of a letter written in 1882 serves as an example. But the writing is described as even more obscure, with capitals for all nouns and no linkage between letters. It is interesting to note that the first changes in style came in 1850 and in 1853.

With such general outlines for a guide, many smaller

methods may be used. Bits of poems were often included in letters, and most of the letters have been dated — not by month, often, but usually at least by a season. *Faith is a fine invention* is quoted to Mr. Bowles in a letter some time during 1862, before its second line had been reworked, reading:

When gentleman can see!

— a much less effective version than:

For gentlemen who see.

To illustrate a method of study:

This poem is numbered LVI (" Life "), coming after the gambling poems, the poem entitled *Success* by Mrs. Todd, " The heart asks pleasure first," " The Soul selects her own society," the poem charactering Mr. Higginson as a " Mighty Merchant," " To fight aloud is very brave," " Pain has an element of blank," " I'm Nobody," " I taste a liquor," " I never hear the word escape," and " Surgeons must be very careful," which all appear by their subject to have been written before and during 1862 — many of them clearly accompanying the great adventure of sending her verse to Mr. Higginson and her bid for success. We know besides that poem XXIX (" Life ") " The nearest dream recedes, unrealized," was sent to Mr. Higginson in the first letter, on April 10. It is close enough to the poem mentioned above to reinforce the dates in each case.

Working with the letters, it is possible to trace the origin of a few poems in an event. For instance, the famous

poem about the railroad train is numbered XLIII
(" Life ") — that is, it comes forty-third in the first division of the first series chosen by Mrs. Todd. This places
it before " Faith is a fine invention," which is numbered
LVI (" Life "), for which we have the general date 1862.
We find that in a letter dated June 20, 1853 Emily mentions the Amherst and Belchertown Railroad, which had
then been running for just a month, a celebration for the
completion of which Emily is describing. Father was chief
marshal of the day, and Emily writes to Austin: " I sat
in the woods and saw the train move off." The poem, then,
has a possible date as early as 1853, if we allow the letter
to guide us, although it is not very likely that Emily wrote
it until her great year of activity, 1862. Most explicit of
all the reasons for rejecting the early date is Emily's own
statement that she wrote little of importance until the
winter of 1862. Could she have written anything as excellent as the railroad train and not thought it vastly
important — really more important, she might have declared, than the invention of the locomotive? Madame
Bianchi dates eleven short poems sent to sister Sue and
later published in *The Single Hound,* also with some show
of chronological order, as early as 1854–5. But Madame
Bianchi's many errors of date and fact so often catch the
eye, in even a casual reading of her biographical sketch,
that we cannot alter Emily's own statement to suit it.

And what shall be done with *Further Poems,* brought
out by Madame Bianchi in 1928? Madame Bianchi says in
her Introduction: " Many pages are difficult to read. Some
of the writing is in the shy character of her girlish habit;

others so bold, there are but two words on a line in ink not yet faded."

But we are given no chronological arrangement, on the basis of faded ink, or script — an arrangement more valuable for a study of the poetry of Emily Dickinson than much of Madame Bianchi's so-called mystical sentence-writing about the poems. A few of these poems can be dated by the letters that first accompanied them; most of them, if dated at all by us, without the manuscripts, must be blocked into periods when the idea was running in Emily's head, shown in her letters — periods producing many poems, successes and failures both, which we may date by any means that count, or often not date at all.

This is one of the most rewarding ways of studying the poems in any case. Sometimes one subject gives off twenty attempts, of which number one may succeed as a whole and contain lines that cannot be omitted in the future from the small body of our permanent literature. It is safe to say that when a prose passage parallels the conception, the prose probably preceded the successful expression in poetry and never came after. The only thing to bear in mind is that Emily kept certain phrases perpetually on her tongue and said certain sententious things at the age of fifty that she had said over and over since the age of sixteen. A few such repetitions must be allowed for; they come uppermost so often that one gets to know them from the others less frequent.

Only the work of a line of poets and students will be able to diagram the interrelation of these knots of ideas.

The description of a few pages cannot exhaust or even enumerate possibilities. One of the most apparent, however, involves a poem which we are compelled to take apart for its singular merit; we will use it and its satellites for an example. First let the reader find for himself the several lines in which Emily describes drunkenness; he will come upon them easily under the first section, " Life," in the *Collected Poems.*

In her third letter to Higginson, Emily remarks: " I had tasted rum before," explaining the ecstasy she felt at a little praise from him. In poem XXXIX (" Nature ") a twenty-four line poem on drunkenness begins: " Bring me the sunset in a cup." This is a very interesting piece of writing, when we study Emily's manner; it is one of the most confused things she ever wrote; and, what is worse, it is really an ordinary poem except for two or three flashes. The confusion comes from the fact that the poem tries to handle far too many ideas supplementary to the tipsy theme, which evidently most interested Emily; but to this she adds a general poeticism, thus:

> *. . . write me. . .*
> *How many trips the tortoise makes,*

and

> *Also, who laid the rainbow's piers . . . .*

The last stanza changes its style and may have been added later. Everything else in the poem indicates a very early origin, coming doubtless when Emily had great technical struggles with her medium, usually ending in surrender to a silly, conventional form — so far as Emily was capable of surrender. It is strange to catch glimpses of Emily bending her back to exterior form; but we are able in a very few early poems to see such traces of the attitude. Undoubtedly she saw that other poems she had written were entirely bad and destroyed them, saving the few we have for the hint that they might grow in the true direction.

And we must remember here Emily's own recital of her difficulties. In writing Higginson she pictures what distressed her. First, the trouble of self-criticism: " The mind is so near itself it cannot see distinctly, and I have none to ask." And again: " I could not weigh myself, myself. My size felt small to me."

And then the attempt to say what led her to try to write: " And, then, far afterward, when sudden light on orchards, or a new fashion in the wind, troubled my attention, I felt a palsy here the verses just relieve."

When Mr. Higginson wished to correct and amend certain lines, and especially, we feel sure, Emily's " off " rhymes, she refused, explaining that she could not " drop the bells whose jingling cooled her tramp."

And then, sending some new poems to inquire if they were more orderly, she said, trying for a power far beyond Higginson's requirements: " I had no monarch in my life, and cannot rule myself; and when I try to organize, my little force explodes and leaves me bare and charred."

After her apprentice days Emily never mentioned such troubles again. Her earnestness about her poetry had met with many rebuffs, had met with casual comment, mis-

THE HON. EDWARD DICKINSON AT THE AGE OF SIXTY
"YOU KNOW HE NEVER PLAYED."
— *From the* HISTORY OF THE CONNECTICUT VALLEY IN
MASSACHUSETTS

MRS. MABEL LOOMIS TODD
— *From an* OLD PHOTOGRAPH

understanding, and indifference. But she fortified herself
by believing that a poet was " exterior to time," and then
in all honesty wrote to Sue a little sentence that shows
how ambitious she was for the honourable labour and
recognition of a genuine poet: " If I could make you and
Austin proud some day, a long way off, 'twould give me
taller feet."

With this picture of difficulties, we return to Emily's
girlish ambitious, conventional, and ineffectual little poem
which started by demanding the sunset in a cup and ended
in demanding escape from the prison of the body. In spite
of all the girlish concessions, the poem was still odd; without the oddities Mr. Higginson could doubtless have got
it in the *Atlantic*. The poem's meaning, doubtless added
later, was suitable.

The poem is almost a total waste, but it hit upon one
fine phrase: " debauchee of dew " — the kind of phrase
Emily could not, for all her false starts, sacrifice to lesser
phrases; and so presently she wrote another poem (we
cannot tell how many she wrote in the mean time) which
did the phrase full justice. Out of this overwritten early
attempt comes one of Emily's most dazzling poems. Despite its number, XX (" Life "), it is obviously later
than " Bring me the sunset in a cup." In twenty-five
years of writing Emily was not going to excel it very
often.

> *I taste a liquor never brewed,*
> *From tankards scooped in pearl;*
> *Not all the vats upon the Rhine*
> *Yield such an alcohol!*

⤙EMILY DICKINSON⤚

Inebriate of air am I,
And debauchee of dew,
Reeling, through endless summer days,
From inns of moulten blue.

When landlords turn the drunken bee
Out of the foxglove's door,
When butterflies renounce their drams,
I shall but drink the more!

Till seraphs swing their snowy hats,
And saints to windows run,
To see the little tippler
Leaning against the sun!

In the earlier poem there are four attempts at the inns of molten blue, the tankard, the vats, the dram, and the landlord of the foxglove. But the effect is cloudy. Emily uses " spun the breadths of blue," and " withes of supple blue "; she makes two of the four stanzas turn on the rhyme *blue* with *dew* and *due*. In the poem given above, the phrase chimed, at last. There are many reasons why. And the second poem is in quatrains — Emily's destined form; the first tries with adjectives and rhymes to make a stanza form of six lines. Many of the early poems resist the quatrain form. Of the successful poem Thomas Bailey Aldrich wrote in 1903, in *Ponkapog Papers:*

" In the first volume of Miss Dickinson's poetical melange is a little poem which needs only a slight revision of the initial stanza to entitle it to rank with some of the swallow flights in Heine's lyrical intermezzos. I have tentatively tucked a rhyme into that opening stanza."

268

Mr. Aldrich's tinkered stanza follows:

I taste a liquor never brewed
In vats along the Rhine;
No tankard ever held a draught
Of alcohol like mine.

Idiotic meddler! What has he dared to do to one of the most delicious lines in the English language! Mr. Aldrich takes one line of Emily's and then writes three nondescript of his own, in the interest of " swallow flights " and " lyrical intermezzos."

" From tankards scooped in pearl " enjoins our attention, after being so vandalized. Quite apart from the sounds received and carried on by it, it runs the voice from the *a*'s in " tankards " to the *o*'s in " scooped " and then produces the word " pearl," on which to let them culminate; the *nk* and the *r* in " tankard " catching all the other consonants as the ripple of tone-colour runs down the line. If anyone needs the pale device of rhyme after such interplay of sound, culminating in " Yield such an alcohol," he is tone-deaf and deserves to be so. But he should be told that, while he was hearing nothing, the stanza as a whole has been giving off the variations on the sound of *l*, firmly placed in the middle of the first line, at the end of the second, near the beginning of the third to culminate in " yield " and the *l*'s of " alcohol."

The next stanza is equally, although differently, inebriate. " Inebriate of air am I " plays with the delicate *i* sound in the first word, repeats it in " air " and then

grounds it in the word "*I.*" Line two is all *e* and *ew*
sound, alliterated and emphasized by the *ee*'s run into
"reeling." Then comes "inns of moulten blue," which
would be only a phrase if the *i*'s of the stanza were not
still in the ear and the *ou* and the *u* in "moulten" and
"blue" did not come as a perfect conclusion, a sensuous
resolution.

Will my reader read the rest of the poem with analyti-
cal eyes?

"I cannot weigh myself, myself." That induced her to
seek out Mr. Higginson. And how was he with scales?
After a time Emily became her own critic and made no
more inquiries. But first she sent her poems on a long
journey.

Mr. Higginson records the names of the poems enclosed in the first letter. They were: *Safe in their alabaster
chambers; I'll tell you how the sun rose; We play at
paste;* and *The nearest dream recedes, unrealized.*

In the second poem Emily rhymes "time" with
"ran." It was like performing a witch-rite before the
gaze of Cotton Mather. Higginson undoubtedly pounced
on the false rhyme at once. The rest of the poem is obedient: "begun" rhymes with "sun," "stile" with "while,"
"gray" with "away." Mr. Higginson must have pointed
out, as all teachers do, that it is improper to compare the
grandeur of nature with a man-made textile:

> *I'll tell you how the sun rose, —*
> *A ribbon at a time . . .*

and

> *The hills untied their bonnets . . .*

270

were doubtless the subject of a pat little paragraph when Higginson answered. *Safe in their alabaster chambers* rhymes " noon " with " stone," in the first stanza. The poem is a little unsure, but it is Emily when she chooses to turn Venetian. It has a rhythm she seldom used, and one line is one of the two obvious results of a long admiration for Browning:

> *Diadems drop and Doges surrender.*

Emily evidently didn't know that she was echoing; for although she speaks about this time of rejecting a passage that sounded like someone else, this was not the passage. Of the first poem in the next group Higginson said: " The slightest change in the order of the words — thus: 'while yet at school a girl,' would have given her a rhyme for this last line; but no; she was intent on her thought." Until modern poetry began to understand what Emily had accomplished by her derelictions, the chief labour of critics was to present Emily with inversions that would fix a rhyme.

The poem concludes with a remark that was associated, in some far way, with either Leonard Humphrey or George Gould.

> *It's far, far treasure to surmise*
> *And estimate the pearl*
> *That slipped my simple finger through*
> *While just a girl at school.*

" Pearl " is one of the words that rang continually in her ear during the sixties.

A bird came down the walk, next, and Mr. Higginson

was probably the first to behold him bite an angle-worm in halves and eat the fellow, raw. It is a poem as rare as a bit from Chaucer, as fine and sweet and nimble and quiet. Mr. Higginson must have capitulated to it; who would not? But his perfectly natural delight may have been a little marred by observing that the third stanza forgot to rhyme itself at all; it was so busy describing the eyes in the velvet head. Emily seldom quotes, but in one letter she remembers that Keats's bird " hops and hops in little journeys," which is itself from the Chaucerian strain. Her bird hops too, but only once, and then she attempts a description no poet had tried:

> *And he unrolled his feathers*
> *And rowed him softer home*
> *Than oars divide the ocean. . . .*

The " home-work " went away to be corrected. Mr. Higginson corrected manfully. But it did no good.

> *You cannot fold a flood*
> *And put it in a drawer.*

No, indeed, you cannot. He corrected, but Emily changed nothing to please him, which of course checked Mr. Higginson's avidity. And she wrote faster than he could correct, and by 1886 there were twelve hundred poems or more — the last as unregenerate as the first.

People who build vacuums and sustain existence inside of them may or may not be wise or clever or valuable. It happens that a vacuum was a perfect place for poetry in New England in 1862. Outside, in the real world, were

Longfellow, Lowell, Holmes, and Whittier, all poor poets. The world had them in its pocket. The laws of Emily's vacuum ignored the literary traditions that so hampered the bearded venerables in Cambridge. She had always been heterodox. If souls were unique and self-sufficient, so should poems be. God was not even — least of all — God of Prosody. Here is Emily's subjective test for poetry:

" If I read a book and it makes my whole body so cold no fire can ever warm me, I know that is poetry. If I feel physically as if the top of my head were taken off, I know that is poetry. These are the only ways I know it. Is there any other way? "

And so her thought allowed itself to be as odd as lightning. Lightning asks no rules the leave to express itself; it strikes. Many of Emily's poems have a like technique, they grumble and gather sound — yellow writing, a rocket. . . .

She describes what seems to have been the preaching of one man she loved, in a poem which ends:

He stuns you by degrees,

Prepares your brittle substance
For the ethereal blow,
By fainter hammers, further heard,
Then nearer, then so slow

Your breath has time to straighten,
Your brain to bubble cool, —
Deals one imperial thunderbolt
That scalps your naked soul.

273

A technique Emily admired.

Shakspere and the Bible and Watts's hymn-book had been absorbed early; their rhythms beat with the beating of her heart. She was heterodox and odd, and so the conventions of poetry were not for her. She had an instinctive splendour in language, she used it like a master. It said what she told it to say, and someone else might count up the cost, add the loss or the profit. So the poet went on in her vacuum.

We think it now the busiest spot in the nineteenth century!

274

CHAPTER XVI

THE POETRY OF BLACKSTONE

I N THE POEM WHICH STANDS IN THE SECTION EN-
titled " Love," we find eight legal words in as many
lines.

> *Mine by the right of the white election!*
> *Mine by the royal seal!*
> *Mine by the sign of the scarlet prison*
> *Bars cannot conceal!*
>
> *Mine, here in vision and in veto!*
> *Mine, by the grave's repeal*
> *Titled, confirmed, — delirious charter!*
> *Mine, while the ages steal!*

In announcing her love Emily used her father's
language.

What could be more like Emily than to take the very
words out of her father's mouth and to put them to such
ends? It was a jest. It was necromancy. People called the
law a dusty profession, factual, unimaginative, and mundane. Emily loved to prove what enchantment she could
extract from stony rubbish. The words in codicils and

briefs and deeds and pleas should be handled to make the salt of phrase. She needed words with a taut resonance; she needed precise, healthy, homely, quaintly formal words. Her verse, veering round rhyme in minor chime, needed words with an odd apt colour. She needed verbs strong enough to suggest adverbs, and nouns brilliant enough to imply adjectives. She needed words with new edges and solemn strangeness; she needed words with enough facets for building on angles; she needed spondaic words to carry the deliberate ruthless pace of plain statement. She needed words that could be dwelt upon until they were poems in themselves. These words she repeated over and over, because she was in love with them. Some of them were legal words. Others were literary words which grew new with Emily's loving use of them — such words as " ample," " scant," " emerald," " punctual," " frugal," and " imperial." To have encountered these words in a poem of Emily's is to possess a new sense of their value.

Subtract Emily's habitual phrases from the world's poetry and survey the damage — where in the nineteenth century was anyone simply remarking the " yellow noise " of sunrise? Who, except some hypersensitive subjective novelist, would describe a dog's footsteps as " intermittent plush." Proust and Dorothy Richardson do such things in novels and we weary of them, because their observations have no form; impression follows impression until the mind is giddy; and sharpness, restraint, position are lost.

Emily's poetry leads one to gloat over words — over their excellent round syllables or high sharp consonants. Bad poetry is written with the same words, sometimes;

but we sense at a glance when the author has not fully valued his currency. Emily seemed to think that this richness was the gift of screws.

When Noah Webster worked on his dictionary in Amherst, he was preparing a book greatly to Emily's taste — to know enough words meant to find the right one possibly and eventually. Mrs. Todd says that often the margins of the best poems had as many as ten or a dozen substitute words standing ready to take the place of the first choice. It is significant that many of these were not synonyms at all; they were delicious variations on a sound-theme, and Emily regretted that she could not use them all. Maggy Mahar's Irish speech pleased Emily's ear; it had flavour. Theological language on the tongue of the visiting minister sometimes had a tang. Emerson, too, had a tang. Thoreau was tart, like a wild apple. They both used nice words.

But father's words became her greatest acquisition. For several reasons Emily found them surging up in her mind when she wrote. The first reason, the most obvious of all, was of course the hypnotism of father's manner — " industrious, laconic, punctual, sedate." That spell began when Emily was very little; her father's manner was the chief fact of her life. Another reason lies in Emily's use of argument as the framework of many poems. Before the bar of heaven, before God, the upright Judge, Emily presented her culprit, Life, and pleaded in accurate syllables for a lenient decision. Argument, even if only one-sided argument, suited her mind. A poem sometimes states only one side, as if to refute an opponent. Then sometimes Emily argues both sides. And in certain of the metaphysical pronouncements Emily speaks with the authority of the person who hands down the law.

This ability to argue two sides of a question is seen when we place these poems side by side:

> *They say that " time assuages ",* —
> *Time never did assuage;*
> *An actual suffering strengthens,*
> *As sinews do, with age.*
>
> *Time is a test of trouble,*
> *But not a remedy.*
> *If such it prove, it prove too,*
> *There was no malady.*

But Emily could take the other side as well, and say with equal point:

> *We outgrow love like other things*
> *And put it in a drawer. . . .*

People who think they have seized on what Emily " believed " have only to turn the page. She will cancel as speedily as she will maintain.

Perhaps the best way to write this comment on Emily's use of legal words is to marshal the words themselves. Here is a very partial, skimming list, by no means exhaustive, from the *Letters* and poems:

audits	abscond	approbation
abdicated	astute	annealed
annulled	ably argued	adjourn
allied	assault	absolute decree
annual	annually	adjure

278

EMILY DICKINSON

arraigns
avocation
amended
affidavit
audits
accredit
auction
accused
abrogate
acquitted
assignable
arbitrate
alibi
bulletins
benefactor
benefits
balance
briefs
bond
bribe
bar
bequeath
boroughs
bond we sign
conjectures
certificate
consummate
confirm
corporeal
convict

counterfeits
compete
counsel
consult
concede
compensations
court-practical
commit a start-
    ling fraud
concomitant
communications
custom
curtail
covenant
ceded
candidate
committed
condign punish-
    ment
cite
currency
cancelled
certified
confirmed
charter
clause
claim
conferred
contested
complaint

certify
codicil
caucus
contract
condemned
detecting
defray
duration
dispatch
decease
deter
defraud
defaulter
destitute
depose
demur
dowries
decree
depreciate
defer
disburse
democrat
exchange of terri-
    tory
espoused
expire
endorsement
estimate
enact
elect

estate
endow
exorbitant
executors
exigencies
estrange
expositor
election
evidence
execute
extorted
elicit
enfranchise
express
enjoin
extant
foreclose
facilities
frauds
fluctuate
formula
facilitate
forfeit
forswear
guaranty
guarantee
hear at price
invalidate
inference
insure

insecurity
identity
interest
investigation
intercede
inventory
insolvency
inviolate
investments
indemnity
invest
inquest
impeach
interdict
interview
income
intermit
justice
jurisprudence
justified
justify
jury
judgment
larceny
lawful heir
licensed
litigants
legacies
lease
legally

minorities
moiety
nomination
negotiate
negotiations
not a party to
optional
option
ordain
ordinance
omit
prospects
premises
principalities
penurious
prevalent
preclude
proclamation
per cents
premium
preceding
proof
perquisite
preferment
precincts
pedigree
perjury
patent
parties in both cases
requite

request
render
requisite
rotatory
redress
render unto
reprieve
reduction
recapitulate
remit
rescind
receipted
recompense
repudiate
repeal
ratified
repealless
rates
restitutes

ratio
specifical
seal
sessions
sue
subjugate
stipulate
specify
sureties of
    staunch estate
salary
shares
stocks
supersede
signed away
sentence
status
trustees
terms

title
transactions
tax
tribunal
treason
traffic
titled
testified
title-deed
usurp
value
vilify
verdict
veto
voted
witnessing
witness

CHAPTER XVII

GOD'S CULPRIT

" — but was not temptation the first zest? "

IN HER OWN EYES, EMILY WAS ONE OF THE WORST
sinners that ever lived.

Could any other kind of intensity culminate in New
England? Calvin was more than a memory of the blood.
The New Englander needed Calvin's evil for stimulus, as
much as he needed hard cider in winter. The extremes of
seasons and their toil widened the scale of his senses;
strong drink and religion fed them; fear and guilt were
calluses on the New England hand, as inevitable to living
as toil itself.

The New Englander feared God. In order to get the
hysterical ability to run towards God he must feel himself pursued. . . . He looked over his shoulder to help
himself run.

Evil pursued. That was Evil's business. This was a
theology of extremes; violent and orderly at one and the
same time. The New Englander had made his theology
to suit his temperament, drawing from the great of the

282

line, Calvin and the Apostle Paul. He craved incredible good and invented profound evil for its sake. This was a work of art, a way of life, a folk-story.

During Emily's lifetime brave mistaken Sir Ralph Waldo Emerson slew Evil, which had lived like a folk-dragon in the forest primeval. And then New England as an idea began to die. Emerson wanted one half of the system without the other half, the sweet without the sour; he struck at the Devil to kill it and, instead, killed God.

But even while he denied evil, Emerson used the old forms, the old dualism: "An inevitable dualism bisects nature, so that each thing is half, and suggests another thing to make it whole. . . ." " It would seem that there is always this vindictive circumstance stealing in at unawares . . . this back-stroke, this kick in the gun, certifying that the law is fatal."

The New Englander knew and indulged in many extremes, but he avoided the extremes of sex, and the sexual powers. The avoidance became a form, a denial as acute as indulgence. And as a result all the other indulgences he practised took on the sexual colour and drew energy from the denied. Evil came to mean either sexual misdemeanour, a defiance of God's law, or open literal defiance of God Himself. Where it was both, as it often was, in the witch-days, the attending sense of guilt blotted everything. A very deep and almost fatal struggle over the nature and exact source of evil, and the impulse to experiment in it, went on endlessly with every process of Emily's living. To a lesser degree it went on in every robust face she saw; only the weak and the insane escaped; it was the only story life had. No New England thinker could hope to free himself and his habits of mind in one decade from such bred-in-the-bone concepts. In enumerating the " inevitable duality that bisects nature " Emerson put " spirit, matter, man, woman," in his list of doubles.

Emerson dimly saw the danger of dwelling confidently on this duality; but it was an old danger, which many philosophers had weathered. To solve the problem, he proposed wrapping God up very carefully and putting Him outside the circle, where He should be safe. And then Emerson intended a thorough house-cleaning of his generalizations; Emerson purposed bringing God back and setting Him in the centre of the swept and garnished place, where His light would shine for all therein. God was to be a unity to enclose the duality.

But the doctrine of duality, which was to have made a rational order in which God might shine, got out of hand. The doctrine was too well embedded in Christianity to slacken its fatal force, once set completely in motion; it made, not the sweep of a broom, but the path of a whirlwind. Emerson's generalizations brought everything, even God, into a heap — the litter of a theology was on the door-step.

There poor Hawthorne beheld it, ready for the dustbin, and complained of the interior: ". . . a dull routine of commonplace prosperity; no picturesque or gloomy wrong."

Emily did not need to complain, for although she took good care not to believe in evil, she lived in the forest primeval and experienced the hazards and horrors of the outlaw. She had, like all her neighbours, felt the kick in the gun after the explosion of God. Fervently enough she wished that both could be abolished. And so she dwelt on every word that came out of the mouth of Emerson. But when she wrote, she was not gratifying desires for a new theology. She felt the disaster of a sinner; she was a major poet beset by a tragic view of life, not a Disciple of Newness. Guilt and sin dye the virginal white of her feeling, and stamp it with undeniable experience in the dismay of living. What Emily recorded, therefore, was something in the realm of Scripture, a Scripture tested by the actualities of the human heart. If this were not so, she would be only the poet of the ethereal prude.

Nevertheless, there is a serious misfortune in many of Emily's attitudes of guilt. Too much of the time she takes the part of the naughty, impudent little girl, sparkling blasphemies at her father; it is a pantomime that wearies; we feel often that Emily was always and only a child.

> *I hope the father in the skies*
> *Will lift his little girl, —*
> *Old-fashioned, naughty, everything, —*
> *Over the stile of pearl!*

That she grew beyond the child we have supreme evidence in certain poems; Emily grew far beyond, but when sore pressed, she collapsed. In the hideous level of her middle years the only relief must have been the playing of this more innocent game of the bad, old-fashioned little girl. In a letter written to Austin during the spring of 1853, there is an exclamation that is, as usual, edited just as Emily opens her mouth to speak her full heart. Emily

285

wrote it before her second engagement with her father, when becoming an adult seemed much more difficult than any pinnacle of being for a good angel:

"I wish we were children now — I wish we were always children, how to grow up I do not know. . . . Cousin J. has made us an Æolian harp which plays beautifully whenever there is a breeze."

She says of woe, as she may have felt of guilt:

> *Softened by Time's consummate plush,*
> *How sleek the woe appears*
> *That threatened childhood's citadel,*
> *And undermined the years!*

> *Bisected now by bleaker griefs,*
> *We envy the despair*
> *That devastated childhood's realm,*
> *So easy to repair.*

Commenting on something he saw in all the New Englanders about him, George Gould said in a sermon:

"But, as I have said, my present purpose is practical rather than speculative. Whatever obscurity technical theologians, in time past, have thrown around the connection between divine and human agency, between man's duty and God's grace in the work of religion, the Bible is responsible for none of it. *The Bible is a practical book; it, therefore, never arrays God's sovreignty and man's freedom in an attitude of antagonism to each other, but always in rational coincidence and in perfect practical harmony.*"

The theory of Creator and created fascinated Emily. She was a metaphysician, not a practical person.

286

God's function was authority; He was male; He ruled. Emily pitted herself against authority until her last breath; creation, love, the fruits of love — these had been a long time, except when carefully supervised, the sins of New England. She criticized father and God, but she felt for ever at their mercies, having committed herself to poetry and love for its own sake.

As a creator, God was at fault.

> *It's easy to invent a life,*
> *God does it every day —*
> *Creation but a gambol*
> *Of His authority.*

Irresponsible God! Emily reproached Him for having made herself, in His perturbless way, to inhabit such an impossible cruel double universe. She rebelled; she said that she would not go on, that she would go back, not merely to childhood, but to that happy, insensible place the " atom's tomb, merry and nought and gay and numb." A unity!

> *My reason, life I had not had*
> *But for yourself. 'Twere better charity*
> *To leave me in the atom's tomb,*
> *Merry and nought, and gay and numb,*
> *Than this smart misery.*

Father's accusing eyes followed her all during her childhood; that we already know. After father died, Emily dreamed of him every night, and always it was a different dream.

" We have had no rain for six weeks except one thunder shower and that so terrible that we locked the doors, and the clock stopped — which made it like Judgment day."

Clocks and the day of judgment had always coincided, ever since Emily was late to breakfast, and Edward waited, compressed and appalling, timepiece in hand.

" Punctual " is a favourite word. Pink, small, and punctual is the arbutus, punctual is the snow, the frost, death; and the railroad train is " punctual as a star." There was a great virtue in punctuality, and a great fault in the lack of it; and Emily couldn't tell the time for years, and she was always being slow, or late, and scolded for being late. Clocks were demons, and Emily was delighted when they stopped or ran down. " The everlasting clocks, chime noon," she says, baffled by their decimals. Once a poem ends on a shout of glee: " Jehovah's watch is wrong." In one of her gayest verses she turns the familiar domestic comment upside-down and has the pleasure of saying:

> Lightly stepped a yellow star
> To its lofty place.
> Loosed the Moon her silver hat
> From her lustral face.
> All of evening softly lit
> As an astral hall —
> " Father," I observed to Heaven,
> " You are punctual."

The little guilts grew into a snowball bigger than naughty little Emily. Not liking Sunday-school, not liking housework, putting the nicked plate at father's place time after time, saying witty things about the heroes of the Bible, wanting to read, and reading, forbidden books, and loving the world that father called evil because it was luring — all these things convicted the young, round-faced Emily in her own eyes. She was used to her role of youthful sinner and she did not take it so seriously as she did exuberantly, for a long time.

And then Emily found Leonard Humphrey and George Gould, and lost both of them.

What happened then? Why, then their ghosts came back, and the colour of guilt deepened to a supernatural hue, and its presence had to be hidden. In guilty loneliness Emily spent the next few years, and nothing happened to break the rack of pain, only thousands of small screws wound it tighter on the bone. Emily grew queer; she avoided people; she brooded; father saw too late that Emily was headed wrong and would soon be the town anecdote. It was too late; yes, Emily embraced her queerness and began to let people think her double when she was merely bored. Father watched; father mourned. He drew near his daughter, his eyes showing his love, compelling, repressed, potent with a million child-memories. It is as if Emily screamed to get away. She began to want to run, to hide, to grow small and invisible — to escape.

> *To my quick ear the leaves conferred;*
> *The bushes they were bells;*
> *I could not find a privacy*
> *From Nature's sentinels.*
>
> *In cave if I presumed to hide,*
> *The walls began to tell;*
> *Creation seemed a mighty crack*
> *To make me visible.*

This is the sensitivity in *Crime and Punishment*.

After Leonard Humphrey's death the design grew in expanding webs of pain and bafflement. Another living man fell before the unnatural spell and became a ghost so far as Emily was concerned. The world was razed and blasted, and the only thriving thing, a tacit understanding between Edward and Emily.

Humbly kneeling, Emily looked up hurriedly, to scan God's face — an oblique scrutiny, as quick as lightning.

She was always suspecting that He would prove to be unjust. Sometimes God was just. Often not. She saw, as she put it,

> *. . . the underside*
> *Of His divinity,*

too well to trust Him, and said:

> *" But I, grown shrewder,*
> *Scan the skies*
> *With a suspicious air. . . ."*

With poor old Moses, God seemed:

> *In tantalizing play*
> *As Boy should deal with lesser Boy*
> *To show supremacy.*

She collected instances of a bullying God. The doubt, the scrutiny, the hope, the disappointment, widen and grow as a theme. The cheated child has a long grievance. God swindles, and God does not " provide." Emily says in a letter what she has said in a score of verses:

" . . . but I seek and I don't find, and knock and it is

not opened. Wonder if God is just — presume He is, however, and 'twas only a blunder of Matthew's."

This is the way God took Leonard Humphrey:

> *God permits industrious angels*
> *Afternoons to play.*
> *I met one, — forgot my school-mates*
> *All, for him, straightway.*
>
> *God calls home the angels promptly*
> *At the setting sun;*
> *I missed mine. How dreary marbles,*
> *After playing Crown!*

In the second loss God used a method more long-drawn-out, a slower agony, as if He knew that Emily had not been quite baffled by death.

" My life closed twice before its close," she said to start one poem, and then, compressing the whole story into eight lines:

> *I never lost as much but twice,*
> *And that is in the sod.*
> *Twice have I stood a beggar*
> *Before the door of God!*
>
> *Angels, twice descending*
> *Reimbursed my store.*
> *Burglar, banker, father,*
> *I am poor once more!*

No wonder Emily ceased to count on publication or to take pleasure in the prospect of it! Her poems were soon so very good — in her own eyes — and so unprintable that she discarded the desire to see them in print and only kept the desire to write more, as ruthless and satisfactory as the little pile in her cupboard. "Publication is the auction of the mind of man." Think of the scholarly and elegant Longfellow, and of Lowell, who was a witty man and very suave, and how they dismissed Whitman and countered Poe. Emily's content had more shattering power than had Whitman's.

Sin is no more now. It has technical names, and the X-ray is employed to locate its dwelling. After the picture is taken, we have only a branching of bones. Which means that sin is no more. Not so in Emily's time. Even Emerson uttered the word at times — Emerson, who skimmed over the dark pool of life like those water-bugs which indent the surface, but never get their feet wet. He made a series of observations about sin. Sin, he said, he who had never sinned in earnest, might well become the point for beginning a wider life. Sin was bone-meal to his thin soil — Emerson wanted to use everything. Melville had seen sin grinning in a whale's jaws; he had spent his early manhood with bad men and the sea's violent tempests; he was sure of sin, but not as a concept. Whitman tried to establish a mood that would empty evil of its terror — his performance came of an impulse like Emerson's, and he indeed succeeded in finding a death without a sting — his poetry seems to be making diplomatic offers of some sort to reality, in a soft boastful voice. Poe exploited evil, giving it a purple lining; he had not the fibre to withstand it, or the ability to describe it in simplicity; the grandiose evil Poe evoked was a wall against the pitiless evil he suspected might snatch at him. . . . Evil as an element in tragedy had come uppermost when Hawthorne wrote the story of a woman who lived her life fully around a carefully embroidered letter A. Hawthorne, like Melville, and unlike Emerson and Thoreau, the theorists of evil, and unlike Whitman, the placater of it, or Poe, its fond fool, had emotional experience to testify to its active, tragic, and devastating power. And of Hawthorne, who represented the same past that had produced her father, Emily recorded her true sensations when she wrote: " Hawthorne appals, entices."

" I never was so rapid in my virtue but my vice kept up with me," said pure Thoreau, who abhorred vice or even the hearing of dirty stories. " We cannot do well without our sins; they are highway of our virtue." Calvin's drama of the soul was quitting hard, and ludicrously. Sin still lingered like heat-lightning in sultry landscape.

Behind Emerson stood the German transcendentalists and romantics, with a credo of emotional self-indulgence. Its corollary was self-expansion. The Germans urged Emerson on his Unitarian way and began in Europe a rationalization that flowered eighty years later — that is, fifteen years ago — in the doctrines of psychoanalysis. Self-expansion, and self-indulgence by means of a series of psychic alibis, motivate most of psychoanalysis so deeply that we have seen its power as a theory already beginning to wane. The relief it gave to a sense of guilt was its chief value — a relief, but it had no solution, since it did not solve what gives rise to the sense of guilt. Guilt remains, sin has gone. In our own time we have seen the culmination of many romantic doctrines, of which this is one. And by their fruits we are able to know them.

The romantics of 1860 made a world-climate of suggestion, and no creature, if sensitive, escapes climate. Emily saw the sky — she noted the prevailing winds — she read the *Atlantic*. If she read further afield and studied the instigators of the new doctrines, we have no memoranda of that reading. Emerson she knew as one becomes familiar with the language and the ideas of the local minister of the gospel.

Indeed, she needed nothing more than a hint, a little rough sketch of a new universal plan, to develop by herself a philosophy, similar at certain points to that of the Disciples of Newness. But the consciousness of a world philosophy was as far away from Emily in Amherst as the world itself, and what of the world came to her came only as iron does in food from the soil of the vegetable garden. Her solution could never have been formulated in our terms. We must forget our terms. We must remember that we are Puritans, in memory, and that Emily is our ancestor.

Her solution was a much-travelled foot-path from her primitive feeling to a dialectic in her own shorthand.

Still the puzzle remains; how could Emily feel all that we find written on paper and still live inside her niche of a mind, and never hint or even seem to know fully the import of what she was saying? It is hard to explain how she could so completely taste a bliss like murder and still possess herself in saintliness, too, without experiencing wonder at herself. And it is hard to see how she could know the darkness and evil of life so instinctively and yet believe so blithely in a good world, and live crisply, as if it were.

What took her off, under her father's roof, on practices, in spirit, for which the Salem witches were caught and adulterous women branded and stamped for ever into the soil of the New England consciousness? And how did she keep her integrity? And how her unsullied self?

Emily was not accused socially of any evil practice; there was nothing wrong, by the code of the time, in tending a father with devotion, in being docile and shy and obedient. In her inner life Emily used and enjoyed her guilt almost as a means of living. And so it did not kill her. There is no denying the significance of her retreat from the world. She feared to meet evil face to face, she feared being forced to combat it outside herself. Emily never allowed anyone in her world of friends to assume that they knew more of the world than she did, and with anyone she would have argued aphoristically against its existence. We find only a few evil objects in Emily's poetry; war was evil — a snake was evil, — it made Emily feel zero at the bone, and she said of it: " Guile is where it goes." For a moment in a very mild way she felt as Melville did when he saw the white whale; the small snake is Evil Incarnate, and Emily later wrote a dream-poem in which the snake is hooded evil, regnant. Emily flees. But the snake in the grass in her father's meadow " wrinkles and is gone." Emily puts it out of mind. The war lingered. The war restated the problem of death, which introduced the argument about evil, and Emily pursued the inquiry on, through death to God. Death, from 1850 ever after, all her life, was the key to the mystery; it would reveal the true nature of God and of the soul; and if death turned out to be good, Emily saw that she could conclude life to have been so. Death would tell the truth about God. Emily tracked evil to its lair and found that it vanished into God. God, who cheated, bullied, swindled, and coerced His children, was the source from which evil radiated — that is, if evil really existed at all. Emily kept an open mind, or, rather, an opening and closing mind.

And then finally Emily pardoned God. She had a vision of a world brilliantly alive, miraculously ordered, atom within atom, built structurally on truth, and so, since God was an important rivet in the structure, she brought herself to God, and was both penitent and proud. Any world so lawfully made could not, for all its pain, be considered evil. God was authority — creation, the soul, had made him. Creation was the principle to which God was a slave.

Emily's role was that of the sceptic; she was God's critic. Without God she would have been nothing. She found her place. She had a work to perform, seemingly, in her New England environment. T. S. Eliot says: " I believe that the sceptic . . . is a very useful ingredient in a world which is no better than it is. In saying this I do not think I am committing myself to any theological heresy. . . . But here I want to make a capital distinction: criticism, infidelity, and agnosticism must, to be of value, be *original* and not inherited. Orthodoxy must be traditional, heterodoxy must be original."

By such a distinction we place Emily in the body of the

Puritan tradition, with her faith and her doubt in daily communication. If her faith had not been so solid that she did not fear to knock it over, or break it off at the base, she would never have swung about in its branches so securely.

And then Emily took all sin and made it petty and childish. Very carefully Emily took sin out of the world of consequences and put it into a laboratory where it could be treated as priceless, and where it could do no harm. It was the stuff of life — the culprit. Then, having pardoned God by a supreme effort of the will, Emily pardoned herself. She felt double when she did it.

Did she travel this argument toilsomely only once in the course of fifty-six years? No, daily. Sin was a blot which rose on the sun when the sun rose, and it had to be scoured off each day, because it never really came off, any more than did the little stain on Lady Macbeth's hand.

" Faith is doubt, sister," said Emily, and talked of the kind of mind that " doubts as fervently as it believes," to explain how simultaneous were her adoration and rebellion. On one page God has " a cordial visage." And on the next He bullies the trusting child. She comes to pray and remains to worship. And with the same hand she is able to write:

> *Bride of the Father and the Son*
> *Bride of the Holy Ghost,*

and then:

> *We apologize to Thee*
> *For Thine own Duplicity.*

Her torment is that she is able to mock God and love Him with the same voice.

Like Penelope's web every night, Emily's faith had to be nearly finished only so that it might be, in the morning, ravelled again.

> *Myself would run away*
> *From Him and Holy Ghost and All —*
> *But — there's the Judgment Day.*

Still, as Carlyle said of De Quincey, " This child has been in hell."

CHAPTER XVIII

BRIGHT ABSENTEE

I tend my flowers for thee,
Bright Absentee.

WITH EQUAL GRAVITY AND CARE SHE TENDED HER love. It must bloom and bloom and never die. A religious zeal, like the love of God, sustained it; the daily use of fancy and self-torment kept it green. It was far rarer than the *Daphne odora* from the Italian Riviera which only grew in Emily's greenhouse by special arrangement. Emily could show her flowers to her friends; she could talk about her love only to a few. Except to Sue, it is said, and then only for a few seasons. At last the story was finished, as a story, and the shades of feeling grew too fine. In order to give it extended reality, to solidify and ramify what was left, Emily began to write about her love. The weight of years fossilized the few facts; so little had happened that she dwelt on each morsel with lonely harrowing detail. Emily grew into a miser gloating over a secret treasure. She confessed herself strictly, lest a grain be lost. She grew impatient of any speech or attitude except the gaunt lovely honesty of great solitude.

299

The world's vague pity was mistaken; she ignored it. After 1862 Emily had two secrets by which she lived: she was — or had been — beloved; she was and would be perpetually a poet. Both joys were illicit; both had been forbidden her. But nothing could keep her stealthy hands from closing over such treasure. If the world had called: " Stop, thief! " at her back and had chased her and wrenched her treasures out of her hand, it would have as promptly tossed them aside with disgust as worthless. What Emily called her experience of love most people would call merely a disappointment; and what she called her poetry most people — indeed, everybody — called queer writing. Both would be — both were, in so far as they were known — pathetic in the world's eyes. For Emily, in everybody's eyes, was only a sorry little spinster, unable even to turn a proper rhyme.

> *My love is of a birth as rare*
> *As 'tis, for object, strange and high;*
> *It was begotten by despair*
> *Upon Impossibility.*

> *Magnanimous despair alone*
> *Could show me so divine a thing,*
> *Where feeble hope could ne'er have flown*
> *But vainly flapped its tinsel wing.*

> *And yet I quickly might arrive*
> *Where my extended soul is fixed;*
> *But fate does iron wedges drive,*
> *And always crowds itself betwixt.*

For fate with jealous eyes does see
  Two perfect loves, nor lets them close;
Their union would her ruin be,
  And her tyrannic power depose.

And therefore her decrees of steel
  Us as the distant poles have placed
(Though Love's whole world on us doth wheel),
  Not by themselves to be embraced,

Unless the giddy heaven fall,
  And earth some new convulsion tear,
And, us to join, the world should all
  Be cramped into a planisphere.

As lines, so loves oblique may well
  Themselves in every angle greet;
But ours, so nearly parallel,
  Though infinite, can never meet.

Therefore the love which us doth bind,
  But fate so enviously debars,
Is the conjunction of the mind,
  And opposition of the stars.

wrote Andrew Marvel, in the year 1650, as if John Donne, who had been dead nineteen years, were leaning down out of heaven to dictate a love-poem as it should be written.

If Emily ever read Marvel, or John Donne, she must have been able to feel less odd. She was always feeling odd, in her own New England. "Myself felt ill and odd . . . the only kangaroo among the Beauty, Sir, if you please it afflicts me." What a happy sigh of satisfaction might have escaped her if she had found the two or three other magnificent oddities of literature! Hard as it is to credit, she probably never read them; the nearest neg-lected poet she mentions is Vaughan. Shakspere con-tained enough oddity, perhaps, to sustain the oddity of herself, and Emily, who could have written, or at least prodigiously enjoyed:

> " *My love is of a birth as rare*
> *As 'tis, for object, strange and high,*"

was reading Mrs. Browning.

For something besides style and substance, her letters make clear. It was Mrs. Browning's life and Mrs. Brown-ing's happy fame — a contrast, with a similarity of circum-stance. Elizabeth Barrett had broken the taboo of a father (whose name was Edward) in the midst of invalidism and spinsterhood and had walked straight out of tyranny into Romance and Italy. Emily's lover had asked her to run away into Romance, too . . . to break the taboo. Eventually he went alone. Eventually he married. Robert Browning and Elizabeth Barrett indicated that they had found paradise in each other and in Casa Guidi in Flor-ence. Emily Elizabeth did not run away, never saw Ro-mance or Italy, and wrote poetry out of a stony fate that would have seemed odd and barbaric to the spirituel authoress of *Sonnets from the Portuguese.* . . .

> " *The banquet of abstemiousness*
> *Surpasses that of wine* . . ."

302

said Emily, those ten years before George Gould married; those twenty after, thinking of what she had missed. She said it to comfort herself, but she also believed it, having a knack for the supper of denial. Missing wealth, which she felt would have ill become her, and banquets and Victorian-Renaissance happiness, she gleaned along the edges after love's opulent harvesters, stooped and gleaned trifles they had no use for.

No one in Emily's day was much interested in her shrewd, apt, near-Freudian themes, unless it was Robert Browning. Emily wrote a poem about being transferred from the arms of father to the arms of a lover. This is the theme of many modern novelists, both good and bad. But such liberals as Margaret Fuller and Elizabeth Barrett would have deprecated Emily's verses, as poetry, if they had seen them. To be sure, if the passage about the father and lover had been decked with obsolete words and a stilted language, no one even in the Victorian age would have denied something " Greek " or " Elizabethan " about it, because of its sharp, high fancy, its headlong speech running with thought. Elizabeth Barrett, in Italy, was writing the flat-footed *Aurora Leigh* and for some unhappy reason was going to spiritualistic seances, after her marriage, and Robert was being accused of running round the room to try to jealously intercept a laurel-wreath manipulated by wires, which had been intended by Sludge the Medium to float over and rest on the brows of Elizabeth Barrett. This sort of real life and romance Emily missed. She missed Ba's kind of life, that went with Ba's kind of courage; she achieved her own kind of life, that went with her kind of courage. She missed knowing Robert Browning, the only poet then living who might have seen the importance of Emily's poetry at first sight. In 1847 he was having *Sonnets from the Portuguese* softly placed in his hand as he stood looking out of his window at the Leaning Tower, in Pisa. . . .

> *I'm wife; I've finished that . . .*
>
> *How odd the girl's life looks*
> *Behind this soft eclipse!*

wrote the Amherst spinster, dramatizing that longed-for separation from the lion rug and the hair sofa, as if it had taken place. The theme overflowed the brim of each successive poem; she used it again and again until she wore it out.

Although by the church records Emily was never christened any more than she was ever married, she wrote about both ceremonies. Vinnie had been christened when Emily was three and a half; and when Emily grew to be a poet, she used Vinnie's holy water. Christened, married, buried — one life, another life, and yet another life — so Emily arranged the stages of the soul; nay, almost believed her design. In her father's arms, to begin:

> *I'm ceded, I've stopped being theirs;*
> *The name they dropped upon my face*
> *With water, in the country church,*
> *Is finished using now,*
> *And they can put it with my dolls,*
> *My childhood, and the string of spools*
> *I've finished threading too.*

My second rank, too small the first,
Crowned, crowing on my father's breast,
A half-unconscious queen;
But this time, adequate, erect,
With will to choose or to reject,
And I choose — just a throne.

These inventions and dramatizations are early poems written when Emily still called herself a wife in spirit. The years taught her that her experience had been too spiritual to be called espousal, and she felt again the chain of the virginity she had wished to put off, and knew that she would only put it off in death. The grave, then, became her appointed marriage-bed, and the body lost hope, and Emily began to decry the body and turned more and more away from her first brief exultation of fulfilment back to the statements of lack and longing . . . and back to spiritual completion, since she craved completion, and the spiritual kind was all she could have. Substituting a ceremony of marriage for a funeral service, she says:

A wife at daybreak I shall be. . . .
At midnight I am yet a maid. . . .
So soon to be a child no more!

She tried on marriage like a bonnet too expensive for her frugal purse, and put it off with a smile and a sigh, having seen, at any rate in the milliner's mirror, how well the pretty thing became her. But she had speculations, perilous to contentment under her celibate vow . . . much as Emily disliked domesticity, railing against kitchens and house-cleaning, one person made her want the shared life, the double fate, the humble labour. " My kitchen I think

I called it — God forbid that it was, or shall be, my own — God keep me from what they call *households* except that bright one of faith," she had once exclaimed.

But there came a time when Emily wanted the satisfactions all of her women friends had. And she speculated:

> *This might have been the hand . . .*
> *[That] played his chosen tune. . . .*
>
> *Your servant, Sir, will weary,*
> *The surgeon will not come,*
> *The world will have its own to do . . .*
>
> *The cold will force your tightest door*
> *Some February day,*
> *But say my apron bring the sticks*
> *To make your cottage gay. . . .*

Emily's renunciations are especially keen because they keep a background of natural desire.

Poem CXLIII in *Further Poems* makes a picture, such as she could fancy, of an outlaw and his bride. It is a ferocious poem and it ends on an appalling discovery which applied to Emily's whole behaviour; it shows how, at times, she loathed her scheme of renunciation, her metaphysic of love. Ten distracted miserable years and a marriage not made in heaven may have been on her conscience. The last three stanzas:

> *And when at night our good day done,*
> *I guard my master's head,*
> *'Tis better than the eider duck's*
> *Deep pillow to have shared.*
>
> *To foe of his I'm deadly foe,*
> *None stir the second time*

On whom I lay a yellow eye
Or an emphatic thumb.

Though I than he may longer live,
He longer must than I,
For I have but the art to kill —
Without the power to die.

But it was not all speculation; things had happened, doors had opened, words, kisses, vows had been exchanged. Trifles of scenes, the black and white of moments, could be relived in memory, beginning with the query:

It was a quiet way,
He asked if I was his.
I made no answer of the tongue,
But answer of the eyes.

Whoever this man was, he took Emily's love with dignity, very firmly, wanting it very much, as if it were, she says, the deed to a great estate, resolved to keep it safe.

He put the belt around my life, —
I heard the buckle snap. . . .

Emily was fully and physically in love, so much in love that some of her imagery is innocently erotic. It was the summer of her life: "Come slowly Eden," one poem begins; another: "Wild nights, wild nights, were I with thee!" Vinnie often quoted this poem to her friends in the nineties.

All these came, doubtless, before she asked Samuel and Mary Bowles to name their child Robert for her. But the game of getting a spiritual child did not work; Emily

307

called him "Robert" for a little while, with quotation marks around his name, and then stopped. There had been no physical love, only dreams and longings and renunciation; children are renounced in renouncing love. Emily transferred her hope of creation to her poetry.

Meanwhile letters went and came. Emily's life was fed and drawn on by letters. Letters for Miss E. Dickinson, and the letters from Miss E. Dickinson, went and came in a steady stream in and out of the old mansion for thirty-six years. Letters from and to dear A., Mrs. Ford, Helen Hunt (later Jackson), Mr. Higginson, Mr. Bowles. But the letters, in a hand Emily cherished above all others, were like immortality.

She had a great zest for detail, the juxtaposition of the small against large; trifles delighted her; little things and little ideas pleased her fancy to be used. And so she loved to pick up the stray threads of her feeling and put them down in words to express the troublesome fact of her futile desire. She says, for instance, as some Shaksperian woman might have said in a scene with her maid:

I envy seas whereon he rides. . . .

Juliet and Cleopatra committed suicide, and so might Emily. It is all a species of playwriting:

> *What if I say I will not wait?*
> *What if I burst the fleshly gate*
> *And pass, escaped, to thee?*
> *What if I file this mortal off,*
> *See where it hurt me, — that's enough, —*
> *And wade in liberty?*

308

> *They cannot take us any more,—*
> *Dungeons may call, and guns implore;*
> *Unmeaning now, to me,*
> *As laughter was an hour ago,*
> *Or laces, or a travelling show,*
> *Or who died yesterday!*

But even in the heaven of supposition she would be forced, she realized, to hide her love, just as she was forced to hide it in her father's house. She reasons it all out, stanza by stanza, saying in the first line of poem VI (" Love "):

> *If you were coming in the fall. . . .*

Three lines follow to say how she would brush the summer aside as a housewife does a fly. The gesture stays in the mind. The next point is:

> *If I could see you in a year . . .*

and then, in three lines, she uses the image of winding the months in balls, as if they were merely worsted.

> *If only centuries delayed . . .*

— oh, well, she could manage centuries, or even, if certain, when this life was out, she would toss life away like the rind of a fruit and " taste eternity." But not even heaven is sure, and Death is very indefinite about his date of arrival:

> *But now, all ignorant of the length*
> *Of time's uncertain wing,*
> *It goads me, like the goblin bee*
> *That will not state its sting.*

The kiss, the angle in the floor, " where he turned, so," the box of letters — a few details like these stand out of the piercing generalizations on love, and death, and life, and pain. One poem of eight lines, about the opening of a door, contains the drama Emily retained after the crisis of her life. It was perhaps an unconscious harking back to Elizabeth Barrett's creaking door. A thousand details of character and circumstance are gone now; we have only the mute gesture of the door. The scene is set, light pours on an empty stage, nothing is illuminated beyond the spot that held the action:

> *What fortitude the soul contains,*
> *That it can so endure*
> *The accent of a coming foot,*
> *The opening of a door!*

Renunciation, which only took a moment of pause in her actual life, had to be approximated gradually, every minute inch of the journey travelled, and searched again and again. Two poems, larger than the rest, remain. They are great poems, written with the ecstasy and freedom of a major poet moved by her strongest passion. The first begins, as perhaps some sentence in life began, then to ring in the head for years:

> *I cannot live with you . . .*

Relentlessly the logic continues: I could not die with you. . . . Nor could I rise with you:

> *Because your face*
> *Would put out Jesus',*

That new grace
Glow plain and foreign
On my homesick eye. . . .

Stanza eight, it is interesting to notice in passing, contains the clearest echo of Browning's monologue style. The lines, still holding the quatrain form Emily got from the hymn-book, are short and sensitive, and they culminate in a more complicated stanza where the rhymes chime and the language is momentous:

> *So we must keep apart,*
> *You there, I here,*
> *With just the door ajar*
> *That oceans are,*
> *And prayer,*
> *And that pale sustenance,*
> *Despair!*

Mrs. Todd put the second poem just next, in her arrangement of *Poems: First Series;* and entitles it *Renunciation.* A facsimile of the poem was included as the frontispiece of *Poems: Second Series.* There is, however, no explanation of the fact that the two poems are not identical, and in view of the fact that this is the only published facsimile of an important poem extant, we wonder what amount of editing, or at least of choice between different versions, Mrs. Todd thought it within her function to exercise. I give the poem from the facsimile version, following, however, Mrs. Todd's punctuation and her line and stanza divisions:

EMILY DICKINSON
(No title)

There came a day at summer's full
Entirely for me;
I thought that such were for the saints
When resurrections be.

[The printed version reads: "Where revelations be."]

The sun, as common, went abroad,
The flowers, accustomed, blew,
As if no soul that solstice passed
Which maketh all things new.

[The printed version reads: "the solstice," and "that" for "which" in the last line.]

The time was scarce profaned by speech;
The falling of a word
Was needless, as at sacrament
The wardrobe *of our Lord!*

[The printed version reads: "symbol" for "falling," does not italicize "wardrobe," and omits the exclamation point after "Lord."]

Each was to each the sealed church
Permitted to commune this *time,*
Lest we too awkward show
At supper of "the Lamb."

[The printed version does not italicize "this" in line two and omits the quotation-marks around "the Lamb."]

The hours slid fast, as hours will,
Clutched tight by greedy hands;
So faces on two decks look back,
Bound to opposing *lands.*

[The printed version does not italicize "opposing."]

And so when all the time had leaked,
Without external sound,
Each bound the other's Crucifix,
We gave no other bond.

[The printed version substitutes " failed " for "leaked."]

Sufficient troth, that we shall rise,
Deposed, at length, the grave —
To that new marriage, justified
Through Calvaries of love!

[The printed version does not italicize "justified" and capitalizes "love."] Several of the underlineations — namely: under the words " opposing," "rise," and " justified " — seem to have been made, not for emphasis, but because the words, as she lettered them, caught the touch of her pencil, almost as if she were drawing on the page. The word " opposing " is a little crowded for room, and a new stanza — which Emily always began in the middle of the page, like the indentation of a paragraph in prose — might have instigated the stroke, for the sake of clarity. " Wardrobe " and " this " in stanza four are underlined for emphasis.

There are, however, four very important changes of words in the printed version. Did Mrs. Todd make these changes, or did she follow one of Emily's many versions? Had she any way of knowing which of these versions came later, and were all four contained in one of the several versions, or are they a combination of variants, chosen by Mrs. Todd? In every case the printed version is less good than the facsimile; we are led to conclude, if Mrs.

Todd chose the words, that her choice here, and possibly
in other poems, where we have no opportunity of comparison, was for the less characteristic image and word.

Twelve years after first love Emily's lover married.
Was the blow " softened by Time's consummate plush " ?
Emily liked to use the momentary cruelty towards herself of telling the truth about her feelings, no matter how
incongruous, and once, in some mood of grim observation,
she noted down:

> *We outgrow love like other things*
> *And put it in a drawer. . . .*

Now, we must examine the report that *Mercy Philbrick's
Choice* was partly either by or about Emily. Vinnie told a
friend that Helen Hunt stayed for two weeks with them
after Major Hunt died, and during that time Emily and
Helen talked literary matters constantly and sent out a
great many manuscripts. Nearly all of Helen's letters to
Emily are destroyed; and there is something of a mystery
about what happened to Emily's to Helen. The house in
Colorado was searched by Helen's widower — to no effect; the letters were grimly gone.

Vinnie said that Helen Hunt first requested Emily to
write *Mercy* with her; and that Emily half consented,
only later to find it impossible — and that Helen, annoyed
by Emily's refusal, worked Emily into the book, after the
first chapters. Does the story bear out such a possibility?
It seems to be as much about Helen as Emily. Mercy Philbrick is an original New England girl, widowed after a
brief marriage, devoted to beauty and poetry and her

mother. She moves into a small town for her mother's health, away from the sea-board. The town described is obviously Amherst; and Helen Hunt uses Ora White's and Seth Nims's names in the book — there was a real Ora, and a real Seth Nims was postmaster in Emily's days, and Emily once had a dream about him. Mercy moves into half of a double house inhabited by a young man named Stephen, who has a jealous, tormenting old invalid mother. The two young people fall in love; but Stephen's mother's morbid power over him makes him request of Mercy an unnatural ascetic love, in which even kisses are forbidden. Mercy is spiritually in love with Stephen, secretly, and love leads her into all kinds of deceit and connivance. She is represented as a normal person incapable of deception unless it is forced upon her. Then into this unnatural atmosphere comes Parson Dorrance, a mighty and godly person, much older than Mercy, who falls in love with her and wishes to marry her. Mercy is represented as being cheated by Stephen's false and selfish hold on her — for Mercy realizes that if Stephen had not forced her heart, she should have found Parson Dorrance her true destiny. All this time Mercy is writing poetry — in secret; her two secrets corrode her very soul. She sends the parson away, and her mother dies. Mercy resolves to break Stephen's power over her and leaves the little town. Poverty has cramped Stephen's life, so that, with his mother on his hands, he can only gaze after her, wistfully. After a time he writes Mercy in great excitement to say that he has found a bag of money in the old fire-place of the house. Mercy is affronted by Stephen's glee over the money because the owner of the house, a queer old woman, who had once inhabited it, is still alive. Legally it is Stephen's; morally, Mercy feels, it is the old woman's. This accomplishes the final rift; and no sooner is it over than Mercy hears that the parson is dying. She goes to his death-bed, feeling that she has missed, between these two men, the perfect love she might have had. Mercy, meanwhile, with little effort becomes a famous poet. The story ends with her death.

How near is this to Emily's life? Obviously, it is not actually her story. Some references sound like descriptions of Emily. On page 84 there is a passage explaining Mercy's reluctance to see company. Another passage reads:

" Mercy combined, in a very singular manner, some of the traits of an impulsive nature, with those of an unimpulsive one. She did things, said things, and felt things with the instantaneous intensity of the poetic temperament; but she was quite capable of looking at them afterward, and weighing them with the cool and unbiased judgment of the most phlegmatic realist. Hence she often had most uncomfortable seasons, in which one side of her nature took the other to task, scorning it and berating it severely; holding up its actions to its remorseful view, as an elder sister may chide a younger one, who was incorrigibly perverse and wayward."

And again: " The loneliness of intense individuality is the loneliest loneliness in the world — a loneliness which crowds only aggravate."

Mercy had a " sensitive, orchid-like face."

Another interesting circumstance turns up in the fact

that we find Mercy at first under the influence of a "teacher," Harley Allen, who loves Mercy, wants her to be a poet, but hopes when he guides her to Stephen that she will find her proper husband in him.

Now for design, despite concrete differences, this fits Emily's life rather well. In her life there was first a teacher, then a lover whom she could not marry because of an unreasonable parent, and then an older man, a minister, who came into her life while she still remained true to her lover. Helen Hunt planned the story on somewhat other lines; she did not resolve to put Emily's life into her book until she had written several chapters. This we know because Vinnie said that Helen Hunt came to Emily expecting her to write the next chapter; and Emily would not. In the first chapters the plot culminating in the incident of the money-bag found in the fire-place is carefully prepared for; at the beginning this was the chief incident of the tale. Stephen's way of failing Mercy, then, had to be his lack of honour in not returning the money to the old woman. In Emily's life the parallel circumstance must have been nothing so like *Silas Marner;* but a quite different, although equally final break, if the story is meant to be hers. — It was, possibly, George Gould's marriage. Parson Dorrance seems to stand for the Reverend Charles Wadsworth, seventeen years Emily's elder. The design is something similar.

Helen Hunt left Amherst in 1846 before George Gould came to college. She never saw him, evidently; she was not, then, drawing a picture of George Gould, but satisfying the requirements of her plot, when she constructed

317

Stephen's character. Emily, if she recognized the similarities in Helen Hunt's story, was of course deeply disgusted and hurt — the story's sum total is false and superficial. It was not the essence of her life, use it as Helen might, to preach her stubborn friend a sermon. Emily's face — the horror and disdain it expressed — when someone asked her if she was the author of *Mercy Philbrick's Choice* is still remembered.

Devious love! Emily went out into her garden. It held how many ghosts she could not say! When Mr. Higginson came to visit Emily after the death of his first wife, Vinnie hoped that he would fall under Emily's spell and want to marry her. One ghost stood near the syringa bush, and another by the tree-box. Others flitted over the lawn. In 1870 George Gould came to Amherst at commencement to receive the degree of Doctor of Divinity. And later the Reverend Charles Wadsworth dropped in, one warm afternoon.

" The last time that he came in life, I was with my lilies and heliotropes. Said my sister to me: ' The gentleman with the deep voice wants to see you, Emily ' — hearing him ask of the servant.

" ' Where did you come from? ' I said, for he spoke like an apparition. ' I stepped from my pulpit to the train,' was his simple reply; and, when I asked ' How long? ' — ' Twenty years,' said he, with inscrutable roguery."

In a sermon George Gould said: " The Dead Sea is dead because it has inlets and no outlets."

How well Emily knew. The only way out was underground.

CHAPTER XIX

"NOR IS DYING DOUBLE"

WE HAVE A LITTLE FRAGMENT WHEREIN SAPPHO apostrophizes an Evening that is systole to Morning's diastole: "O Evening, who brings together again all Morning disperses!"

Emily awaited such an evening. Morning had not scattered her as Sappho's translator examples — the lamb from its ewe, and the child from its mother. It had, instead, divided herself from herself. Evening, with the dwindling light, would gather together again all the diverse colours of life and fold them into one hue, and, in folding, fold the life of Emily Dickinson so that it would seem very slender indeed, incapable of division. "All things are double, one against another," strophëd Emerson. This double had been the engine of life, the energy, the strife, the heart-beat, the suspense, never-ending. This double evoked Emily's poetry, one voice calling to the other, urging, arguing, balancing, and striking. It made a multiple world full of events. She delayed to resolve her truth, lest she kill it; to marry her opposites, lest she mislike their offspring; to tamper with the delicate engine, lest she stop it. The emphasis of truth lay in its counterpoint; straight lines required the nuance of irregularity. First let earth speak, and then listen while heaven rejoins. In such a mood Bach wrote the *Concerto for Two Violins, in D Minor.*

If the voice of heavenly vision had spoken alone in Emily, she would have been a mystic poet. She is not a mystic poet. She constantly corrects vision by another faculty. Vision is not her truth. What is her truth? She named it " fact " — the truth perceived and then anatomized. The real mystic experiences an ecstasy, and his invariable report is that life is single and divine; he abhors a double. Against her primary impulse, which is something akin to the mystic intuition, Emily constantly placed her correcting fact, and her conclusion is always in the mood of the observed fact. There are only four or five poems of desire for something that is not, in the entire collection of her hundreds of poems. The mystic, who sees a divine reality, speaks with the serenity of that vision; the romantic, who aspires beyond himself, is full of the beat of wings — all true things for him are the things he has not touched, but, rather, desired. Emily has the calm of the mystic; but it is a grave calm; she speaks of things as they are:

> *Faith is a fine invention*
> *For gentlemen who see;*
> *But microscopes are prudent*
> *In an emergency!*

In order to embody her opposites, Emily divided herself (or life divided her) into this and that. She gave her secret away when she called herself shy and bold. She is both. And she is everything else by pairs. It was the logic of a lawyer in her blood, perhaps; the conception of argument in all things. If she was afraid, she was also brave. If she was proud, she was also more humble than the consistently and wholly humble. If she was subjective, she maintained herself by being also objective to a degree astonishing and strange. If she was a little mad, she was also a little beyond necessity sane. If she was rebellious, she was also meek. If she was frugal, she was also greedy. If she was vain and self-enticed, she was also too much in love with all her lovers for their comfort. If she was sensuous, she was also chaste and virginal and silver. Expansiveness had its check; passion its resignation; and every bitterness its wit. Thus she climbed, from opposite to opposite, growing by experience thus: by being one thing, and then the other. Thus no crevice in experience escaped her thorough method. It was the technique of double; it was the device of keeping attracted opposites far enough apart to use their tension. It was a control of life that depended on spinning everything between two poles. Her intensity had its equal in restraint, could not have been such pure intensity but for its balance; her drunkenness was matched by a power to abstain. So she lived; and her poetry gathered from the poles, north and south, as sky gathers to make rain. This is why Emily speaks with the authority of a great poet; she is the thunder and lightning of universal humanity.

All this took place in Emily's secret life. This world of yea and nay — her spiritual existence, as it may be termed

— had its balance-wheel, besides, to keep it steady and in motion.

E. M. Forster says: " So daily life, whatever it may be really, is practically composed of two lives — the life in time, and life by values — and our own conduct reveals a double allegiance." Emily's life in time kept her other life poised. One life was theme, and the other counterpoint. Emily borrowed intensity from one life to pay back the other. Often they seemed to run parallel; but more often one was what the other was not. They might not be severed, at the peril of double death. Emily kept them both going.

But now the design was worked and two parted threads must be twisted and carefully threaded back through the eye of the one needle, Death, in order to take the last stitch together. At the moment of death there must be only one Emily. Indeed, for Emily, to be one was to die; and to die was to be one. *Life* was the culprit.

She had many figures for death; and from the time of Leonard Humphrey's going she had not neglected to employ them all in daily meditation.

She knew that she would be no novice in his array. She prepared perpetually. She watched Death on his repeated visits to those about her; and rehearsed, for years before he came, her own encounter. It was her only exercise in single being; she wanted to know how to be, when the time came. She had died several times in expectation. Once a fly buzzed when she died — that is, when she lay on her bed imagining the ordeal. His loud husky voice said that the lowest, crudest form of life was better than eternity in God's barren sky. Another voice answered, and the two voices argued. We catch the argument in the poems. Emily let them speak out fully through her.

Meanwhile she saw Death's value. He should be her focus; not her woe. He should solve what she had lost the art to solve; and he would be lordly when he came, requiring no double of her. Only those dualists who accept a miracle to solve the contradiction of the double they find are holy people. Those who love their double and accept no miracle are damned.

Emily was not tired. She had experienced too much, perhaps, with her displaced fancy; still she felt no fatigue. In 1882 she spoke of an old grief that tired her; but life itself was refreshment. Her way of living had yielded her endless energy; and she was able to repeat her old, old intuitions in every letter, with an air, each time, of a first discovery. And the dozenth verification of a *fact* was as fresh as the new-risen sun.

For the reason that life's greatest secret lay in its last breath. In that moment of mutation from mortal to immortal, Emily would find something more to be desired than God. She had scrutinized that moment whenever she could—watched for the thin edge of eternity as it cut into actual life; listened for the click of change. She saw much, without seeing all. She might watch on trigger for years and not see quite all.

But when it was too late to make poetry of it, she should have her own experience, her quicksilver instant; and then she should know, although she might not tell.

No, nor reach for a pencil, nor even shutter the eyes with strange lightning.

Emily saw everyone growing old. It is necessary now to make a new picture of Edward Dickinson. He is a gaunt old man. It is necessary to put a film of age on the face of Emily's mother, and bow her figure slightly, in a little ice-wool shawl — bow her head, too, and give her voice a querulous note. Vinnie has taken her mother's place. Come into the kitchen and see Vinnie at the preserves, rustling about her work in her full print dresses, a spinster, now, not a belle. Austin is now middle-aged, brusk, and able; he and father walk to the office together, lawyers, citizens, business men. Amherst, too, must change; the mud-hole that used to be the Common became a lawn, planted with elms. The Improvement Society, of which Austin is the chief spirit, has discovered him digging them up, weeks after planting, to put a few of them either a little to the left or to the right. Austin strove to avoid the set effect of the straight line.

It is about time for Edward to die. But he spends no effort worrying about his soul. There is trouble with the Massachusetts Central Railroad, and so Edward goes to the legislature once again to get the affairs of the road in running order before he has to quit.

" We were eating our supper the fifteenth of June, and Austin came in. He had a dispatch in his hand, and I saw by his face we were all lost, though I didn't know how. . . . While horses were dressing, news came he was dead."

" Between twelve and one o'clock on a cruelly hot day,"

said Mrs. Todd in a letter to Mr. Higginson, " Edward
Dickinson was making a speech at the State House in Boston, discussing, for the railroad, the state management of
the Hoosac Tunnel. In the midst of his speech he felt
faint, and sat down, and the House adjourned. He walked
back to the Tremont House, and began to pack his bag
for the trip home, when a physician came, pronounced it
apoplexy and gave him a dose of opium or morphine
which killed him."

Emily dreamed of her father every night and woke up
exclaiming: " Where is he? "

It was exactly like father to contrive to die on his feet.
Edward's privacy was so august; to die at home, in bed,
would have humiliated and embarrassed him, the faces of
his family too near, and his ignored soul awkwardly fighting for exit. Better never to let his children see him in
death's throes. But for Emily this was hard. She could
have been trusted not to come too near her father, no
matter what his extremity. If he had wished it, she would
have refused to note what had become an obsession to
note with her — the dying eye running round and round
the room, recognizing Death, pondering and deliberating
and then consenting, before Death took possession. Not
to know how a person died denied her what she wanted
most to know. But if father desired it, she would have consented to see nothing.

Still, an unhurried soul — in this instance, at least, imperial — was the only fair soul in death. This was the only
right way for Death to come, courteously, with true pomp.
Leonard Humphrey had fallen on the street, stricken by

an angry God; and father fell in the State House, in the midst of petty affairs. Neither had consented. Such brutalities beset her.

Father's power diminished not at all with death; it was merely reinforced by translation. To find the mortal father, Emily searched the spring days before he died, and came on one Sunday afternoon where she might dwell. She wrote of it to Mr. Higginson, to whom it was easy to tell a little of her experience, only half knowing how well she pictured the last of a long companionship expressed in silence, a few embarrassed words — a great constraint — a perfect intimacy.

" The last afternoon that my father lived, though with no premonition, I preferred to be with him, and invented an absence for mother, Vinnie being asleep. He seemed peculiarly pleased, as I oftenest stayed with myself; and remarked, as the afternoon withdrew, ' he would like it to not end.'

" His pleasure almost embarrassed me, and my brother coming, I suggested they walk. Next morning I woke him for the train, and saw him no more."

Exactly one year from the day father died, Emily's mother was paralysed. Emily nursed her for seven years. Mother reversed father's sudden going, lingering in a ghastly and childlike daze. This was realism, for Emily; and all the tedium of the sick-room chained her down as she had never been chained before. Now, for love's sake, she must tend the woman of whom she had remarked: " I never had a mother " ! Emily noted honestly that mother grew larger with her affliction. At length the notice came, and mother became a part of that drift we call the infinite.

George Eliot died. " Now *my* George Eliot," Emily exclaimed, as if she had lived in the other world, waiting for her to die. Mrs. Higginson died. Little Gilbert, Austin's son, died. Mr. Bowles died shortly after Edward, of whom he had said in his paper that Edward had never understood himself, and so perchance no one had succeeded in understanding him. Dr. Holland died. Helen Hunt Jackson died. The Reverend Charles Wadsworth died, and when Vinnie sought to break the news, which Emily had known for days, Emily exclaimed: " How *can* the sun shine, Vinnie? "

Maggie's brother died. " Dr. Stearns [a neighbour] died homelike, asked Eliza for a saucer of strawberries, which she brought him, but he had no hands."

One Saturday morning in May, Emily was making a loaf of cake with Maggie when she saw a great darkness coming, to use her own words. She fainted for the first time in her life and lay unconscious for several hours. The doctor called it nervous prostration — *revenge* of the nerves; but who, cried Emily, but Death had wronged them?

The darkness hovered for the last two years of her life, very imminent and near. The phantasmal event, the event long awaited, prepared for, dwelt upon, and enlarged, often cast a shadow and darkened what was to come. So came this great darkness, the precursor. Emily had often longed to return to the atom's tomb, to that merry, gay, and numb locality before consciousness. Here was her

327

invitation. But she would not yield. She fought off " mental trouble " and died of Bright's disease.

Her mysteries, intuitions, doubts, faiths, and " facts " were in full company about her, like children attending, when she died. She lost not one of them all, relinquished not one, and scanned Death intently and curiously before she consented. Now is the eye single, and the whole body full of light.

Mr. Higginson noted in his journal as he rode away on the railroad train after one final look at the woman he had only imperfectly seen:

" To Amherst to the funeral of that rare and strange creature Emily Dickinson — E. D.'s face a wondrous restoration of youth — she is 54 and looked 30, not a gray hair or a wrinkle, and perfect peace on the beautiful brow. There was a little bunch of violets at the neck and one pink cypripedium; the sister, Vinnie, put in two heliotropes by her hand ' to take to Judge Lord ' (an old family friend). I read a poem by Emily Brontë. How large a portion of the people who have most interested me have passed away."

Certain of Emily's friends were already in heaven. But one remained on earth. He could not even come to her funeral.

CHAPTER XX

VINNIE'S LAST TASK

VINNIE KNEW PERFECTLY WHAT REMAINED TO BE done. Mending and preserves did not matter any longer. She must bury Emily and she must ensure her immortality.

But even while Emily lay dead in the parlour, Vinnie played one of the games they had played together so adroitly and with such pleasure for so many little years. At certain games Vinnie and Emily were notorious— games with flowers and cryptic words flung at visitors and friends. Visitors never quite learned the vocabulary, nor sent back the right reply, although a few tried.

Games were done now. But first Vinnie went out and chose three flowers from Emily's garden for Emily's adornment. When Mr. Higginson came, he looked down at Emily and asked why Vinnie put heliotrope in Emily's hand; and Vinnie said: "To take to Judge Lord." But it was not for Judge Lord. Another person was associated with heliotrope. Emily would know how well Vinnie decked her. The violets and the pink cypripedium denoted two others.

Then Emily was gone, and it was incredible.

Vinnie and Maggie sank beneath the emptiness. And Vinnie grew wholly tired to think of her one more task above-stairs. She must open and sort and destroy — quickly, before it was too late — some of the letters. She must obey quickly.

It was much harder than arranging to have Emily carried away across the fields in her white gown. Vinnie shut her eyes and burned letters, rolls of manuscript, packages unopened. Then her first hasty resolve blindly to obey, wavered; and when, with the pull of a drawer, Vinnie saw the store of Emily's writing, she considered and could burn no more. How devious Emily was! How contradictory! No one knew so well as Vinnie! Vinnie had played the game of no that meant yes, and the game of yes that meant no, too long and too well.

How often Emily had exclaimed: " My work, Vinnie! How shall I ever do my work? " Sitting in Emily's western chamber, with the sunlight striking the floor, with this formidable mass of poetry before her — not, as she had suspected, a handful of verses — Vinnie knew that she must ignore her sister's words and remember her real desires. This work of a lifetime, done in snatches and odd hours, was enough to imply a professional routine — full day-labour. Emily had not destroyed a scrap. And Vinnie doubtless knew that Emily knew that Vinnie would know that Emily wanted it saved.

How strange to see her sister face to face! Here was Emily, but never the Emily who lived on the downstairs level with the pussies and the flowers. This was the Emily implied but never stated so long as she lived. Vinnie had

330

THE REV. GEORGE H. GOULD
— *Courtesy of* MRS. JOHN W. GOULD

THE DOORSTEP OF THE DICKINSON HOUSE AS IT LOOKS TODAY
— *Photograph by* LINCOLN W. BARNES, *of* AMHERST, MASS.

seen the outward Emily and known somewhat the nature of the inner one. But here was a person she had only seen out of the corner of her eye.

The resolve to disobey (for obedient Vinnie a very serious resolve) was more than a sisterly act. As Vinnie sat in Emily's room, she became her first reader; she appraised the poetry and knew that it should be her chief concern. She was not herself a poet, but she could bear witness of a poet; and that she did.

Mrs. Todd will tell how Vinnie came:

" Soon after her death her sister Lavinia came to me, as usual in late evening, actually trembling with excitement. She told me she had discovered a veritable treasure — quantities of Emily's poems which she had had no instructions to destroy. She had already burned without examination hundreds of manuscripts, and letters to Emily, many of them from nationally known persons, thus, she believed, carrying out her sister's partly expressed wishes but without intelligent discrimination. Later she bitterly regretted such inordinate haste. But these poems, she told me, must be printed at once. Would I send them to some 'Printer,' and how quickly could they appear?

" Having already had some experience with publishers, I told her that no one would attempt to read them in Emily's own peculiar handwriting, much less judge them; that I should copy them all, then have them passed upon like any other literary production, from the commercial stand-point. . . . Her despair was pathetic.

" ' But they are *Emily's* poems! ' she urged piteously.

" I asked her how many there were; but that she could

not tell. Afterward we found that almost six hundred were in the box first discovered. Later many more were found in other boxes and envelopes. But from a printer's point of view they looked hopeless. The handwriting appeared to consist of styles of three periods, absolutely different from one another — although none were particularly difficult to decipher, they were usually written on both sides of the paper, and the number of suggested changes were baffling. In the so-called 'copied' poems, tiny crosses written beside a word which might be changed ultimately and which referred to scores of possible words at the bottom of the page were all exactly alike, so that only the most sympathetic and at-one-with-the-author feeling could determine where each word belonged. . . .

"One evening she [Lavinia] arrived just before midnight, making a still stronger appeal; she was more than ever certain that I *must* undertake the work. One or two incidents had stirred her to even more than her usual vehemence. . . . Lavinia almost went on her knees to me that night, and it hurt me to see her so intensely in earnest over what might prove a disappointment. But at last I did promise to put the poems in shape and try to find a publisher; to begin the very next day and to have them in order as soon as possible. So my daily occupation was clearly indicated, as it turned out, for almost four years; and the results were overwhelming."

Indeed, they were. The first volume, with Mr. Higginson's preface, was published on November 12, 1890.

Vinnie wrote Mr. Higginson:

"If you knew my disappointed endeavors for 2 years

before Mrs. Todd & yourself came to my rescue, you would realize my gratitude to you both. Mrs. Dickinson was enthusiastic for a while then indifferent & later, utterly discouraging. I naturally looked to her first (with you) for help, supposing it would be her highest pleasure, but I found my mistake. She wished the box of poems *there* constantly & was unwilling for me to borrow them for a day, as she was fond of reading them (the verses) to passing friends. Mrs. Dickinson has fine ability but lacks now the energy to complete. . . . But for Mrs. Todd & yourself, 'The Poems,' would die in the box where they were found. After my brief talk with you (2 years ago last summer) I resolved (if your life was spared — your interest continued, the poems *should* be published. I have (from that time) never mentioned the subject to my neighbours — preferring the *new deal* to take their own way, satisfied in their hands the end would be *success*. . . . I have had a ' Joan of Arc ' feeling about Emilies poems from the first. Their reception convinces me I was right. As all Emilies possessions were given to me years before her death, I recognize the right to magnify her name as she deserved."

Vinnie's " neighbours," as she called them, had caused her much annoyance and had blocked for years the hope of any publication. Not so Austin, who wanted the poems published before he died. Mr. Higginson himself knew of some of Vinnie's difficulties, for he had requested Sue's goodwill when he first consented to do what he could for the manuscript. Sue's little piece about Emily, written shortly after she died, and published in the town paper, was to have stood as preface and appreciation of her poetry.

333

But when the book of poems, with Mr. Higginson's influence, seemed about to become a reality, Sue withheld her paragraphs.

He did not know that Vinnie was struggling against heavy odds. He did not know that Austin, after father died, controlled all the family funds — paid his sisters' bills, but allowed them not one penny of actual money. He did not know that Emily's habit of doubling up one letter inside another came from the limitation on postage stamps. He did not know that Vinnie, now, must implore people to work for her and the poems without being able to offer them any pay whatsoever — nothing, indeed, but flowers and gratitude, and future fame.

The first volume sold six editions in five months. Mr. Niles, who had coaxed Louisa Alcott to write that best seller *Little Women*, was amazed at the sale. Extravagant praise in metropolitan dailies and monthlies ruffled the tempers of the townsfolk who had known the Emily legend too well to take her poetry seriously. It became the sport in academic circles to write parodies of Emily's silly verses. At one dinner-party Mr. Frank Moore Colby produced as parody to *Belshazzar had a letter:*

> *Leviathan ate Jonah,*
> *He never ate but one,*
> *Leviathan's indigestion*
> *Concluded and begun*
> *In that immortal stomach. . . .*

Mrs. Todd records that she was often irritated by the jests at the expense of this queer, queer stuff written by the illiterate female who had become a fad.

By 1894 the poems were famous and had sold everywhere. Mr. Higginson had arranged for a special English
edition. Bliss Carman, William Dean Howells, Louise
Chandler Moulton, and many others had testified to the
literary value of what Emily had written and Vinnie
had saved. Mrs. Todd edited the *Letters,* without Mr.
Higginson's help; and again the reviews exclaimed that
something of value had been preserved. How did George
Gould adjust himself to the publication of the poems so
long cherished in secret by himself — Emily's letters, so
they had seemed — her astonishing self bewitched on to
paper and sent under a government stamp to sustain him
against the petty years?

We have a little hint in one public utterance made by
Dr. Gould just after the *Letters* were published in a volume. In 1891 he had seen in the *Atlantic* Mr. Higginson's
article giving Emily's letters written to Higginson and
referring to George Gould, though not by name. In 1894
they reappeared, with many others — flirtatious, sententious, captivating, demure, and often all too fond; letters
declaring devotion and affection and love to ever so many
scattered persons — to Mr. Higginson and Mr. Bowles
and Dr. Holland and to the friend of C. H. Clark who
was the Reverend Charles Wadsworth. In May 1894
George Gould attacked Colonel Higginson in a public
address and scornfully described his "rhetorical rose-
water" in treating of Oriental religion. Now, it is interesting to note that George Gould admired Colonel Higginson
until about this time; or so we would infer, for in his note-
books he quotes bits from Higginson's writings to use in

his sermons. It is also interesting to note that George Gould's note-books are full of references to the sayings of Buddha, chosen to make nearly the same point in his sermons that Higginson had made in his speech. It is, therefore, interesting that Dr. Gould should have said what he did just when he did. Especially when we remember that in all his sermons there is not a like scorn for any other person. Dr. Gould is everywhere remote and tender — until we suddenly behold him saying:

"Colonel T. W. Higginson, addressing the world's fair last autumn on 'The Sympathy of Religions,' in faultless elocution and golden English told his polyglot audience, that for us in America, the door out of sin and superstition was called 'Christianity,' but it was only a historical name, the mere 'accident of a birthplace,' while other nations had other 'outlets,' he assured them, equally safe and inviting; and with a dash of rhetorical rose-water right and left, over heathendom in general, he retired from the platform in a blaze of millennial eloquence." My correspondent X heard George Gould speak shortly before he died and remembered how distinguished he was. One day she called on Vinnie, after having at Vinnie's request copied the manuscript now entitled *Further Poems*. The copying had made the query, which trembled unspoken on her lips, very natural indeed; for after *Further Poems'* graphic accents who would not wonder: "*What manner of man was it Emily loved?*"

"When Vinnie told me the name of Emily's lover, we were in her sitting room, on the right, as one enters the hall. She handed me a miniature of Emily, saying, '*This*

336

is Emily. No one on earth could paint her face, because no one could possibly catch the light in her eyes, nor the spirit behind them, but this gives a *faint* idea of how Emily looked.' Voluntarily, she then told me that her father was a stern man, with any affection that he might have, frozen in his heart. He was bitterly opposed to either daughter marrying, and was the cause of much suffering — perhaps unconsciously — when he forbade a certain man to see Emily. He thought of all evils that could befall his daughters, to marry a poor minister was about the worst!

"I asked, 'Why did not Emily marry after your father's death?'

"'Because,' she replied, 'we were just as much afraid of father's wrath *after* he died as we were when he was alive, and Emily would not dare to go against his will."

"After a few minutes, and while I held the miniature, Vinnie said, 'George Gould is the man that Emily loved.'

"I told her that I had heard him preach several times and that I admired him tremendously. She was much surprised, and when I was about to leave her she put her hand on my arm saying, 'I have trusted you with a great secret, — I know that it will be safe with you.'"

Four months before Vinnie died, George Gould lay down one evening feeling the hand of death upon him and remarked to his wife that his life had been a disappointment. This was a startling thing for a man to admit, even to his wife, when all his public utterances had glorified God's way of life, and when his demeanour had never failed of cheer and resignation. Nellie Grout, who had married George Gould forty years before, and who

337

married someone else just a year afterwards, remembered that remark as something significant and included it in the few lines of preface to a privately published edition of his sermons after he died. It was not a worthy sentiment; a dying clergyman should never speak in such a manner. Nevertheless George Gould felt in some respects that his life had been a disappointment to him.

And besides, he said: "For one of my intellectual furnishings I should at least have written a book. There is so little to *show* for it all."

He who had been Emily Dickinson's literary stimulus, from the early days when they read Dickens and *Jane Eyre* and Emerson together, felt now that he had done nothing.

In this mood George Gould died and entered heaven, where Emily already dwelt with God and Squire Dickinson.

Vinnie had been Emily's hands and feet, her servant and her sister. And she, too, was going to die and go home, to father and mother, and Austin and Emily. She doubtless expected very little change in heaven; in that respect, Vinnie was provincial — she should be a servant still, she supposed, and she should have to whisper, not shout, in some interval of the formal reunion, the news, to Emily, that her poetry was "alive" on earth. Father had never known that Emily was a great American poet. His scorn and wrath at having fostered such a child would have to be gently avoided. And while God — that is, father — asked them kindly to come in before the dew fell, Vinnie would not be able to tell from Emily's face or her eyes how much or how little she was amused.

In the name of the bee
And of the butterfly
And of the breeze, Amen!

Antibes, France
Amherst and South Hadley, Mass.

APPENDIX I

BOOKS USED

Poems, 1890; *Poems, Second Series,* 1891; *Poems, Third Series,* 1896
Letters, ed. Todd, 1894. 2 volumes
Life and Letters, 1924
Complete Poems, 1924
Further Poems, 1929

Carpenter and Morehouse: *History of the Town of Amherst, Mass.,* 1896
William S. Tyler: *A History of Amherst College,* 1895
Frederick Tuckerman: *Amherst Academy,* 1929
Frances M. Smith: " The Dickinson Family " from *Colonial Families of America*
Samuel F. Dickinson: *Oration in Celebration of American Independence. The Connection of Civil Government with Manners and Taste,* printed by William Butler, Northampton, 1797
George William Montague: *The History and Genealogy of the Montague Family of America,* 1886
Scrapbook compiled by Lucius M. Boltwood

Anna Phillips See: *The Naughty Girl of Amherst, Helen Hunt Jackson,* 1923; manuscript in the Jones Library

Mrs. Thomas L. Eliot: " Memoir," Portland *Oregonian,* March 19, 1899

Catalogue of the Trustees, Instructors and Students of Amherst Academy, 1847

Nathan Haskell Dole: Report of a paper given by Mrs. Todd, published in *Book News, Book Buyer,* Vol. IX, no. 4 (May 1892), pp. 157–8

George S. Merriam: *Life and Times of Samuel Bowles,* 1885

Richard Hooker: *The Story of an Independent Newspaper,* 1924

Susan L. Tolman: Journal, written at Mount Holyoke Female Seminary, September 1847 to May 1848

Beth Bradford Gilchrist: *Life of Mary Lyon,* 1910

" Letter to a Young Contributor," *Atlantic Monthly,* April 1862

Emily Dickinson's Letters, October 1891

Atlantic Monthly, 1860–91

Mary Thacher Higginson: *Thomas Wentworth Higginson. The Story of His Life,* 1914

Thomas Wentworth Higginson: *Contemporaries,* 1899

—: *Cheerful Yesterdays,* 1900

—: *Part of a Man's Life,* 1905

—: *Carlyle's Laugh and Other Surprises,* 1909

—: Articles in the *Congregationalist* and the *Christian World*

—: *Atlantic* Essays

—: *Letters and Journals,* 1921

Galatea Collection, Boston Public Library, Of Books relating to the History of Women

Charles W. Wadsworth: *Sermons* (Roman & Co.)

Reminiscences of Aaron Colton. The One Hundred and fiftieth anniversary of the First Church of Christ, Amherst, Mass., Nov. 7, 1889; Amherst, 1890

The Indicator, Amherst College, 1848–9, 1849–50, in files of Converse Memorial Library

Rev. George H. Gould: *In What Life Consists, and Other Sermons*

—: Note-books, dated 1867, 1877, 1881

Franklin P. Rice: *The Worcester of Eighteen Hundred and Ninety-Eight*, 1899

Commemorative Exercises of the First Church of Christ in Hartford, 1883

George Leon Walker: *History of The First Church of Hartford*, 1884

Robert S. Fletcher and Malcolm Young: *Amherst College Biographical Record*, 1927

William Henry Allison: *Inventory of Unpublished Material for American Religious History in Protestant Church Archives and Other Repositories*, 1910

John B. Gough: *Autobiography and Personal Recollections*, 1870

Obituary Record of Graduates of Amherst College, 1899

The Congregationalist, May 1899

A few pages of a diary by John B. Gough, American Antiquarian Society, Worcester

Genealogies of Hadley Families. Northampton, 1862

Emerson: *Journal*

Legal files

Town records

Files of the *Springfield Republican*

Files of the *Hampshire and Franklin Gazette*

343

Files of the *Amherst Record*

McElroy's Philadelphia Directory, 1853

Helen Hunt Jackson: *Mercy Philbrick's Choice*

Elizabeth Barrett Browning: *Aurora Leigh*

Henry James: *William Wetmore Story and his Friends*

Letters from Helen Hunt Jackson to Botany; Jones Library

Letters in manuscript from Helen Hunt Jackson to various persons; New York Public Library

Letters in manuscript by Higginson, New York Public Library

Mabel Loomis Todd: " Emily Dickinson's Literary Début," *Harper's Magazine*, March 1930

APPENDIX II

NINETY—NINE YEARS' CALENDAR OF DATES PERTAINING TO THE LIFE AND WORK OF EMILY DICKINSON

(Compiled while working on her life; here included for those readers who wish to correlate events in the *Letters*)

1830, December 10. Emily Elizabeth Dickinson was born at 50 Main Street, Amherst, Massachusetts.

1833, February 28. Lavinia Norcross, her sister, born. Samuel Fowler Dickinson left Amherst during this year for Cincinnati, Ohio.

1833, August 4. Vinnie baptized, First Congregational Church.

1840. The Edward Dickinson family moved to the Deacon Mack house, from the homestead at 50 Main Street. The Deacon Mack house was a frame house on the east side of Pleasant Street; a gasoline station now stands where it used to be.

1844. Helen Fiske, later Helen Hunt Jackson, left Amherst.

1845, February 23. First of Emily's letters preserved written to " Dear A." — Mrs. A. P. Strong.

1846, August. Leonard Humphrey gave valedictory address, Commencement, Amherst College, " The Morality of States."

1846, September 8. Letter from Emily written in Boston, where she visited Mt. Auburn, Chinese Museum, etc., returning too late to enter Amherst Academy. First mention of Leonard Humphrey, principal of Amherst Academy, in next letter.

1846, October. George Gould entered Amherst College, living at 25 North College.

1846, December. Emily entered Academy, second term, one week after Thanksgiving.

1846–7. Emily attended spring and summer term at Academy, term ending August. Letter describing school, March 15, 1847.

1847, September. Emily entered Mount Holyoke Female Seminary.

1847–8. Leonard Humphrey studied at Andover Theological Seminary.

1848. Emily returned home sick after Valentine's Day.

1848, May. Emily returned to Mount Holyoke for spring term.

1848, autumn. Emily at home. Leonard Humphrey, tutor at Amherst College, spring of 1849, fall of 1849, and spring and summer of 1850.

1849, June. George Gould edited the first number of the *Indicator*.

1849. Leonard Humphrey took M.A. degree.

1850, February. " Valentine " copied in the *Indicator*. Another rhymed valentine verse sent to Mr. Bowdoin, who was studying law in Edward Dickinson's office.

1850, May 7. Invitation to ride in the spring woods.

346

1850, August 8, Thursday. George Gould was graduated from Amherst College; entered Union Seminary that fall.

1850. Edward Dickinson joined the First Congregational Church under the Rev. Aaron Colton.

1850, November 30. Leonard Humphrey died of congestion of the brain after one week's absence from Amherst, North Weymouth, Massachusetts.

1850, December. George Gould left Union for Andover, to take Professor Park's course on systematic theology. Emily wrote letter about Professor Park to Austin.

1851, January 2. Emily Dickinson's letter regarding Leonard Humphrey's death (omitted from 1924 edition of the *Life and Letters*).

1851, September. Emily visited Austin in Cambridgeport.

1852. Emily wrote valentine to Mr. William Howland, Leonard Humphrey's best friend, later published without Emily's consent in the *Springfield Republican.*

1853, May 9. Railroad between Palmer and Amherst completed. Jubilee for Amherst and Belcherton Railroad, June, of same year.

1853, August. George Gould graduated from Union Theological Seminary; invited to take post of collegiate pastor under the Rev. Albert Barnes, First Presbyterian Church, Washington Square, Philadelphia.

1853. Emily and Lavinia went on the cars to visit Dr. and Mrs. Holland in Springfield.

1853, December 5. Edward Dickinson went to Washington, member of the 33rd Congress.

1854, March 13. Letter from Edward Dickinson at Washington, requesting Austin to bring the family to the capital.

1854. Letter from Emily Dickinson in Philadelphia to Dr. and Mrs. J. G. Holland.

1854. Emily returned to Amherst before June. George Gould went west, dates given in several places as early as 1853.

1854, spring. Edward Dickinson expressed jealousy of Emily's books.

1855. The Edward Dickinson family moved from the house on Pleasant Street to the mansion at 50 Main Street.

1856, July 11. Austin Dickinson and Susan Gilbert married in Geneva, New York.

1857, July 14. George Gould sailed with John B. Gough for Liverpool.

1857–60. George Gould spent " one year in England, four months in Edinburgh, six in Paris, two in Rome, several in Germany, besides two summers in Switzerland." From *The Worcester of Eighteen Hundred and Ninety-eight,* an account of Dr. Gould, evidently written by himself, one year before his death.

1860, August 22. Gough and party returned home. (For evidence that Gould was with him, see Gough: *Autobiography,* p. 526.)

1861, April 17. News of the firing on Fort Sumter reached Amherst.

1861, June 19. First child born to Austin and Sue, Edward Dickinson, junior.

1861. Hon. Edward Dickinson nominated by Republican party for office of Lieutenant Governor. Declined.

1862. " Faith is a fine invention " included in a letter to Mr. Samuel Bowles.

1862, March 14. Frazer Stearns killed at battle of New Berne.

1862, April 14. Six-pound brass cannon presented to Amherst College in memory of Frazer Stearns, Hon. Edward Dickinson presiding at meeting.

1862, April 15. Emily sent a note to Thomas Wentworth Higginson containing four poems.

1862, April 25. Emily wrote a second letter to Mr. Higginson in reply to his answer.

1862. Mr. Bowles's first trip to Europe.

1862, June 7. Emily's third letter to Mr. Higginson.

1862, October 15. George Gould married Nellie Grout of Worcester.

1862. November 12. George Gould was ordained and moved to Springfield to take pastorate of the Olivet Church.

1863, September 30. Major Hunt mortally hurt in accident at Red Hook Point, Brooklyn, while experimenting with his invention, the Sea Miner. Accident reported October 3 in *Springfield Republican.*

1864, April. Emily went to 86 Austin Street, Cambridgeport, to be treated for her eyes by the Arlington Street doctor, staying six to eight months.

1865. Emily went to Boston, staying from six to nine months.

1864–70. The Rev. George Gould pastor of the Old Centre Church, Hartford. Preached in Boston and Providence from time to time.

1865. Mr. Bowles's first trip to Pacific coast.

1866, February 14. " The Snake " poem printed in *Springfield Republican.*

1866. Mr. Samuel Bowles made trustee of Amherst

College, largely through Edward Dickinson's influence.

1868. Emily stated that she should go to Boston for another treatment, but could not because her father wished her to stay at home.

1868. Mr. Bowles went to Colorado and San Francisco with Mrs. Bowles.

1870. The Rev. George Gould given an honorary degree of D.D. at 49th Commencement, Amherst College, in June.

1870, August 16. Mr. Higginson went to Amherst to see Emily Dickinson.

1874, June 16. Emily's father died in Boston.

1875, June 16. Emily's mother paralysed.

1876. *Mercy Philbrick's Choice* by Helen Hunt Jackson published.

1878, January. Mr. Samuel Bowles died in Springfield.

1881. Dr. Holland died.

1882. Rev. Charles Wadsworth died.

1882. Emily's mother died.

1883. Death of Emily's dear nephew Gilbert, aged eight.

1884, about May. Emily saw a great darkness. Doctor called it nervous prostration. •

1885, August 12. Helen Hunt Jackson died in San Francisco.

1886, May 15. Emily E. Dickinson, fifty-five years, five months, five days, died. Cause of death, Bright's disease (from old Death Records, Town of Amherst).

1886, May 18. Emily buried in the West Cemetery.

1886, summer. Lavinia went to Mrs. Todd to ask her help in preparing for publication of the poems found at Emily's death.

350

1890. *Poems,* edited by two of her friends, Mabel Loomis Todd and T. W. Higginson, Boston, Roberts Brothers.

1891. *Poems,* Second Series, edited by two of her friends, Mabel Loomis Todd and T. W. Higginson, Boston, Roberts Brothers.

1894. *Letters* edited by Mabel Loomis Todd, Boston, Roberts Brothers.

1896. *Poems, Third Series,* edited by two of her friends, Mabel Loomis Todd and T. W. Higginson, Boston, Roberts Brothers.

1895. William Austin Dickinson died.

1896, May 25. Lawsuit filed by Lavinia Dickinson vs. Mabel Loomis Todd. Decision for plaintiff. Appealed. Confirmed.

1899, May 8. George Gould died of a failure of the vital powers in Worcester.

1899, August 31. Lavinia Norcross Dickinson died of heart-disease, aged sixty-six years, six months, and three days.

1913, May 12. Death of Susan Gilbert Dickinson.

1914. Publication of *The Single Hound,* edited by Madame Martha Dickinson Bianchi.

1924. Publication of *The Life and Letters of Emily Dickinson* by Madame Martha Dickinson Bianchi.

1925. Publication of *Complete Poems of Emily Dickinson* by Madame Martha Dickinson Bianchi.

1929. Associated Press carried news story about the " discovery " of *Further Poems.*

1929. Publication of *Further Poems, Withheld from publication by her sister Lavinia,* by Madame Martha Dickinson Bianchi.

NOTES ON BOOKS ABOUT EMILY DICKINSON

THE LIFE AND LETTERS OF EMILY DICKINSON by her Niece
Martha Dickinson Bianchi. Boston: Houghton Mifflin
Company, 1924

1. Madame Bianchi gives the date of Emily Dickinson's birth as December 11, 1830 (page 12).

On the tombstone, at the office of the town clerk, and in brief biographies of her life by Mrs. Todd and Mr. Higginson, the date is given as December 10, 1830.

Madame Bianchi corrected this error in subsequent editions.

2. Madame Bianchi gives Emily Dickinson's middle name as " Norcross " omitting " Elizabeth."

Emily herself all during her lifetime signed herself from time to time Emily Elizabeth, or Emily E. She signs herself so on legal papers. *The History of the Montague Family in North America* gives her middle name as Norcross, however. On Lavinia's tombstone the name is given as Lavinia N. Dickinson. Mrs. Todd in the 1894 edition of the *Letters* says: " It will be seen that the name Emilie E. Dickinson is sometimes used. The *ie* was a youthful vagary, and the second initial, E., stood for Elizabeth, a ' middle name ' entirely discarded in later years." In the *Catalogue of the Trustees, Instructors and Students of Amherst Academy, 1847*, the names are Emily E. and Lavinia N. In the 1929 edition of her *Life and Letters* Madame Bianchi corrects the name to read Emily Elizabeth Norcross Dickinson. Not once in my reading have I found the Norcross used in Emily's name during her lifetime.

3. Madame Bianchi gives the date of Emily's winter

in Washington as 1853 (see *Life and Letters,* page 45).

Edward Dickinson was in Congress and in Washington in 1853 to 1855, but he did not request Austin to bring his mother and his sister Lavinia with him, " and Emily, too, if she will come," until March 13, 1854. By May she was again at home, in Amherst. Cf. letter dated spring 1854 and headed Philadelphia, saying: " We were three weeks in Washington . . . and have been two in Philadelphia." There was no " winter in Washington."

4. Madame Bianchi tells of Emily's flight to her home, after meeting the man with whom she fell in love. This was 1853 by Madame Bianchi's account. Lavinia was supposed to come next door to beg Sue to prevent Emily from running away from home with " that man " (cf. page 47). But Sue was not married to Austin until July 11, 1856. If Sue was visiting at the family house, there is no mention of this, and no allowance for the mistake as it was recorded by Madame Bianchi. Madame Bianchi inserted a note in the 1929 edition in an attempt to explain this difficulty. She does not explain how a house could be building three years before a marriage, when a last-minute change in plans kept the Austin Dickinsons from going west.

5. Madame Bianchi says that Emily Dickinson wrote to Colonel Higginson after reading an article entitled " The Procession of Flowers " in the *Atlantic Monthly.* Emily Dickinson wrote to Mr. Higginson so that he got his note in Worcester on April 16, 1862. " The Procession of Flowers " was not published until December 1862. The article Emily read in the *Atlantic* in April was an unsigned " Letter to a Young Contributor," of which a photostat is given in plate 14.

6. A picture of Mr. Samuel Bowles in the 1924 edition is wrongly named J. G. Holland. This is corrected in a subsequent edition.

7. Madame Bianchi gives the date of Emily Dickinson's death: May 16, 1886. Amherst Old Death Record gives May 15.

This is corrected in the 1929 edition.

8. On page 27, Madame Bianchi dates Emily's stay at Mount Holyoke Female Seminary as in 1849, instead of 1848. This is corrected in the 1929 edition.

9. Madame Bianchi says that Emerson came to Amherst in the winter of 1857 — as Austin's guest (cf. page 82). Emerson makes no mention of such a trip in his very full account of all his sojourns and travels, recorded in his *Journal.* He came on two other occasions to Amherst and stayed with distant relatives of his.

10. "Dickens was always a favorite of her father's." Madame Bianchi, page 81.

The 1894 edition of the *Letters,* edited by Mrs. Todd (page 122): "Father was very severe to me; he thought I'd been trifling with you, so he gave me quite a trimming about 'Uncle Tom' and 'Charles Dickens' and these 'modern literati' who, he says, are nothing compared to past generations who flourished when he was a boy. . . ."

Emily's interest in Charles Dickens seems to have started about the time that she knew George Gould. It is interesting to note that she mentions the Brownings only after his trip to Italy, where he may have met them through the Storys.

11. Madame Bianchi (page 83): "When her father died in Boston during the summer of 1879. . . ."

Edward Dickinson died June 15 or 16, 1874.

⌐ APPENDIX ⌐

Further Poems Witheld from Publication by her Sister Lavinia. Cf. letter in Galatea Collection, published herein, page 333; and testimony by X.

THE LETTERS OF EMILY DICKINSON edited by Mabel Loomis Todd, in two volumes. Boston: Roberts Brothers, 1894.

Pages 1 and 2: ". . . oldest yet found, dated when Emily Dickinson had but recently passed her fourteenth birthday."
First letter, next page, dated: Amherst, Feb. 23, 1845.
From Mrs. Gordon L. Ford's reminiscences of Emily Dickinson, in a passage describing Emily's schooldays, 1846–50: " The Atlantic Monthly was a youngster then " (page 127). The *Atlantic Monthly* was started in 1857.

EMILY DICKINSON, FRIEND AND NEIGHBOR, by MacGregor Jenkins. Boston: Little, Brown and Company, 1930.

Of Lavinia (page 26): " She was born on the twenty-ninth of February and always regarded the fact that her birthday. . . ."
Her tombstone gives February 28, 1833, which was not a leap year.

EMILY DICKINSON, THE HUMAN BACKGROUND OF HER POETRY, by Josephine Pollitt. New York: Harper and Brothers, 1930.

On page 169 it is implied that Emily knew from the *Springfield Republican* the identity of the author of a

"Letter to a Young Contributor," published in the *Atlantic*, April 1862.

Two persons, one of them myself, have found not one line in the *Springfield Republican* concerning the authorship of this article.

" The letter was postmarked ' Amherst,' and the stamp had been put on so hastily that it was almost in the middle of the envelope, covering the word ' Mr.' (page 174)."

Mr. Higginson gives no such account, and the following telegram from the Reference Room of the Boston Public Library, where this material is kept, would indicate that the envelope is lost:

" Boston Mass Feb 24 1930
" No envelope with April sixteenth letter.
                    Harriet Swift Librarian."

APPENDIX III

My dear Miss Taggard: —

One bright sunny day when doors and windows were open Miss Vinnie took me into the front part of the house — I often just stayed in the kitchen — probably so as not to be overheard by Maggie. As I recall it, some one had prophesied that a certain student would not amount to much. I think it was something said about her beloved — —. There in a room I almost never went into, the room on the right of the front entrance being the familiar one, she told me the following story of her sister Emily. She told of a brilliant student to whom her sister Emily became engaged, a George Gould. Mr. Gould insisted on going to her father to ask for the hand of his daughter. The father, however, refused to give his consent because of the poverty of the young man and the prospect of a long engagement while the young man was preparing for the ministry. She gave me the impression that Mr. Dickinson felt that a poor minister was a wholly unsuitable husband for Emily. Anyway Mr. Dickinson forbade the young man to see Emily again and forbade Emily to see the young man, and then Miss Vinnie said he became a prominent minister. This was the only time that Miss

Vinnie ever told me anything of the tragedy of Emily's life. . . .

Cordially yours

Z

I am very glad to respond in every way I can to your request in regard to the love episode in Emily Dickinson's life, so distorted and complicated in recent publications.

Mrs. Austin Dickinson and my mother were friends, and long before Emily Dickinson became known to the public and before her " love affair " was of interest to any but friends and neighbors, Mrs. Dickinson told her — my mother — *that the man in question was a young lawyer* who afterward became prominent in Boston, and that Emily's father, the old-time austere parent, though of a most kindly nature, objected to her marriage to a man unestablished in life. The name of the man was never given to us, but I see no reason why it could not have been that of the Amherst student you refer to. That he was Helen Hunt's husband seems inconceivable. In fact it was a distinct shock to read in " Life and Letters " Mrs. Bianchi's version, that he was a married man. You no doubt noticed that the story told in the preface to " Further Poems " differed from the one in " Life and Letters."

I, myself, have never attributed Emily Dickinson's secluded life wholly to her broken love affair, though her work is so deeply colored with it. She was a poet and she sounded the depths of feeling. She came naturally by her shrinking nature from her mother, who was a most retiring and diffident woman — the old-school meek wife of the old-school dominant husband, rarely seen outside her

358

family circle — almost a recluse herself, in fact. Emily Dickinson's was a preternaturally sensitive organism for whom seclusion was a necessity.

I heartily sympathize with you in your effort to get at the actual facts of the matter and do away with fanciful and sensational accounts of it. If I can be of further use to you I hope you will let me know.

Very sincerely

February 15, 1930   (Signed)   Y

Note

Some persons say that Maggie Mahar did not begin to work for the Dickinsons until about 1860. This would put the letters from George Gould, delivered to Maggie by Deacon Luke Sweetser, and carried by her to Emily, much later than I have placed them in my book. Since the arrangement must have been made during the 50's, if made at all, we conclude that either Maggie worked at the mansion before that time, or that she inherited the practice from some other maid.

G. T.

APPENDIX IV

I

July 1849

FROM *The Indicator:* A LITERARY PERIODICAL, AMHERST COLLEGE

" Dr. Townsend's Sarsaparilla put up in quart bottles six times cheaper pleasanter and warranted superior to any sold; its progress to fame is marked by a long line of facts and cures which stand out as beacons and headlights pointing the way to heaven and health, lassitude want of ambition and premature decay can be entirely restored by this pleasant remedy; liberal discount made to travelling agents and literary associa — " " Hold on you plugless wordspout! "

II

Unsigned Article Written by Some One of Emily's Friends [1]

January 1850

DESDEMONA

Beneath the very summit of Vesuvius, the Campagna, that Eden of Italy stretches away; and in tropic isles, where the tornado sweeps at times, and the Earthquake buries thousands, the softest breeze of evening will play, and the mildest moonbeams sleep.[2] Just so, strange elements seem to mingle in the social world. The Poets of old married Vulcan and Venus, and the closest of all observers of human nature has given us Othello and Desdemona. What could be stranger, if we look only at outward circumstances, than that a maiden of beauty and fortune and high birth in Venice, in the days of Venice's glory; who had looked with disdain upon the noblest youth of her native city, should cherish so ardent a passion for the dark-browed Moor? The case is well set forth *by the indignant father* — [3]

"A maiden never bold;
Of spirit so still and quiet, that her motion
Blushed at herself; and she — in spite of nature
Of years, of country, credit, everything —
To fall in love with what she feared to look on!
It is a judgment maimed, and most imperfect,
That will confess — perfection so could err."

---

[1] Italics mine throughout.
[2] See Emily's use of these proper names.
[3] Indignant father?

Yet to our mind, her affection is one of Shakspeare's best conceptions of earthly love, and is brought out by that skillful painter of life in his liveliest coloring. For he makes us feel that the source of her affection is the esteem of true excellence: and he does it as it has been so well done since in " Jane Eyre," by denying to Othello all exterior attractions.[1] A great mind lives, and a large heart beats beneath the tawny skin and rough exterior of the Moor. If our business were with the character of Othello, it were easy to show this, even from the intensity of his jealousy and the agony of his remorse. And the Poet has not given us a boarding-school Miss for the heroine of his tragedy. We have something more here than an imagination excited by the story of an adventurer. Curiosity indeed prompts her at first to listen, but it is soon succeeded by admiration of the man, and a Woman's pity for his sorrows; and all are blended at the conclusion in a deep and earnest love. She tells us herself, in her decision to accompany him to Cyprus: —

> " I saw Othello's visage in his mind;
> And to his honors, and his valiant parts,
> Did I my soul and fortunes consecrate."

She cannot mean that high alliance was her object. It is, indeed, a pleasure to know that the great qualities of one we love are appreciated by others; and if any pride be pardonable, it is a wife's pride in the renown of a loved husband. But had the source of Desdemona's affection been ambition, it could not have out lived the loss of Othello's fame, and been warmer than ever on the very eve of his return to Venice in disgrace.

[1] *Vide* jests at the expense of George Gould's " exterior attractions."

And while the love of Desdemona is so far from the sensual on the one hand, it is equally far from the Platonic on the other. It *is* pure, but it is warm. It is a love of greatness and goodness; but it is of *personal* greatness and *personal* goodness. It is no abstract love of bravery and generosity and truth as illustrated in Othello; but a sincere, absorbing affection for Othello himself.

It may be inferred from his position in the state and the glimpses of his life which we have, that Othello was of an age much disproportioned to the maiden's. It is true that, generally, Youth is the time of ardent affection. But we cannot admit the oft-repeated sentiment of that licentious poet of our own age: —

> " *O what* without our youth
> Would love be? What would youth be without love?
> *Youth* lends it joy and sweetness, vigor, truth,
> Heart, soul, and all that seems as from above;
> But languishing with years it grows uncouth,
> One of the few things, experience don't improve."

Such love may do for the masses, — the great masses, to whom life is valuable principally as a means of personal and animal enjoyment. For if the sentiment be stripped of its beautiful verbiage, it amounts to nothing but this. Such is the affection which our Poet has created in Romeo and Juliet. The love smothered in the tomb of the Capulets would have died away with the lapse of years in the palace of Montague.[1] But no lapse of youth could change the love of Desdemona, for such affection knows no old age. The frame may totter in life's autumn, but the great qualities that make the man never lose the bloom or the charm

---

[1] Montague?

of spring. The world, indeed, ever accounts such unions unnatural; and sympathizing friends speak sadly of the sacrifice. In the vineyards of the South, the experienced Peasants wisely join the tender vine to the green young plane tree; and both grow old together; but does the union seem unnatural, where the tendrils creep, untaught, round some storm-beaten monarch of the forest, and bide their blushing clusters in his rough old arms?

If the beating heart of youth finds oftenest its response in the breast of one who looks on life from the same point, and with the same bright hopes, yet Nature and Nature's God alike approve the union of those who truly love, although years intervene between their starting points in life. For why should a few brief summers separate *immortal* beings, when theirs are kindred souls? Ah! those are in truth, the unnatural unions, and they are many, whence mutual sympathy has fled, and neither can appreciate the other; though they be formed in Youth's high bloom, and blest with every outward seeming. So, two fair rivers of the West, that sparkle in the same glad sunshine, and roll through the same bright land, join their swift floods, and side by side flow on, but their waters mingle not. And if instances of true affection between those whose only sympathies flow from the great and good in each other's characters are rare, it is only because the qualities necessary to such affection are rare.

Such is our Desdemona's love in its source; pure, yet glowing; — kindled by graces only visible to the mental eye, only tangible to the throbbing heart; we shall find it in its progress, unshaken by misfortune; uninterrupted by coldness — a love stronger than death.[1]

[1] The text of Emily's life.

Under cruel taunts she utters no word of complaint. She never tells Othello of the happy home she had left for him, nor of the broken-hearted father now cold in death. His strangeness and waywardness but make her love to plead in his extenuation and find excuses for his altered bearing.

> " O good Iago,
> What shall I do to win my lord again?
> Good friend, go to him; for, by this light of heaven,
> I know not how I lost him.

> Unkindness may do much;
> And his unkindness may defeat my life,
> But never taint my love."

And in that death-scene, everywhere so marked with Shakspeare's genius, the last words of Desdemona are still like herself. To the question:

> " O! who hath done this deed? "

with her last breath, she answers:

> " Nobody; I myself; farewell; [1]
> *Commend me to my kind lord;* O! Farewell."

Surely our assertions need no stronger proof; and 'twere vain to try to set in livelier colors a character delineated by such touches as these. We cannot forbear pausing to remark how the drama of Othello as a whole, and the last scene especially, illustrate the peculiar glory of Shakspeare.

---

[1] Emily quotes this in a note to Sue.

The genius that shines out in Macbeth and Richard III may be compared with the gloomy splendors of the Grecian tragedians; but the literature of the world may be challenged to produce a picture of domestic life, at once so beautiful and so awful and so true to Nature. He has no heart who can read it without emotion, and who has felt the full force of its simple, Saxon words, — no matter how warmly he may love the classic pages, will yet never regret that he speaks the language of Shakspeare.

We hardly dare to say, that at one part of this splendid painting we are disposed to carp. *Othello insinuates that the lady, Jane Eyre-like, popped the question herself:* —

> " My story being done,
> She gave me for my pains a world of sighs;
> — " In faith, 'twas strange, 'twas passing strange;
> 'Twas pitiful, 'twas wondrous pitiful:
> She wished she had not heard it; yet she wished
> That heaven had made her such a man: she thanked me;
> And bade me, if I had a friend that loved her,
> I should but teach him how to tell my story,
> And that would woo her. *Upon this hint I spake.*"

That hint *we cannot like. It sounds too much like the " encouragements " given by " sweet girls " now-a-days. A true woman may indeed unguardedly betray her love in a thousand ways; but she will ever seek to guard it. Beautiful is the struggle between native frankness and guilelessness, and innate shrinking modesty.* Ever would she

> — " Be woo'd,
> And must unsought be won."

And he who can appreciate such a woman will not ask for the dark eye that flashes back to his, more than the love he offers on his bended knee; *better, the soft, trembling hand should be half withdrawn, and nothing but the embarrassed silence and the crimsoned cheek, show the glad fluttering of the heart within. Better to seek himself into the depths of that heart unfathomed before; and* draw *forth from the inmost sanctuary, the silent confession which all the world beside could not have won. Never can ambition have place in such a woman's heart. Never will she talk of " woman's rights ";* — *her whole soul shrinks back from moving a hair's breadth from her sphere. If she be gifted with a brilliant imagination, that Gothic window of the mind that turns the light of common day to softest tints of beauty, they will play only around her quiet home. If endowed with that true fire from heaven, the poetry of heart which is thrillingly alive to every great and generous sentiment, and worships, with whole-souled devotion, the nobleness of self-denial, and the bravery that dares, through every danger to pursue the right, yet he who has won that noble heart and can draw forth its secret thoughts, will find it trembling to enter upon the voyage of life* — *fearful lest she fail to realize the high ideal she has formed of what the chosen of her love merits at her hands.*[1] — But where have we got to? and how " literary ladies " and " social reformists " would pounce upon us, if they only thought us worthy of their notice.

We would fain think that from our subject, is deduced the true Philosophy of Love. And why should it not have its Philosophy? True, many sneer at it as a disease, that like the measles, seize upon youth, and when once well

[1] Truly, a digression.

over, never troubles man again. There is such love, to be sure; and there are such men who catch it, or *fall in* it, rather. We well remember hearing an old lady, whom we venerate, describe this affection, and give it the expressive name of " calf-love "; — and so long as the fear of " calf-love " then impressed upon us, remains before our eyes, we think that we are in no danger of bringing sorrow to the gray hairs of Alma Mater, by contracting matrimony, while tied to her apron strings. *But we do believe, and will believe in love, the same in kind as that which binds the angels and the spirits of the just; — for both are founded on high esteem; both are fixed on loveliness and goodness and nobleness, living and personified. It is indeed, in some respects, peculiar; — it has its home on earth; its path lies through a wilderness world;* [1] *it meets sore sorrows; and lavishes on one dear object an affection that is in Heaven the common property of all.* But more deeply and tenderly they love who have wept together over buried hopes; and though conjugal affection be so exclusive as to shut out all the world from its peculiar joys, yet it is not necessarily a narrow love; for the heart that is large enough to hold it, must be large enough to take a world beside, into all its due regard.

And as Love has its true Philosophy, so it has its peculiar treatises. And why should it not have its treatises? Does not the subject come home closely enough to " men's business and bosoms "? True, many works of fiction are world-wide of the mark. Bulwer has sought to breathe love's burning words; — but " Zanoni " and " Ernest Maltravers " are strange fire. James has tried to picture it; — but his is only outward ministering; — he never was within the veil. A

---

[1] " Wilderness world " crops up in Emily's language.

host of less distinguished men have mistaken sensuality for its warmth, or sentiment and unearthly romance for its *purity and poetry of heart*. The great and good are divided in their opinions of works of fiction, and of the propriety of putting them into the hands of youth.

But taking the question's dark side, and admitting the dangers of such works, yet, if these dangers are surmounted, there must be profit from them. We do not think novels the worst of books; but even if they were, " the worst books are sometimes the best; they compel us to think." For, one who has learned to judge of works of fiction, has learned to judge of human nature in some of its most important earthly relations. He reads Bulwer and James, and even Scott, and *thinks* he loves just such ideals. The danger is, that he may stop short in his error, and take a step that will render life unhappy. But if the delusion passes off, he will be less liable to be deceived in real life; — he has found out what is not suited to him; and what is more, he has found out what he is not suited for. He will come to seek in some walk of every-day life, our Desdemona, or the originals of those pictures drawn by that Shakspeare of novelists, Currer Bell. — " But these are unreal pictures of life. Can such characters be found? " Truly they can. Few are the characters depicted in novels, which cannot be found somewhere in life; though the circumstances into which their subjects are thrown, are often unnatural or uncommon enough. There *are* noble men and noble women on Earth, and many of them not far from our homes. Many a " Caroline " lives among the pure-browed maidens of New England; there is many a " Shirley " among the wild, warm-hearted daughters of the South; and the heart of " Jane Eyre " herself, is beating in many an original, sterling woman of the West.

Our subject warrants us in thinking that the idea of a " love marriage " is neither Utopian nor silly. And we cannot believe that any circumstances in life can make it a duty, to promise solemnly to " love, cherish and protect " one, for whom no higher sentiment than respect, is entertained. It is not every one whom we esteem and whose excellent qualities we acknowledge, that we can admit to our secret heart. Forms of good character are greatly varied; and love demands that both its subjects be alike, and yet unlike; — each of a different nature, but who yet can be the same; — this mild and meek, but capable of rousing to noble deeds, all man's sterner soul; — that, strong and steady on the battle-fields of life, but gentle at his fireside; and able to make, with softest touch, the wild, sweet music of a woman's heart. Surely, no claims, — not even those of religion, come in such shape as to debar those worthy, from this precious boon. From that same sacred page, where we read, " Thou shalt love the Lord thy God with all thy heart," we read also, " Rejoice in the wife of thy youth." We cannot think a marriage of convenience, duty, even though it be of religious convenience. True, they who have for life's great object its only grand and glorious end, will often meet on the highest ground of sympathy and love; but even such, whether breaking the bread of life on distant shores, or living as strangers in their native land, and though their dearest portion is above the stars, *should yet have by their side their hearts' best choice on earth; — for they, of all our race most need it.*

We have hardly room for a single reflection on the broken words of Othello:

" My wife! my wife! what wife? — I have no wife:
— I pray you in your letters,
When you shall these unlucky deeds relate,
Speak of me as I am:
— then must you speak
Of one that loved not wisely but too well,
— of one whose hand,
Like the base Judean, threw a pearl away
Richer than all his tribe."

If the sacred oracles and the voice of experience alike
warn us to lay up no treasures on earth, because they pass
away, yet the very frailty of earthly ties should make us
careful of underrating them. These ties, when such as we
have attempted to describe them, cannot indeed be severed
here. For it is the imperfect wall on which the ivy takes its
firmest hold, and the blast that breaks the outer branches
of the oak, only shows how firmly it is set; and true affection is ever the stronger for bearing with the infirmities of
its object. But though our loved ones cannot be estranged,
they are mortal; and the silent reproach of the grave is
agony to the generous soul. Our friends are with us but to-
day; therefore should gentleness and courtesy mark all our
bearing towards them. The hearts all our own to-day, are
cold to-morrow, and we go mourning many years, for we
cannot follow them for forgiveness to the land where they
are gone.

APPENDIX V

From the *Sunday Oregonian,* Portland, Oregon, March 19, 1899

Portland people will be interested in learning that Emily Dickinson, the New England poet, was warmly attached to the family of a Portland woman, Mrs. Thomas L. Eliot. Mrs. Eliot, indeed, was *born in the old colonial house that is now the Dickinson place in Amherst, Mass.* Her grandfather bought the house from the Dickinsons about 70 years ago, and 30 years later her father sold it back again to them. A close friendship existed between the two families, both Emily and Lavinia, her sister, conceiving, as children, a romantic devotion for Mrs. Eliot's father and mother. As this incidentally reached the ears of a reporter of the *Oregonian,* Mrs. Eliot was sought for further information on the subject. She said:

" I am afraid I cannot tell you anything of interest, since my father moved West when I was only two years old, so that I knew Emily Dickinson only during my visits at Amherst when I was a child.

" Edward Dickinson, their father, was a Puritan of Puritans in his ways, very reserved and undemonstrative. When I went east eight years ago, I had a long talk with Lavinia, who said of him: ' My father would have died for either of us, but he would never let us know it. He never kissed either of us goodnight in his life.' She told me, moreover, that one of the most charming memories of her own and Emily's childhood was the children's parties my mother used to give them.

" Emily, as I remember her, had beautiful auburn hair, but she was not pretty, and was never attractive to me as a child. She was about 15 years older than I. She was very shrinking and sensitive in disposition, and this finally led her to seclude herself entirely from society; she never went beyond her family garden, so morbid did she grow, and out of tune with the world. When my father died, 32 years ago, my mother went east. Emily, at this time saw no one, but so romantic had been her attachment for my parents, that she insisted upon meeting my mother, who accordingly went to her home to see her. After being shown into a room that adjoined Emily's, she was seated next to a door which stood ajar, on the other side of which was Emily, and thus the conversation was carried on without either seeing the other's face.

" As for her verses, although there was the ethereal quintessence of poetry in her lines, they were disjointed and erratic, for she would suddenly lose all sense of rhyme and drop into prose.

" Lavinia, who was nearly the same age as Emily, is now the sole surviving member of the family. She was also very talented, somewhat eccentric, and like her sister, remained unmarried. She was especially brilliant in conversation, quick at repartee, more attractive in appearance than Emily, and passionately fond of flowers.

" I remember when I visited in Amherst just before my marriage Emily had already entered upon her retired life,

373

seeing no one and never going outside the family garden: but Lavinia came to see me and brought me the most beautiful flowers. She seemed to have a personal affection of these, speaking to each flower individually as she lifted it from the basket, caressing it as though she hated to part with it, and all this was done so simply and spontaneously as to be absolutely free from affectation.

" Their mother before them was eccentric; she was a very dainty, exquisitely neat housekeeper, so much so, indeed, that her neatness rather oppressed those around her."

William L. Brewster, of this city, who entered Amherst College in 1886, two or three months after Emily Dickinson's death, was acquainted with the Dickinson family. He says that no one at that time in Amherst had any idea of the real value of the little poems that she had been in the habit of sending to friends in return for small gifts of fruit and flowers. No one had yet discovered the touch of genius in her work. The two sisters had lived alone in the fine old New England house, with only a servant for companion. They were very fond of cooking and enjoyed good living. Most of their time, however, was spent in the garden, which covered several acres of ground and contained many choice flowers and noble elm trees. They had no close neighbors except their brother, who lived in the adjoining house, but *even this they never visited.*[1] This brother, who has but recently died, was a lawyer of much ability and influence in the town, treasurer of Amherst College, and invariably elected moderator of the town meeting. He was a man of keen wit, brusque and autocratic, rather than lovable, but entertaining in conversation, with a fund of good

[1] Italics mine.

stories always at his command. The Dickinson family had for generations back been respected as the aristocrats of the place, and the eccentricities of the two girls were therefore passed over as simply part of the general " queerness " peculiar to the family. In Mr. Brewster's opinion, however, both were slightly tinged with insanity.

EMILY DICKINSON'S PERSONALITY

From the *Book Buyer,* Vol IX, no. 4 (May 1892), pages 157–8

In a recent letter from Boston, published in *Book News,* Nathan Haskell Dole gave an interesting summary of a paper by Mrs. Mabel Loomis Todd, on the late Emily Dickinson and her poems.

" Mrs. Todd," said Mr. Dole, " was one of the comparatively few who were admitted to anything like intimacy with the weird recluse of Amherst. Her friendship began in this way: Mrs. Todd, wishing to send Miss Dickinson a little gift, painted a panel with the pale Indian pipe. It happened that this delicate flower was a particular passion with the poetess, and the gift went straight to her heart. This incident explains the appropriate employment of the flower as a decoration of the cover of the first volume of her poems. Indeed the drawing was made from the very panel which always stood in Miss Dickinson's room.

" Mrs. Todd exploded the popular notion that Miss Dickinson was always a recluse. When her father was in Congress she spent several winters in Washington, and mingled in gay society, which she enjoyed, though still feeling that she had no real part in it. It was only in the last years of her life that she lived in her own home, somewhat like a dear ghost, seen but scarcely tangible, dwelling among her favorite flowers and in the shadows. She had once played the piano in a most individual manner, but this practice she gave up while still retaining her love for music. She delighted to have her friends sing or play to her at twilight. She herself would not come into the music room, but sat outside in the entry, and rewarded the performer, not with praise, nor even speech, but with some dainty refreshment of cream or cake or with a higher guerdon of a slip of paper with a poem written on the spot during the music.

" Mrs. Todd never, in all the years of her acquaintance with her, had a face-to-face conversation about commonplace, mundane affairs. She dressed always in white, but such was her dislike to being ' fitted ' that her sister was obliged to act as her model. In spite of the white dresses, she was neither morbid nor an invalid, but possessed of a keen sense of humor, which sometimes betrayed itself in grotesque plays upon words, and always in the queerest, quaintest turns of expression. Her letters are full of daring originalities, which, if they were not so evidently the coruscations of her individuality, would be affectations. She was always doing odd, undreamed-of things. Once, when her father desired her presence at church, she stoutly refused. A conflict of wills ensued, such as is possible only in an old New England ' orthodox ' family. In the end Mr. Dickinson went to church alone. When the family returned home Emily was nowhere to be found. She did not appear at dinner. At last, toward the close of the day, she was discovered sitting in the cellar bulkhead, calmly reading a book, and her only remark was that she had not cared to discuss the question of going to church, and so had retired underground.

376

⟩ APPENDIX ⟨

" It happened that once in her service of laying the table she put at her father's place a plate that had a bad nick in it. This annoyed the old gentleman very much, and he rather sternly forbade her ever again to let him see that plate. But perverse fate brought it about that twice in succession again the offending plate, with the old nick in it, fell to Mr. Dickinson's share, who was very indignant. It did not happen again, for after that last dinner Emily disappeared and was found back of the barn under a big tree with a hammer and a stone, between which she was reducing the plate into the most infinitesimal fragments, and she remarked that now she hoped she should remember not to put it on the table again.

" After her death her sister and her friends were amazed at the immense amount of literary material which she had left behind her. Besides the poems collected in the first volume, which is now in its eleventh edition, and in the second series, which has reached a sale of over five thousand since November, there are at least twelve hundred poems catalogued, and no one knows how many more in a mass of notes and manuscripts found among her possessions — enough to make several stout volumes. Mrs. Todd is engaged in preparing and editing a volume of her letters which were written to Dr. and Mrs. Holland, Mr. Samuel Bowles, Colonel Higginson and others of her friends. She was a voluminous letter-writer, and these precious documents reveal her personality in a surprising way."

An estimate of Edward Dickinson written in 1873, a year before his death.
From *The History of Amherst College,* by W. S. Tyler, page 539.

Mr. Dickinson, (Hon. Edward), has made enemies by his unbending firmness of purpose and his great freedom and boldness of speech under excitement; but no enemy, whether personal or political, has ever questioned the integrity of his character, the purity of his life, or the breadth, depth and intensity of his public spirit. A liberal giver for public objects from his private purse, his vote may always be relied on in the town, the parish or the State, for the largest appropriations for public improvements. The best financier in the corporation has publicly announced, as the result of a careful examination for many successive years, that, as Treasurer of Amherst College, he has never lost a dollar. And one of the sharpest and shrewdest of the Board of Overseers declares that after the most prolonged and patient scrutiny of his books and accounts, only a single error of less than a hundred dollars could be detected and that error was *against* himself. At the age of threescore years and ten Mr. Dickinson still stands erect, perpendicular, with his senses of seeing and hearing unimpaired, with his natural force and fire chastened and subdued but scarcely abated, one of the firmest pillars of society, education, order, morality and every good cause in our community.

INDEX

i